About Island Press

Island Press is the only nonprofit organization in the United States whose principal purpose is the publication of books on environmental issues and natural resource management. We provide solutions-oriented information to professionals, public officials, business and community leaders, and concerned citizens who are shaping responses to environmental problems.

Since 1984, Island Press has been the leading provider of timely and practical books that take a multidisciplinary approach to critical environmental concerns. Our growing list of titles reflects our commitment to bringing the best of an expanding body of literature to the environmental community throughout North America and the world.

Support for Island Press is provided by the Agua Fund, The Geraldine R. Dodge Foundation, Doris Duke Charitable Foundation, The Ford Foundation, The William and Flora Hewlett Foundation, The Joyce Foundation, Kendeda Sustainability Fund of the Tides Foundation, The Forrest & Frances Lattner Foundation, The Henry Luce Foundation, The John D. and Catherine T. MacArthur Foundation, The Marisla Foundation, The Andrew W. Mellon Foundation, Gordon and Betty Moore Foundation, The Curtis and Edith Munson Foundation, Oak Foundation, The Overbrook Foundation, The David and Lucile Packard Foundation, Wallace Global Fund, The Winslow Foundation, and other generous donors.

The opinions expressed in this book are those of the author(s) and do not necessarily reflect the views of these foundations.

Ignition

Ignition

WHAT YOU CAN

DO TO FIGHT

GLOBAL WARMING

AND SPARK A MOVEMENT

Edited by

Jonathan Isham Jr.
Sissel Waage

ISLANDPRESS

WASHINGTON • COVELO • LONDON

Barry G. Rabe, "Second Generation Climate Policies in the American States," *Issues in Governance Studies*, no. 6 (August 2006) : 1–9. Available at brookings.edu.

WorldWatch, "Climate Change: What the World Needs Now Is . . . Politics," January/February 2006.

Eban Goodstein, *Fighting for Love in the Century of Extinction: How Passion and Politics Can Change the Future* (Burlington: University of Vermont Press, 2007). Used with permission.

ISLAND PRESS is a trademark of the Center for Resource Economics.

Library of Congress Cataloging-in-Publication Data

Ignition : what you can do to fight global warming and spark a movement / edited by Jonathan Isham and Sissel Waage.
   p. cm.
 ISBN-13: 978-1-59726-156-2 (pbk. : alk. paper)
 ISBN-10: 1-59726-156-4 (pbk. : alk. paper)
 1. Climatic changes. 2. Global warming. 3. Environmental protection. I. Isham, Jonathan. II. Waage, Sissel A.
 QC981.8.C5I338 2007
 363.738'74--dc22
                            2007001881

Printed on recycled, acid-free paper ✪

Manufactured in the United States of America
10 9 8 7 6 5 4 3 2 1

To the young leaders

of the climate movement,

who are making history

and shaping entirely

new possibilities for

the generations to come

CONTENTS

ACKNOWLEDGMENTS

WHILE IN GRADUATE SCHOOL, we both studied the process of social change under the guidance of several remarkable mentors. With Grace Goodell at Johns Hopkins University, Jon learned the value of thinking critically about social change and the institutional determinants of well-being. With Louise Fortmann, Nancy Peluso, and Jeff Romm at the University of California, Berkeley, Sissel studied the challenges of effecting change within complex social, economic, and ecological systems.

In many ways, this book began with Hilary Bradbury at Case Western Reserve University. We are thankful she asked Sissel in 2003 to collaborate on a dialogue focused on social and organizational principles related to sustainability-oriented transformation. This book is truly an unexpected ripple from that original stone thrown into the pond. Sissel also owes a debt of personal gratitude to Catherine Gray, George Basile, Eric Olson, and Ruth Rominger at the Natural Step for supporting that initial work. A special thanks goes also to Bryant Rice, a consultant to the Natural Step, who actually suggested the title *Ignition* for another book!

Beginning in 2004, we codirected a collaborative research project to help concerned citizens share, critique, and build strategies for the new climate movement. At a meeting over coffee at Middlebury College in the spring of 2004, Nan Jenks-Jay and Bill McKibben not only offered their critical support for this risky project; Bill also succinctly christened it "What Works."

The first outcomes of the What Works project were two coordinated events that took place in January 2005: a Middlebury College winter-term course called Building the New Climate Movement and a three-day workshop called What Works? New Strategies for a Melting Planet that took place at Middlebury as the class ended. During the course, we were fortunate to work with six wonderful service-learning partners: Ben and Jerry's, Clean Air–Cool Planet, Energy Action, Environmental Defense, the Green House Network, and the Middlebury Area Global Warming Action Coalition. We could not have presented this workshop without generous funding from many sources, including the BPB Foundation, Christian A. Johnson Foundation, Mellon Foundation, Schumann Foundation, Seventh Generation, Vermont Campus Compact, and the following contributors from Middlebury College: Ada Howe Kent Fund, Alliance for Civic Engagement, Charles P. Scott Spiritual and Religious Life Center, Office of Environmental Affairs, Program in Environmental Studies, Pooled Enrichment Fund, and Rohatyn Center for International Affairs.

The workshop itself proved to be inspiring in large part thanks to the leadership of the twenty Middlebury College students in the winter-term class who helped pull it together and set the tone. Diane Munroe, Jon's Middlebury colleague, was equally instrumental to the workshop's success. Rob Hartz and Joni Parker-Roach did a masterful job of coordinating and documenting the workshop. The inclusion of filmmakers Judith Helfand and Daniel Gold, taking footage for their documentary *Everything's Cool*, added a feeling that history was turning right before us, as did the enjoyable breakfast that featured a conversation among Bill McKibben, John Passacantando, Ted Nordhaus, Michael Shellenberger, and Peter Senge, another trusted ally in our work. We were also immensely fortunate that Mary Lou Finley and Bill Chaloupka, who had participated in the social change dialogue at Case Western in December 2003, helped lead the workshop. Two Middlebury faculty members who attended the workshop, Christopher McGrory Klyza and Rebecca Kneale Gould, later became chapter authors for this book. During the event, Gary Braasch's photos enabled us to see climate change—literally—through the melting, eroding, and (in some parts) collapsing world in which we now live. In addition, the roster of other participants who so memorably shaped this workshop reads like a climate movement all-star team: Will Bates, May Boeve, Meg Boyle, Gary Cook, Liz Cunningham, Peyton Fleming, Jihan Gearon, Eban Goodstein, Anne Hambleton, Jamie Henn, Rev. Paul Mayer, David Merrill, Susanne Moser, Jeremy Osborn, Billy Parish, Bill Shutkin, Michael Silberman, Tom Stokes, Mike Tidwell, and Jon Warnow, just to name a few.

Following this workshop, the third outcome of the What Works project is this book, *Ignition*. As our work on this volume began in earnest, we were incredibly fortunate to be supported by Brendan Bechtel, who helped us secure a grant from the S. D. Bechtel, Jr. Foundation. The foundation's generosity was a much needed and important sign that this project was worth undertaking. We also received invaluable advice from our colleague Jean Black about how to shape and market the book. Adam Markham and Roger Stephenson at Clean Air–Cool Planet were also immensely helpful as the book began to take shape. During the summer of 2005, Thomas Hand and Julia West provided invaluable research assistance, thanks to the financial support of the Middlebury College Office of Environmental Affairs. During the Fall of 2006, Jon received generous support from the Mellon Foundation.

We are honored to have collaborated with our chapter authors, who will surely continue to inspire us with their amazing work in the halls of academia, in the corridors of the U.S. Capitol, and in the diverse places around the United States and the globe where this movement is being strengthened. They were remarkably understanding and patient with us.

Todd Baldwin, our editor at Island Press, has left us speechless with his ability to provide diamond-sharp comments. His work immensely improved the manuscript, and we are fortunate to have worked with him as well as his colleagues at Island Press. Sincere thanks also go to Joe Spieler for helping us get over the finish line.

It has been a pleasure to collaborate with each other. Since meeting at the Case Western workshop in December 2003, we have been able to shape a common vision about contributing to the nascent climate movement. At various times, we have leaned on each other for ideas, energy, and counsel.

Finally, we are mostly indebted to our families, whom we are honored to personally praise here.

I thank my husband, Steven, for being unflaggingly supportive, kind, and generous. I cannot imagine a more fun fellow traveler through life. Ultimately, though, this book is for Leif, as he literally came into being along with it. I was newly pregnant at the What Works conference, and he has grown as the manuscript emerged. I hope that our small efforts here will contribute to a sound future for you, Leif, and all children everywhere.

—SISSEL WAAGE

I thank my wife, Tracy, for being the best possible friend, spouse, and parent I could imagine. I am constantly in awe of her abilities to manage the demands of work, family, and household. I am particularly thankful that she was willing to forgo a job she loved in Washington, D.C., so that we could take our lives in a new direction in central Vermont. Our girls, Faith, Katie, and Lily, are thriving here, in large part thanks to Tracy. I owe her, big time.

—JONATHAN ISHAM JR.

Ignition

Introduction

BILL MCKIBBEN

IN MID-SUMMER 2006, I HAD a feeling of despair (a strong one) and an idea (a bad one). I imagined walking from my home in central Vermont fifty miles to the state's main city, Burlington, and, once there, getting myself arrested on the steps of the federal building while protesting Washington's inaction on global warming. I wasn't sure what good that would do, aside from make me feel a little less helpless, but that didn't stop me from e-mailing friends and neighbors, asking if they wanted to go along.

Surprisingly, a good many did. Better yet, many wanted to help out. Those colleagues proved to be more astute planners than I was; it took them only a few phone calls to figure out that you really couldn't be arrested in Burlington, not without breaking something, which was not our style. So we jointly evolved the idea of a march across the same fifty miles, but with a different aim: we would ask all Vermont's candidates for federal office in the fall election to meet us by Lake Champlain and pledge to support strong climate legislation.

Thus began a month of nonstop organizing, most of it done by people more competent than me: Will Bates, for instance, a recent Middlebury College graduate with a quiet knack for getting things done; Becca Sobel, a Greenpeace organizer who was already in the state working on global warming and who now joined our efforts; Connie Leach, who at the very first coffee shop meeting said, "I'll take care of the food" and proceeded to do just that; Steve Maier, our local state representative, who started calling his fellow politicians; Jon Isham, a Middlebury College colleague; and on and on and on.

Here's what we learned in those weeks. Many people want to do something about climate change, something real and large and meaningful. They've already put in some compact fluorescent lightbulbs, and maybe they've even bought a Prius. Yet they realize that those moves are small stabs in the dark, that if we have a chance at dealing with global warming, it's going to require quick and decisive political change. Almost everyone we asked said either "Count me in" or "If I wasn't going to be away on Labor Day weekend, I'd be there." Many were overjoyed to be asked, and people thanked me repeatedly for giving them the "opportunity" to trudge across the late summer countryside. That should give us a clue: the climate movement is rich in scientists and economists and engineers; we have no shortage of answers, of analysis. Until now, however, we've never bothered to build the *movement* part of the movement. There's been no way for people to really engage in the process of fighting for change, no way to make very deep fears and hopes public and powerful.

Given the opportunity to be part of the movement, however, three hundred people showed up on Thursday noon to start the walk. That may not sound like many folks except that it was a workday, we were gathering in one of the state's smallest and most remote towns, and we were planning to go eleven miles before supper. We listened to a few talks, most notably John Elder, one of Vermont's most beloved writers, who dressed as an endangered maple tree and read from Robert Frost's poem "The Road Not Taken." It was in homage to Frost that we'd come to this small burg of Ripton; the great poet's summer writing cabin was a few hundred yards from the roadside turnout where we stepped off. With his words ("I took the one less traveled by/And that has made all the difference") ringing in our ears we hit the road, with a crew of real pros from Greenpeace out front to slow down traffic and keep us safe.

And what do you know? Three hundred people walking two and three abreast down a winding country road turns out to be one hell of a long line. We felt buoyant from the very start, a crowd of kids and elders and moms and college students and golden retrievers on a perfect late summer day, walking through a landscape we loved and also knew to be threatened by a warming atmosphere.

By late afternoon we'd reached the town of Middlebury's green, where more people were waiting for us, waiting with banners and music and food. We heard speeches from our Middlebury College president, Ronald Liebowitz, and from a chief aide of Patrick Leahy, one of our state's two senators. Then came dinner—a potluck pulled together by one of the local churches—and sleep.

That was the rhythm of the next few days: long walks (ten miles on pavement is much more tiring than ten miles on mountain trail), long conversations (with the whole day stretching out, there's no reason to give the short version of any story), and a steadily growing sense of optimism. We mostly hiked along Route 7, western Vermont's main north-south thoroughfare, on the left shoulder, facing traffic, which meant that we could see drivers as they passed. They'd read our signs, and by the time they were halfway down the line of marchers, three-quarters of them would be honking or waving or both. (The great danger was overexcited hybrid car drivers veering wildly in their enthusiasm.) It was clear that, at least on this road, climate change was not an iffy proposition or a hard sell; the reaction fit those public opinion polls showing that 80 percent of Americans understand that we have a problem (even if they might not be willing yet to march themselves, or even to countenance higher gasoline prices). Every night we'd have a wonderful meal: a wheat farmer used a newly built cob oven to bake us pizzas by the score, an activist opened her waterfront home not only for supper but for a much-needed swim in the lake. We got used to stirring welcomes, such as a rock band on the lawn of the senior center. And as we walked, and as our numbers grew, we began to pull in rumors that many of the politicians we wanted to hear from were actually planning to come to our final rally.

Sunday morning began with a church service so crowded that people were spilling out of every door of the sanctuary, so crowded that the communion wine ran out before everyone was served. That didn't matter much, though, for there was a communion of song and spirit that rocked the halls. That night we bedded down at Shelburne Farms, one of Vermont's great institutions. This conserved farm on the shore of Lake

Champlain features, among other things, the northern hemisphere's largest wooden building, originally built to breed horses to pull cabs, but this night put to use for a dance and for talks from local business owners, local farmers, local clergy. In the morning, a bagpiper waked camp. By now, there were six hundred of us wrapping blisters and munching bagels, ready to take our cause from the small country towns into the heart of what passes for urban Vermont. As we marched by the car dealerships and strip malls, the line kept growing. Soon, more than a thousand people were marching, with television crews and wire service photographers hustling to get their pictures. Vermont is a small state—this march was its largest political demonstration in many years—and as we wound through the streets of downtown Burlington in a line too long to see from any one corner, we could feel our power.

This power was confirmed when we finally reached the rally site. There, along with many supporters, were all the major state candidates for federal office, and they were not just the obvious suspects like Bernie Sanders, Vermont's progressive representative who was now seeking a Senate seat. Also there were the state's Republicans: Sanders's opponent Rich Tarrant, for instance, who for weeks had been running vile ads about immigration, and Martha Rainville, the former commander of Vermont's National Guard, who only weeks before had declared at her first campaign press conference that she wasn't sure global warming was even caused by humans, that maybe it was just a natural cycle and perhaps we should do some more research (she seemed to have changed her mind now).

One thing we had decided from the start was that we didn't want vague declarations of concern, nicely worded promises of shared worry and possible action, from our politicians. Rather, we wanted them to sign on to the legislation that our retiring U.S. senator, Jim Jeffords, had offered earlier that summer. The companion to California Rep. Henry Waxman's House bill, Jeffords's legislation called for 40-mile-per-gallon cars, 20 percent renewable energy by 2020, and 80 percent carbon reductions by 2050. These steps are not enough to solve global warming, but this bill was the most ambitious one introduced in Washington so far. Not even the House Democratic leadership was embracing it, but we were. We had the key points written on a huge sheet of paper, and we had the youngest marcher who'd gone the whole distance, thirteen-year-old Schuyler Klein, ready with a giant felt-tipped pen to hand to the pols as they stepped to the microphone.

First, though, came a word from the future. Three of the nation's most dedicated climate activists, college students May Boeve and Jamie Henn and recent college graduate Jared Duval (a contributor to this book), stepped up to the mike. They had walked every inch of the trail, and now they asked the other young people in attendance to join them on the stage. Toddlers toddled, high school kids sidled shyly up, and soon there were approximately 120 young people standing on the stage. The three leaders took turns saying pretty much the same thing: these people are the ones who will deal with the effects of your decisions the rest of their lives. Look them in the eyes, damn it, and then tell them that you're not ready to take real action.

After that, it was kind of spooky. One by one, the candidates came forward, took the pen, made their mark, spoke their piece. Sanders, of course, delivered big time; he promised to a mighty roar that he'd reintroduce the Jeffords bill on the very first day of the next Congress. Tarrant was almost as vigorous; ditto Rainville and her Democratic opponent, Peter Welch. Only the incumbent governor didn't show, which was his mistake because the crowd was generous to a fault, cheering everyone no matter their party label. They were cheering, but not kowtowing, for that afternoon we had the unmistakable sense that for once the political leaders were responding to our agenda, not the other way around. We let each of them speak for three minutes only; we'd walked far enough, we'd acquired enough moral capital that we got to set the ground rules. It was a true Vermont town meeting, with business to accomplish, not a set-piece photo op controlled by the candidate's advance team.

What stood out was how easy it was to get agreement from even those candidates who had never made the issue a priority. It reminded me of a political truth that's easy to forget: you don't need everyone. You don't even need 51 percent. All the moaning about how "the average guy" doesn't really understand climate change is beside the point; 5 percent of the population is plenty to roll politicians as long as that 5 percent is committed, as long as that 5 percent is willing to get up and walk. We've won the battle of the science and even the battle of perception; today, most Americans believe that human's effect on climate is a real problem. Now we've got to win the political battle, the one where we're pitted against ExxonMobil. That company made a $36 billion profit in 2006, which buys plenty of politicians, but only if there's no one pushing from the other side. One thousand people are enough to push back and win three votes in Congress. Sure it's Vermont; sure it will be harder in Texas. Yet it's worth a try anywhere; in fact, it's worth more than a try.

One of the small secrets was that we had fun. There was much music along the way—a good reminder that most of the movements that have worked in this country have been singing movements—and lots of religion, too. I kept haranguing the pastors who joined us to march in their collars, to demonstrate that the faith community was finally understanding the centrality of these issues.

The other secret, the really crucial one, is that people get it. Twenty years ago, climate change was hard to understand and obscure, but not anymore. Plenty of people, more than enough to constitute a movement, understand what's going on and feel it in their hearts. And plenty more, even if they lack that commitment, will wish us well. We've been banging our heads against this wall for so long that we've become accustomed to thinking that change is impossible, that the forces on the other side are just too strong, that ExxonMobil will always carry the day. Indeed, we've intimidated ourselves into not even trying; at best, we try to work out "partnerships" with industry. All that is fine and useful work, but history indicates that the best partnerships happen when both sides have reason to be on board. Our job is to be noisy and joyful and footsore and clever and devoted enough to create that reason. Onward!

PART I:

It's Time

1. Igniting Action for a New Movement

JONATHAN ISHAM JR.

SISSEL WAAGE

Could the next grassroots revolution in
America be over climate change?
Economist, March 18, 2004

We need a grassroots movement.
Thomas Friedman, *New York Times*, February 13, 2005

"CAN WE REALLY WIN THIS FIGHT against global warming?"

We often hear that question from college students, business leaders, and civic groups as we go around the United States spreading the word about climate change solutions. If you've seen *An Inconvenient Truth* or had an eye on popular magazines lately—remember that *Time* magazine cover story that told us all "Be Worried. Be Very Worried"?—you too may be asking yourself, Can we really do something about global warming? Can we really shed our fossil-fuel dependence for a clean-energy future?

Our answer—and the resounding message of this book—is, Yes, we can.

We can do it if we engage neighbors in our coffee shops, our church and synagogue and mosque basements, and our chamber of commerce meetings, making a mutual pledge to protect places and people we cherish. We can do it if we then reach out to like-minded allies, building tough-minded coalitions of civic, religious, and business leaders who want to do the right thing. We can do it if we forcefully demand that our elected officials become champions of visionary legislation that will promote rapid investments, in the United States and around the world, in a clean-energy future. Above all, we can do it if we begin to "build the world anew" around the things that matter: our families, our communities, and our shared stewardship of this earth.

Winning this fight will be an immense challenge. To stop the accelerating growth of greenhouse gas emissions, to reduce those emissions to a small fraction of their current levels over a mere generation, will require unprecedented social and economic transformation. To succeed, a sustained movement of engaged citizens to lead the fight will be needed. Quoting *Ignition* coauthor Gus Speth (chapter 2), we need a groundswell.

As we document throughout this book, such a groundswell is growing. If *you* decide to get involved, you will be joining a diverse band of engaged activists: Republicans and Democrats; leaders of businesses, environmental groups, state agencies, places of worship, parent-teacher associations, Native American tribes, colleges, universities, and business schools; and rural grandparents, urban parents, and schoolchildren everywhere. Some see global warming as a form of intergenerational injustice or as a religious affront, some see it as a significant business risk, some are acting to ensure a hopeful future for their children and the landscapes they love. All understand the gravity of the crisis and are committed to doing their part to bring about change.

As this groundswell builds, it will face challenges unlike past efforts to change society. Leaders of past social movements—the civil rights movement immediately comes to mind—could rally the nation by pointing to a clear villain and sympathetic victims. Leaders of today's climate movement have a tougher sell: they must convince fellow citizens that global warming—where each of us is at once victim and oppressor, where the greatest damages will be to those not yet born—is nevertheless worthy of national resolve.

So yes, it will be hard work.

Ignition is designed to help. Here are assembled the voices of top scholars and inspiring young leaders, including academics who have studied social movements and politics for decades and new civic leaders who are developing tactics for today's climate action. This book is neither a cook-book nor a handbook of, say, "Fifty Ways to Save the Planet." Rather, think of it as an ongoing workshop, a gathering of like-minded citizens who are sharing their personal experiences and learning from one another. In the pages that follow, they present insights and strategies designed to build an even larger, even more diverse community of activists. Each chapter of this book is focused on ideas and actions that can tip the balance towards a clean-energy future, and together these chapters provide a comprehen-sive view of what is being tested and what has worked.

A Fresh Perspective on the Climate Crisis

In the last several years, the two of us been lucky enough to get to know hundreds of fellow citizens who are building the climate movement. If you're not sure whether you can play a role, we can assure you: becom-ing active in this new movement does not require expertise, only a com-mitment to making a difference.

We are unlikely editors of a book on climate change. Neither of us has formal training in the science of the issue. Neither of us has spent the last decade or two dressed in suits exhorting policy makers to take action on climate change. In fact, neither of us has been actively engaged with cli-mate change issues at all, until very recently. The reason was simple: it seemed to be the domain of natural scientists, engineers, and policy ana-lysts. As social scientists, we were both drawn less to the corridors of the United Nations than to diverse places around the world where we tried to make a difference in the lives of others: the dirt pathways of villages and towns in Africa and the Pacific Northwest and the hallways of universi-ties and conservation nongovernmental organizations (NGOs).

By the early 00s, we—like many others—finally realized that climate change had the potential to override all other environmental and eco-nomic development gains. So we stepped back to consider the story of how the world got to this point. The story begins at the dawn of the Industrial Revolution, when the world's growing use of carbon-intensive forms of energy—first coal, then fuel oil and natural gas—began to help much of the world's population dramatically improve their lives. Coupled with human ingenuity and growth of international markets, the world's use of fossil fuels unleashed unprecedented levels of well-being. Since the late 1800s, the average human lifespan has almost doubled in much of the world, and the quality of that life has similarly improved. Well over four billion of the six-and-a-half billion people now living on our planet are much healthier, are much better educated, and have many more choices than just about everyone who was alive in the early 1800s.

Yet many have not benefited. More than one-and-a-half billion people still live on the equivalent of one or two U.S. dollars a day, with little access to clean water and other essentials of a dignified life. Malaria and HIV/AIDS devastate the lives of millions. In addition, the extraction of fossil fuels, in too many cases, concentrates power in the hands of a few and damages the environment—and the natural capital—on which the poor depend daily.

In the last several years, the two of us—perhaps like many readers of this book—have finally come to understand the rest of this story. For as the world's fossil-fuel–driven economy has grown, the burning of all that carbon has thickened the heat-trapping blanket of greenhouses gasses in our atmosphere. Consequently, the global mean temperature (which over the earth's longest time spans has moved up and down with natural variation of heat-trapping gasses) has gone up approximately one degree Fahrenheit in the last one hundred years. Although this change may sound modest, the earth's delicate balance has already been affected, as have large segments of the world's population. In this age of global warming, one can't say definitively that any given natural calamity is "caused" by climate change. As an indicator of what is occurring and what awaits, however, simply think of the victims of Hurricane Katrina.

If we continue as usual in the decades ahead—if those of us in the developed world keep driving our gasoline-powered cars, flipping on our coal-powered lights, and turning up the thermostats of our propane-heated homes, soon joined by families in China and India and elsewhere around the world who are pulling themselves out of poverty—we will double the width of the world's heat-trapping blanket. The temperature increase by the end of the twenty-first century will then be at least four degrees, maybe eight, resulting in a world that, by just about every measure, will not resemble our own. Unless the world community takes action, experts foresee a struggling global economy, an unprecedented increase in the number and magnitude of natural disasters as well as deaths and injuries from heat waves, asthma, and insect-borne diseases. Vulnerable populations, including the poorest households in the developing and developed world, will bear the brunt of these changes in the decades ahead.*

By 2003, after years of being immersed in work to alleviate poverty and promote sustainability, we began to focus on solutions to the climate crisis. Our collaboration started at a small workshop convened by Sissel and Hilary Bradbury at Case Western Reserve University. Twenty workshop participants, mostly social science professors and NGO-based change advocates, came together to ask how we can fundamentally change the ways in which we live together—with all living beings and systems—so that future generations not only survive but thrive. Knowing that the path to a more sustainable future would require the mobilization of many, we discussed recent successful examples of social change, such as women's growing empowerment globally, the anti-apartheid shift in South Africa, and the political "green" movement in Europe.

On the last day of that conference, we gathered with others, including future *Ignition* contributors Mary Lou Finley, William Chaloupka, and Julian Agyeman, to share our fears about global warming. With lessons from successful social movements still fresh in our minds, we soon agreed on the need for a strong, diverse, and broad-ranging climate movement within the United States and beyond. As the coffee flowed, we realized that we could share some hopeful signs about the birth of just such a movement. We noted that the Green House Network, under the inspired leadership of Eban Goodstein—a Lewis and Clark College economics professor by day and a dedicated activist by night and weekend (and author of chapter 11)—was training climate activists nationwide, using the successful methods of the earliest civil rights organizers. The Massachusetts Climate

---

* To learn more about the science of global warming, we recommend two indispensable books that began as articles in the *New Yorker*: Bill McKibben's classic *The End of Nature* (now available in a revised edition) and Elizabeth Kolbert's *Field Notes from a Catastrophe* (see the References at the end of this book). Regular updates on climate science can be found at www.realclimate.org.

Action Network was helping residents conduct greenhouse gas inventories and rally political commitment for clean energy statewide. Groups such as Ceres, Businesses for Social Responsibility, and the Society for Organizational Learning were nurturing climate leadership in corporate boardrooms. Students on college campuses nationwide were mobilizing through the Climate Campaign and the Sierra Student Coalition, building pragmatic, creative initiatives to support their goals of a clean-energy future and a more just society.

Reflecting on these promising efforts, our group asked what could be done to ignite more widespread action. We came up with no immediate answers that day, but the two of us believed that it was a conversation worth continuing.

In the following months, we took stock of who was doing what. By the spring of 2004, we had seen a proliferation of initiatives, including citizen petitions, public education campaigns, and e-mail alerts, by national environmental groups such as Environmental Defense, Natural Resources Defense Council, and Union of Concerned Scientists. We also began to uncover innovative approaches by new groups on the state, regional, and national levels. For example, the National Religious Partnership for the Environment, a coalition of Jewish, Catholic, Eastern Orthodox, and mainline and evangelical Protestant leaders, had begun to help concerned persons of faith "strengthen their efforts and amplify their voices in the public square and the halls of government."[1] Activists working on issues as diverse as human rights and the health of the world's oceans were getting into the act, as was Hollywood. All this promising activity was suggesting the birth of something new.

By the summer of 2004, we joined two dozen other concerned citizens for a three-day Green House Network workshop on an island in Boston harbor and learned how to reach out to family members, neighbors, and coworkers. Inspired by that gathering, we made a commitment to start the "What Works" project (www.whatworks-climate.org) to use our own resources and know-how to jump-start this new movement. The project's first major activity was a four-week winter-term seminar at Middlebury College in January 2005 titled "Building the New Climate Movement." In this course, students studied theories of social change and led service-learning projects with a representative sample of leading climate groups, including Clean Air–Cool Planet, Energy Action, Environmental Defense, and the Green House Network.

The class culminated in the second major activity: a three-day workshop at Middlebury College titled "What Works? New Strategies for a Melting Planet" that included the participation of more than a hundred students, scholars, leading climate activists, and citizens. During the workshop, which was covered in a front-page article in the *New York Times* and elsewhere in the national media and filmed for the documentary *Everything's Cool*, participants had the opportunity to share, test, and build their movement strategies. They were also challenged by leading thinkers (many of whom became contributors to this book) to reassess their assumptions about how to fight global warming. Eban Goodstein kicked off the event with a call for focused political action at the national level; Michael Shellenberger and Ted Nordhaus, coauthors of *The Death of Environmentalism*, made a strong case for tapping into American aspirations; William Chaloupka, a long-time observer of the environmental movement, declared that it was time for traditional environmentalists to shake things up; Mary Lou Finley, who helped organize Martin Luther King Jr.'s work in Chicago, offered an analytical overview of movement building; John Passacantando, executive director of Greenpeace USA, called for a new generation of pragmatic "troublemakers" making good and necessary kinds of trouble; and Bill McKibben concluded by saying that it was time to experiment and find the things that work. The Middlebury workshop, in large part thanks to the leadership of many determined college students, offered us all a vision of hope.

The Birth of a New Movement

Since the What Works project, we have seen the climate groundswell come into its own. Activists are framing the potential of runaway climate change as undercutting the healthy, spiritual, and community-based future that we all want for ourselves and our children. In addition, as people begin to realize the effects of global warming, they are mobilizing nationwide in civic and professional groups.

The best news of all is that these mobilization efforts are creating political opportunities. Consider, for example, these events from 2005 and 2006:

- National media coverage finally highlighted the undeniable risks of climate change, as illustrated by *USA Today*'s cover story in June 2005 ("The debate's over: Globe *is* warming") and hour-long global warming reports on MSNBC, CNN, and Fox News. In the spring and summer of 2006, the film *An Inconvenient Truth* was shown in thousands of theaters. As 2006 came to an end, the DVD dissemination of that film was launching hundreds of conversations nationwide, in living rooms and community meeting places and on college campuses, about how to affect change.
- In 2005, evangelical leaders throughout the United States began to speak out about climate change and to organize their own base. On February 8, 2006, eighty-six of these leaders signed the Evangelical Climate Initiative, which declared that "the need to act now is urgent. Governments, businesses, churches, and individuals all have a role to play in addressing climate change—starting now."[2]
- Fortune 500 companies began to rally for predictable, cost-effective climate legislation. In April 2005, Duke Energy, the third-largest burner of coal in the United States, announced its support for a carbon tax. In April 2006, Paul M. Anderson, Duke Energy's chairman and a member of President George W. Bush's Council of Advisors on Science and Technology, joined dozens of other business leaders at a conference to call for mandatory federal action to reduce greenhouse gasses.
- On February 16, 2005, the day that the Kyoto Protocol took effect for 141 countries, Seattle Mayor Greg Nickels challenged mayors across the country to take local action to reduce greenhouse gasses. By December 2006, 339 mayors representing more than fifty-four million Americans had accepted this challenge.
- On December 20, 2005, seven states—Connecticut, Delaware,

Maine, New Hampshire, New Jersey, New York, and Vermont—announced an agreement to implement the Regional Greenhouse Gas Initiative, a regional program designed to reduce carbon dioxide emissions from power plants. Massachusetts and Rhode Island soon followed suit.

- On September 27, 2006, Governor Arnold Schwarzenegger signed the California Global Warming Solutions Act, which is designed to cap that state's greenhouse gas emissions at 1990 levels by 2020.
- After the November 2006 elections, Sen. Barbara Boxer (D-Calif.), the new head of the U.S. Senate's Environmental Public Works Committee, vowed to champion federal legislation after California's new law.

As 2007 got under way, Bill McKibben and six recent Middlebury College graduates announced Step It Up (www.stepitup2007.org), a national day of climate action scheduled for April 14, 2007. As people mobilize support for innovative clean-energy policies, these and other leaders are seeking to transform the societal, economic, and political landscape well into the election year of 2008. It is an exciting time, full of possibilities.

Fighting Global Warming and Sparking a Movement

Winning this daunting fight will take every strategy we can muster. Why should *you* get involved? Why not let others lead? Here's what the two of us have discovered over the last few years: as people begin to get engaged in the growing climate movement, they join conversations about changing their lives for the better. When someone then speaks and acts—for example, by addressing fellow worshippers at a church, synagogue, or mosque about the moral obligation to be a steward of the earth or by helping a local community college switch to compact fluorescent lightbulbs—these words and deeds provide symbols of a new, more promising world. In this way, small, humble efforts are more important than they may first seem, and as the climate movement grows, this process of face-to-face persuasion and collaboration is building robust social networks. These networks will not only help in the fight against global warming, but they will also enhance our daily lives. Joyful outcomes of the growing climate movement include the connections, friendships, and newly found meaning that people discover as they take action.

So, can we really win the fight against global warming? With a new groundswell—a new kind of movement, tailored to the opportunities of this new century—we believe we can.

In this age of polarized politics and civic disengagement, skeptical observers may view this kind of widespread citizen action as naive, outmoded, or even irrelevant to the biggest issues that we face such as climate change. We remind skeptics, however, how it has been done before, on other fronts. Citizen-powered groundswells, time and time again, have taken on seemingly impossible challenges and have proved successful. Think of Dr. Martin Luther King Jr. and the civil rights movement. Recall Gandhi and the struggle for an independent India. Remember the fight for women's suffrage in the United States.

Over the past few years, people have asked how we can remain upbeat given all that we know about the threat of climate change. We both unhesitatingly reply that we cannot imagine anything more fulfilling than working on one of the most important issues of our time, alongside old and new friends. Even though the challenge is immense, we agree with Bill McKibben's words in *Ignition*'s preface: there is much inspiration and joy to be had on this road.

2. *Groundswell*

JAMES GUSTAVE SPETH

Climate change is the most severe problem
that we are facing today—more serious even
than the threat of terrorism.
Sir David King, Chief Scientist of the United Kingdom

SINCE THE FIRST EARTH DAY IN 1970, I have been involved in what
we call, with some exaggeration, the "environmental movement," and since
1979, when I was working for President Jimmy Carter, I and many others
have done everything we could think of to spur action to stop global warming. Those of us who have been in this fight can attest that our nation's som-
nolence in the face of a growing climate crisis has been deeply frustrating.

That is why I am so heartened by the recent public and congressional
awakening and by stories of the new climate movement documented
throughout this book. These developments are truly causes for celebration. In the last few years, we have seen the expansion of a diverse network of Americans who are acting on their vision of a climate-friendly
energy future. Thanks to these efforts and to excellent media coverage
(finally!) based on first-rate science, a resurgent Al Gore, the impresarial
genius of producer Laurie David (see www.stopglobalwarming.org), the
American public has turned an important corner in acknowledging global
warming as a real and serious threat.

We must be honest, though. If we Americans take the next step and ask, OK, Al Gore is right, so what do we do now? we must see a massive job ahead. If we want to avoid leaving a ruined world to our children, we are going to have to reduce greenhouse gas emissions by approximately 60 percent globally and 80 percent in the United States and other developed countries, both by 2050. To do that, global emissions must peak around 2020 and decline steadily thereafter. Developed country emissions should already be declining.

Right now, the United States is clearly on the wrong path. Emissions are rising, and the Energy Information Administration currently projects that both U.S. coal use and carbon dioxide emissions will increase by 40 percent by 2030. The bottom line? The issue is not only real and important, it is genuinely urgent. The actions we take in the next few years will be critical.

So, it is time—indeed, past time—for something different. It's time for a strategy that moves us rapidly forward into a period of profound change. This strategy must mobilize all the possible resources at local, state, and national levels, reward climate-friendly businesses, and help us elect politicians, including a new president, Republican or Democrat, who are prepared to address the climate crisis issue as an urgent national priority.

A Ten-Point Plan of Action

Fortunately, the outlines of a climate strategy we can implement now are highly visible, in part because of the extraordinary efforts already being made by so many Americans to move the United States in the right directions. What follows is a ten-point agenda of action that builds on the many positive, encouraging initiatives are already under way. Many of these strategies are presented in greater detail in the next four parts of this book.

1. State and Local Action

Up to this point, the path forward has been blocked in Washington, although the 2006 midterm election appears to have changed that to some degree. The good news? Many states and localities across the country have moved to fill the breach. More than half the states have developed or are developing initiatives that will reduce greenhouse gas (GHG) emissions. Many of them, such as programs in New York and New England, focus on reducing GHG emissions from power plants. Nine northeastern states are developing a market-based cap-and-trade program—the Regional Greenhouse Gas Initiative (RGGI)—aimed at reducing GHG emissions from more than 600 power plants by 10 percent by 2020. Several western states are building a similar trading scheme. Other states, such as New Jersey and, most notably, California, have ambitious legislation that seeks to reduce overall emissions in the state. Governor Arnold Schwarzenegger has also announced a California goal of reducing that state's GHG emissions to a level 80 percent below the 1990's emissions level by 2050, and California has also taken the lead in regulating GHGs from vehicles, a lead that some states in the East have started to follow. New York is committed to having 25 percent of its power from renewable energy by 2013, and some twenty other states also have renewable energy goals for their power sectors.

Cities are also taking remarkable steps. The mayors of many U.S. cities have announced that they pledge to have their cities meet the requirements of the Kyoto Protocol. By late-2006, 339 mayors representing more than fifty-four million Americans have accepted this challenge (although, it must be admitted, with varying commitments to success).

The goal in the years immediately ahead should be to strengthen and deepen state and local commitments and actions. Until we have a fully adequate national program, we should work to get every state to adopt an overall GHG reduction plan, a renewable energy portfolio standard, the California plan for vehicles, and an energy efficiency program that covers everything from much tighter building codes to transportation and land use planning. We should work to build state participation in regional cap-and-trade programs and to increase the number of cities joining Seattle and others in achieving Kyoto's goals. Most important is to ensure that goals set at the state and local levels are achieved. (For more on progress at the state and local levels, see chapter 16.)

2. Carrots and Sticks with Business

Scores of major corporations are not waiting for federal action on climate and are taking significant, voluntary initiatives to reduce their GHG emissions. They anticipate they will be regulated one day, and they are also acting because of shareholder pressure, consumer pressure, the threat of eventual liability for damages, pressure from insurers and lenders, and public image and corporate responsibility concerns. The strategy regarding business should be to escalate on all those fronts that recognize and reward positive performance by business as well as those that put serious pressure on business to reduce emissions.

3. Greening the Financial Sector

The financial and insurance sectors are waking up to climate dangers. Investors representing more than $4 trillion in assets have formed the Investor Network on Climate Risk organized by Ceres (www.ceres.org). These investors, large lenders, and insurers are becoming increasingly sensitized to financial risks (and opportunities) presented by climate change. Such developments should be encouraged. The Securities and Exchange Commission should be forced to require companies to disclose fully the financial risks of global warming. Fund and other investment managers should be pressed to develop climate-risk competence and to support climate-risk disclosure and action.

4. A Sensible National Energy Strategy

Congress should move beyond the current impasse and write energy legislation that gives priority to energy efficiency and renewable energy. The imperative is to simultaneously meet several national objectives: decreased dependence on problematic oil imports, clean air, climate protection, and new jobs and industries based on advanced technologies. Our goal must be national energy legislation that puts the United States squarely on the road to a low-carbon economy, including legislation that steadily increases the fuel economy of cars, SUVs, and all trucks. In doing so, we should keep in mind that energy efficiency gains provide the cheapest, cleanest, and quickest path ahead. (For more on breaking congressional gridlock, see chapter 14.)

5. Ambitious and Cost-Effective Climate Policy

The McCain-Lieberman Climate Stewardship Act proposal, first introduced in 2003, was a start. Yes, it was modest even by the standards of the Kyoto Protocol, and still it did not pass, but its market-based approach of establishing a national cap-and-trade program, which would be cost effective for the American producer and consumer alike, is the best way forward. The bill introduced in 2006 by Vermont's retiring Sen. James Jeffords is more promising, and it has been reintroduced by Senator Barbara Boxer (D-Calif.). The Jeffords bill called for an 80 percent reduction in carbon emissions by 2050, 20 percent renewable power by 2020, and cars that get at least 40 miles per gallon. The goal here must be to build broad public support to get such legislation passed into law, the sooner the better.

Right now, although action is beginning in Congress, we are not yet near the legislation we need. Moreover, our political leaders and others in Washington are not being held accountable for failing to address so serious a threat. Therefore, it is time for this issue to become highly salient in electoral politics. Those alarmed about climate change—and that should be everyone—can start voting the issue in national elections. (For more on the importance of mobilizing voters at the national level, see chapter 11.)

6. Hands Across the Seas

Europe is taking the climate issue seriously, and it can press the United States to start a credible program of GHG emissions reduction and join the climate treaty process. Prime Minister Tony Blair of the United Kingdom has made a strong effort in this area. In the summer of 2006, he announced, alongside Schwarzenegger, the possibility of inviting California to participate in a cap-and-trade GHG market.

It would be comforting to think that the international community used the last two decades to build an effective international framework for climate action, but it would be wrong. Scholars have lately been developing the concept of treaty "ossification," and they cite as an example the climate treaty and its well-known offspring, the Kyoto Protocol. One reason is that the North-South divide has deepened in the negotiations. There has been no agreement yet on how to achieve equity in the greenhouse. Another reason, of course, is U.S. intransigence. A huge effort is now required from the United States and others to revitalize international negotiations with the aim of moving beyond the Kyoto Protocol and realizing emissions cuts such as those mentioned in the opening part of this chapter.

7. Climate-Friendly Cooperation with Developing Countries
With China's emissions now rising rapidly and soon to exceed those of the United States, future agreements under the climate treaty should provide for commitments from developing countries on climate and GHGs. Such agreements need not seek (yet) actual reduction in GHG emissions from the developing world as a whole. They should, however, vigorously promote measures to achieve rapid decreases in developing-country GHG releases per unit of gross domestic product or, as it is sometimes put, reductions in the carbon intensity of production.

To support these efforts, the international community, including the World Bank, should launch major new programs for large-scale capacity building, urgent transfer of green technology, liberal access to low-cost capital for climate-friendly investments, support for renewable energy and "carbon capture and storage" for any fossil development, programs to aid firms in industrial countries to receive credit for climate-saving investments in developing countries, and tropical forest conservation (moving from net deforestation to net afforestation).

8. Climate-Friendly Consumers and Institutions
We each must do our part to reduce our own carbon emissions. Individually, it is satisfying; collectively, if a lot of us get moving, it's significant. Spurred more by higher gasoline prices than climate fears, consumers are already voting with their pocketbooks for hybrids and other high-mileage vehicles and against SUVs. What if all U.S. colleges and universities joined in a commitment to reduce their GHG emissions impressively below 1990 levels by 2020? What if all U.S. religious organizations made a similar commitment? And all fraternal organizations? And all medical centers and hospitals? And all environmental, consumer, civil rights, and other organizations such as private foundations with commitments to the public interest? We can make a big difference by getting the institutions with which we are associated to take climate action, starting locally and then expanding regionally and nationally. (For more on transforming institutions, see chapter 12.)

9. Limits on Coal

Plans are being laid to construct more than one hundred coal-fired power plants in thirty-six U.S. states, and American coal use is projected to go up by more than 40 percent over the next twenty years. Launching a new generation of coal-fired power plants without plans for capturing and storing the carbon is the worst possible thing we could do climate-wise.

We will need a combination of national, state, and local efforts to ensure that climate and other environmental risks are taken into account in decisions regarding new coal plants. The momentum must be stopped or must be redirected to carbon capture and storage. Environmental, public health, and other citizens groups and foundations can collaborate on such a strategy. In Congress, the prospect of all these coal plants should spur the so-called four-pollutants bill, which would regulate not only sulfur, nitrogen, and mercury emissions, but also carbon dioxide.

10. Movement Building

Items 1 through 9 now bring us to the tenth and most fundamental area: building a powerful grassroots movement for change. To press forward with rapid progress on the other nine fronts requires a new movement of citizens and scientists, one capable of dramatically advancing the political and personal actions now urgently needed. We have had movement against slavery, and many have participated in movements for civil rights and against apartheid and the Vietnam War. Environmentalists are often said to be part of the "environmental movement." Now we need a real one. It is time for we the people, as citizens and as consumers, to take charge. As Bill McKibben recounts in the introduction to this book, politicians will follow if we do take charge.

The best hope we have for a new force for change is a coalescing of a wide array of Americans. It begins at the grassroots level: concerned families, engaged communities, and the nation's many civic groups, be they scientific, environmental, religious, student, or other organizations. These dedicated leaders must team up with climate-friendly business leaders and forward-thinking politicians, demanding action and accountability from corporations and governments, taking steps as consumers and communities to act on these values in everyday life.

A new movement of consumer and households committed to sustainable living could drive a world of change. Young people will almost certainly be centrally involved in any movement for real change. They always have been. New dreams are born most easily when the world is seen with fresh eyes and confronted with impertinent questions. The Internet is empowering young people in an unprecedented way, not just by access to information but by access to one another and to a wider world.

One goal must be to ignite the spark that can set off a period of rapid change, like the flowering of the domestic environmental agenda in the early 1970s. Part of the challenge is changing the perception of global-scale concerns like climate change so that they come alive with the immediacy and reality of the domestic challenges of the 1970s. In the end, we need to trigger a response that in historical terms will come to be seen as revolutionary, a new environmental, social, and economic revolution of the twenty-first century that will transform our communities, institutions, and politics. Only such a response is likely to avert huge and even catastrophic losses.

Building the Groundswell

Can we really build such a response and in such a hurry? An important body of scholarly literature on political change in the United States can give us guidance and hope. In their book *Agendas and Instability in American Politics*, political scientists Frank Baumgartner and Bryan Jones make a distinction between normal periods characterized by incremental change, when negative feedback stalls proposals for large changes, and those special periods when proposals for change generate positive feedback and major change sweeps through the system. They write:

> Our primary thesis is that the American political system . . .
> [has been] continually swept by policy change. . . . During
> quiet periods of policymaking, negative feedback dominates;
> policy innovations seldom capture the imagination of many
> individuals, so change is slow or rare. During periods of rapid
> change, positive feedback dominates; each action generates

disproportionately large responses, so change accelerates. . . . Punctuated equilibrium, rather than stability and immobility characterizes the American political system.[1]

Clearly, protecting the global environment from climate disruption has been addressed incrementally in American politics, whereas we want and need major change, a rapid shift to a new equilibrium.

When does that happen? In analyzing periods of major shifts in American politics, Baumgartner and Jones conclude that sweeping policy change happens when a major wave of new and previously apathetic citizens are attracted to an issue. These newly activated participants almost all enter on one side of the issue. They are motivated to enter the fray because the issue has been redefined, with new dimensions added that the new participants find attractive and compelling.[2] A major event or "crisis" can help redefine the issue and attract wide attention.

When the perception of an issue is systematically altered to engage a new and broader audience, perhaps by a crisis or major event, far-reaching change becomes possible. A new vocabulary or way of discussing the issue can help it along. No group could be better suited to undertake such a redefinition and new articulation than the young people I see on campuses across the country. I hope they can lead in making the grand challenges of today have the same immediacy as the local environmental threats of the 1970s.

Paul Ehrlich has observed that "our global civilization had better move rapidly to modify its cultural evolution and deal with its deteriorating environmental circumstances before it runs out of time."[3] He notes that the potential for conscious evolution is evident in great social movements that societies have already experienced.

I think we are seeing the birth of something new—a new movement for change—in the initiatives under way at the state and local levels, in the far-reaching and unprecedented steps being taken by climate-friendly corporations and investors, in the strength and vitality of civil society organizations, in the growing advocacy for sustainable consumption patterns, in scientists speaking up and speaking out, and in the outpouring of environmental initiatives by the religious community and others. What they all share are the realizations that it is business as usual that is utopian and that building a new world is the pragmatic necessity.

The Global Challenge That Requires Local Action

At times, the immensity of global-scale challenges, their seeming remoteness from everyday life, and the inaccessibility of the policy processes that address them make it hard for individuals to believe they can make a difference.

New York Times columnist Thomas Friedman has noted that globalization is shrinking the world, linking events here with those far away.[4] The great and legitimate fear of many is that the globalization process is homogenizing and hollowing out local economies, communities, and cultures. Yet today's technology is also empowering individuals to combine their forces in unprecedented ways and to link up with others seeking constructive change around the world. Web-based resources, outstanding organizations, and other levers make it possible today, as never before, for citizens to affect the outcome of global challenges. Positive local change can go global, spreading, seeking larger goals, and asserting itself until the world is changing.

The biggest threat to the environment is global climate disruption, and the greatest problem in that context is America's energy use and the policies that undergird it. So in terms of bottom-up, citizen-driven action, there is no riper target than the U.S. energy scene. Indeed, the energy-climate problem provides the best example available of how citizen initiative and local action are beginning to address a global-scale problem. We can imagine goals being set for renewable energy use and for reductions in greenhouse gas emissions by businesses and universities, by communities and states and then by groups of states and national associations and organizations of many types, all supported by worried insurers and institutional investors, to the point that local actions are indeed going to change the world and, in the end, force national and international action. It is not a distant vision: it is a process that has already begun in the United States. We are not powerless to affect even the most remote and global challenges.

There is much to be done. As I reflect on the challenges ahead, I hope some of the grassroots networks that grew in the presidential campaign of 2004 will turn more of their attention to building awareness and action on climate. Religious organizations also have a big role here, as the National Religious Partnership for the Environment is already proving. The entertainment industry and the media also need to do more.

Educators and scientists can no longer content themselves with publishing and lecturing. (See www.focusthenation.org and chapter 11.) The scientific community has the credibility to take the climate issue to the public and to politicians. The various intellectual and policy communities—such as the foreign policy, consumer, and social policy communities—should come out of their silos (we're all in silos) and take up this cause.

With a cascading of many initiatives, we can build our movement. With a strong movement, we will not fail. Changing U.S. energy and climate policies has proven extremely difficult in the face of powerful industry opposition, which is why a powerful popular movement for change is so essential.

3. Shaping the Movement

MARY LOU FINLEY

> Perhaps a spark will ignite a
> massive uprising of popular will.
>
> Ross Gelbspan, *Boiling Point*

Change is in the wind. As the United States recovers from the effects of Hurricane Katrina, as we face the reality of how climate change is changing so many of our sacred places, groups dedicated to fighting global warming have formed all around the country and we are starting to see the potential of this groundswell. In September 2006, Governor Arnold Schwarzenegger signed the California Global Warming Solutions Act, a clean-energy bill that puts a cap on that state's greenhouse gas emissions. In November 2006, the change in congressional leadership in Washington, D.C., brought the promise of the consideration of such a bill to the national level.

The first sparks of this climate movement remind me of an earlier time, the fall of 1965 to be exact. Having just graduated from Stanford University, I joined Dr. Martin Luther King Jr.'s staff that autumn as he launched his campaign in Chicago. Congress had just passed the Voting Rights Act, and we were excited to tackle northern forms of segregation, injustice, and poverty.

It was a heady moment. Within a year, I had participated in my first nonviolent action campaign. In retrospect, what I find quite astonishing is what we were able to accomplish. We were no more than a small group from the Southern Christian Leadership Conference, about twenty-five or so people: King, other well-known leaders and veterans of the southern campaigns, and young folks like me who mostly brought eagerness. When we joined up with a mature civil rights movement in Chicago, however, we managed within less than a year to force the City of Chicago to confront its own segregation. Soon, political, religious, and business leaders were at the conference table with King and other civil rights leaders, designing a plan for change. At the time, we achieved less than we had originally hoped. Nonetheless, it was a significant launching, both for long-term change efforts in Chicago and for King's work against poverty, the central focus of his precious few remaining years. It was during this time that I came to understand the power of a clear vision, the power that can be found in the courage to take bold public action against injustice, and the power of nonviolent action as a strategy.

During that time, I met Bill Moyer, a staff organizer on housing issues for the American Friends Service Committee. His earlier work on ending housing segregation was foundational for King's summer open-housing campaign, in which Moyer played a key role. For the next thirty-seven years he served as an organizer and trainer for activist groups, first in other civil rights efforts and the Poor Peoples Campaign, and later for peace and environmental movements. Were Moyer still alive, he would be very pleased to witness the growth of the climate movement because supporting activists in their work on environmental crises was close to the heart of his life's work.

In this chapter, the current state of the climate movement and its long-term potential are examined. To do so, I'll use Moyer's movement action plan (MAP) model of social movements, which he developed over many years of training activists and eventually summarized in *Doing Democracy* (a book he and I coauthored with two others).[1] The MAP model includes principles describing the fundamental dynamics of social movements, the four key roles for social movement activists, and the eight stages of successful social movements. Specifically, I use the MAP model as a guide for thinking about two questions: If we are to successfully jump-start the climate movement, what is now called for? Can the strategies of past decades, including those I witnessed during my days in the civil rights movement, help us move forward?

The insights of the MAP approach, based on the experience of many activist groups and nonviolent movements over several decades, can provide important guideposts for this new groundswell. As I detail here, the model can help develop strategic thinking, build new initiatives, and maintain the morale of activist groups over the long haul.

The MAP model begins with eight principles. As I summarize here, these principles can guide the development of movement strategies and tactics that are detailed throughout this book.

1. *Social movements have brought significant societal change, although even activists may be unaware of it.* It's sometimes easy to lose sight of what can be achieved through citizen-based action. Victories of earlier movements have been monumental and include clean air and water laws, women's right to vote, the eight-hour workday, social security, unemployment compensation, civil rights for African Americans, disability rights, and rights for gays and lesbians.

2. *The people hold ultimate power.* The theory and practice of nonviolence, as embodied by Martin Luther King Jr. and Mahatma Gandhi, are based on the fundamental insight that people hold ultimate power. It is also the foundation of democracy.

3. *Movement goals should be framed in terms of widely held values.* Movements should clearly articulate the connection between current issues and values such as democracy, the protection of children, preservation of life, love of nature, and social justice.

4. *Powerholders may profess to honor widely held values, but their actions often conflict with those values.* Revealing violations of widely held values by powerholders, such as recalcitrant oil companies and national politicians, is a key strategy for mobilizing the public in support of change.

5. *Every movement needs analysis, vision, and strategy.* A wide range of strategies is needed for reaching many different sectors of society and pressuring recalcitrant powerholders.

6. *Movement activities must seek to awaken and mobilize the public.*
   Movements can measure their progress by observing shifts in
   public opinion. An awakened and mobilized public can demand
   change and begin to implement change in its own communities.
7. *Building coalitions across communities is critically important.* Building bridges among social justice groups, business groups, a wide
   range of religious groups, and others in broad coalitions is critical. As a movement grows, it gains adherents from the societal
   mainstream, who in turn should be welcomed to the movement.
8. *Change emerges from empowered people in motion, and they can
   become virtually unstoppable.* As people win even small victories,
   they begin to feel more empowered. The movement builds
   momentum, drawing people to it as it gains strength and visibil-
   ity. Training, education, and community building for movement
   participants can support the process of empowerment.

Building on these core principles, the work of activists and leaders in the
civic, business, and public sectors will need to take many different forms
as the climate movement grows. The MAP model outlines four roles for
activists, all critical for movement success: the citizen, the rebel, the social
change agent, and the reformer.

The Citizen

Activists in the citizen role show how the movement advocates for the common good and stands for widely accepted values such as justice for all and
a livable future. In the civil rights movement, Dr. King was acting in the
citizen role when he called on the United States to honor its commitments
to democracy. Climate activists can articulate a vision for a renewable
energy, postcarbon society that will serves the needs of all, preserving a
livable world for our children and grandchildren as well as for others
around the world.

The Rebel

Rebels protest injustice, often through nonviolent direct actions such as
marches, rallies, petition campaigns, and civil disobedience or, more

frequently, through simple efforts such as street-corner vigils, informational leafleting, and group visits to public officials. Rebel actions call public attention to the issue, stimulate public dialogue, and sometimes play a crucial role in confronting recalcitrant powerholders. Civil rights activists in the rebel role organized sit-ins and boycotts, rallies and marches, and myriad other public actions. Rebel actions among climate activists have included a hunger strike in the summer of 2005, led by members of Energy Action; a sit-in and organized arrest in the spring of 2006 in the home state office of Senator Max Baucus (D-Mont.), led by members of GlobalWarmingSolution.org; and a protest and organized arrest in the fall of 2006 at the Maryland headquarters of the National Oceanic and Atmospheric Administration, led by members of the U.S. Climate Emergency Council.

The Social Change Agent

Social change agents are the movement's organizers. They focus on public education, organize new segments of the community in support of the movement's goals, and nurture new leaders. As they adapt the framing of movement issues to the needs of disparate constituencies, they build the movement's strength. They also continue to deepen their analysis, encouraging others to seek underlying causes and be open to a major paradigm shift. Civil rights field workers were the social change agents of that movement as they worked with different constituencies in towns and cities across the South; other social change agents organized support in the North. Social change agents in the climate movement include the leaders of Chesapeake Climate Action Network, Clean Air–Cool Planet, Climate Crisis Coalition, Energy Action, Evangelical Climate Initiative , Focus the Nation, Step It Up, and Massachusetts Climate Action Network.

The Reformer

Reformers work closely with mainstream institutions, negotiating for change by filing lawsuits, testifying at hearings, lobbying, participating in official meetings, and carrying out other such tactics. Reformers often play an important role near the beginning of a movement, trying to make the official channels work. In the later phases of a movement, they help craft the laws and agreements that codify the movement's success. Reformers also nurture and support other activists by providing educational materials, research, trainings, and consultation on both organizational and technical issues. In larger professional opposition organizations, paid staff often play this role. In the civil rights movement, the NAACP Legal Defense Fund played the reformer role very effectively when, for example, it filed school integration court cases. It also filed a court case on behalf of the Montgomery bus boycott, the success of which brought the boycott's victory. Reformers in the climate movement include James Hansen at NASA, who has forcefully testified about the perils of global warming; Mayor Greg Nickels of Seattle, who has lead the Mayors' Climate Change Initiative; the public and nonprofit leaders of twelve states and thirteen environmental groups that sued the Environmental Protection Agency to classify greenhouse gasses as a pollutant that must be regulated under the Clean Air Act; and business leaders in groups such as Ceres, Businesses for Social Responsibility, and the Society for Organizational Learning, which are bringing the message of the need to transform our investment priorities into the corporate world.

Some movement activists and leaders may play all four roles; others may specialize. Both approaches can be successful. Nonetheless, tensions often arise in movements between people and groups playing different roles. Reformers and rebels are particularly prone to conflicts. A larger understanding of the importance of all four roles can help diminish these tensions and support the cooperation and collaboration essential for movement success.

As social change agents and rebels emerge to complement the long-term work of reformers and citizens, the climate movement appears to be in the midst of a major shift in relation to these four roles. This shift is an important signal of the movement's progress and strength. Reformers have done much of the work in the past, toiling through government and United Nations forums, seeking to bring international agreements to fruition. It has been, for all its limitations, powerful work. The scientific consensus building has been particularly critical in convincing the public that the global warming crisis is real. In addition, scientific research and analysis has helped make visible to the public the interrelationship between pine beetle infestations in northern forests, the melting tundra, and the growing strength of hurricanes, for example, as well as clarifying, at least for those who have been attentive, the potential for climate catastrophe. Climate change reformers, in collaboration with activists in the citizen role, have also worked at the state and local levels with government officials willing to initiate and support change, with growing success. The California Global Warming Solutions Act of 2006 is an especially notable victory, building on the collaboration of Russell Long of the Bluewater Network, Representative Fran Pavley, and many forward-thinking leaders in the private, public, and civil sectors.

A base of grassroots activists doing social change agent and rebel work has only recently begun to develop. Since 2001, local climate change and global warming groups have formed and now do the organizing work of social change agents. The Massachusetts Climate Action Network and the Chesapeake Climate Action Network were early innovators, as was the Green House Network, with its training workshops for activists (modeled after the early civil rights movement nonviolent workshops), and Energy Action, with its inspiring campus-based mobilization of college students.

In the years ahead, more grassroots work will be needed. Activists need to take on a range of institutions, in the automobile industry and the electric utilities, for example. Then they need to take on many locally specific projects, such as improving agriculture and forestry in ways that can alleviate global warming; organizing businesses to change their fuel practices; strengthening public transportation, bicycling, and other car alternatives; building a biodiesel industry; and working with people in communities to make the changes that they personally can make, such as changing their driving habits. This work needs to pervade every institution in society as we seek to make the needed transformations. Social change agent activists can take the lead in these organizing efforts.

The climate movement also needs to strengthen its rebel contingent; at some point, it will be necessary to confront entrenched power that refuses to change. The movement will need to confront utility companies forging ahead with building new coal plants, governments that refuse to adopt emission reduction legislation, and automobile manufacturers who refuse to switch to low emission vehicles. As Ross Gelbspan, author of

Boiling Point and *The Heat is On*, has said, we "should be outraged" that our government leaders have refused this work, and, in many instances, actively attempted to undermine it.[2] A contingent of climate activists needs to study nonviolent campaign building and prepare to bring the issue to public attention in dramatic ways. More and more people will be needed, in their everyday lives as citizens, to advocate for climate-stabilizing changes in their own communities.

Eight Stages of Successful Social Movements

Moyer's MAP model also describes eight stages in a movement's progress, and each stage has its own strategic requirements and pitfalls. In addition, activist roles shift in importance as the movement progresses from stage to stage.* Seeing the climate movement through the lens of MAP stages can provide strategic suggestions for today's climate activists and may help activists recognize the successes along the way as the movement gains strength.

Stage One: Normal Times (Mid-1800s to 1979)

During stage one, the problem exists, but it is largely unrecognized, invisible, and not publicly discussed. The buildup of carbon dioxide in the atmosphere began with the use of coal in the Industrial Revolution in the nineteenth century. Working in the 1890s, Swedish chemist Svante Arrhenius understood that coal burning increased carbon dioxide in the atmosphere and anticipated an eventual temperature increase on the earth as a result, but he believed such as change would take three thousand years to occur.

After World War II, a massive increase in the use of fossil fuels occurred, spurred by the increasingly widespread use of oil. Scientists Gordon MacDonald and Friends of the Earth president Rafe Pomerance called attention to global warming in early 1979. Together, they asked the Carter administration to address global climate disruption. The National Acad-

---

* For a chart depicting the relationship between movement stages and activist roles, see B. Moyer with J. McAllister, M. L. Finley, and S. Soifer, *Doing Democracy: The MAP Model for Organizing Social Movements* (Gabriola Island, BC: New Society Publishers, 2001), pp. 84–85.

emy of Sciences Charney Report of 1979 confirmed initial scientific reports, indicating that there was "no reason to doubt that climate change will be the result."[3] The period of ignorance was over.

Stage Two: Proving the Failure or Limitation of Existing Institutions (1979–2001)

In stage two, the problem has been recognized by a few and efforts are made to resolve it through mainstream institutional channels. Citizens and experts may testify at public hearings, file lawsuits, introduce legislation, and otherwise seek to bring change. The movement may win modest local victories, but full-blown success is unlikely.

Following the initial discovery of the problem of global warming, the United Nations became active at the international level. Although widely opposed by the "carbon lobby" (largely the U.S. oil and gas industry), the consensus about global warming continued to grow among scientists. Important landmarks in this stage include the alarming testimony on Capitol Hill in 1988 by climate scientist James Hansen, the publication in 1989 of Bill McKibben's *The End of Nature*, the signing in 1992 of the Framework Convention on Climate Change, the publication in 1995 of the first Intergovernmental Panel on Climate Change report, and the Kyoto Protocol, signed in 1997 and entered in force in February 2005. Work throughout this stage was eventually successful in awakening the public in Europe and in other nations, such as Canada.

A significant amount of international collaboration occurred during this period. In addition, the science of global warming was repeatedly in the news and the American public became aware of the issue, if not overly concerned about it. Some segments of the business community, particularly the insurance and banking industries, began to pay attention to the risks inherent in global warming (the insurance industry after suffering significant losses caused by a series of major climate-based natural disasters such as floods, droughts, and forest fires).

For all its strengths, however, this international work had two critical limitations. First, the United States refused to support the growing international consensus, and, in 1997, the Senate voted against signing the Kyoto Protocol. Close U.S. government ties to U.S. oil companies resulted in the government echoing corporate arguments that challenged the science of global warming and cited negative effects on the U.S. economy that would result from any new regulations. The lack of agreement from the United States, source of one-quarter of the world's greenhouse gases, was a major limitation of this work. Second, the Kyoto treaty does not begin to go far enough. The Kyoto Protocol targets call for only modest reduction greenhouse gases worldwide, whereas preventing climate catastrophe will require cuts of 80 percent within a generation.

An increasing sense of urgency led to discussions about global warming at the state and local levels in the early 1990s. By the late 1990s, when it became clear that the Senate was not going to approve the Kyoto Protocol, work began in earnest in some states. New Jersey, surprisingly, became a leader, with a comprehensive program for lowering greenhouse gas emissions. Nebraska passed regulations on agricultural practices that were geared toward decreasing climate effects. Other states passed new requirements of some sort. These state-level initiatives represented important victories and laid the groundwork for future work to come. A number of states, led by Michigan, however, passed resolutions that "decried any future efforts to reduce greenhouse gas threats" as a risk too great for the economy.[4] These resolutions, along with the limited nature of the successes, indicate that the movement was still in stage two.

This stage ended with President George W. Bush's withdrawal from the Kyoto process in 2001, indicating the limitations of working through existing institutions, most notably the federal government. Further, this definitive change alarmed leaders on college campuses, in businesses, in local communities, and elsewhere. In their organizations and networks, these leaders began to build new activities, signifying the beginning of the next stage.

Stage Three: Ripening Conditions (2001–2006)

During stage three, a growing number of citizens become aware of the problem. Activists mobilize existing organizations and networks, such as churches, synagogues, and mosques; local civic groups; and business and professional associations. It is a time of much public education, small-scale protests, local victories, and widening public concern,

Beginning in 2002, the evidence of global warming became more visible. In the spring of 2002, the Larson Ice Shelf B in Antarctica, approximately the size of Rhode Island, collapsed. In September 2003, the largest ice sheet in the Arctic ruptured. Scientists reported that the earth was warming much faster than earlier anticipated. In the summer of 2003, thirty-five thousand Europeans died as a massive heat wave struck the continent. Pulitzer Prize–winning journalist Ross Gelbspan reports:

> Ironically the year 2003 also seemed to mark a sea change among many segments of American society on the climate issue. The failure of the world's diplomats to enact meaningful solutions has generated a groundswell of grassroots and voluntary climate action around the country. Some 30 states—and more than 100 cities—have initiated plans to reduce their own carbon emissions. Hundreds of colleges and universities have embarked on "green campus" programs. Growing numbers of religious leaders and their congregations are responding to what they see as the ethical challenges embedded in climate change. A number of large environmental groups have taken up the climate as their central issue. And [as documented in Chapter 1] grassroots activist groups dedicated to the climate crisis have sprung up all over the country.[5]

In 2004 came the release of the film *The Day After Tomorrow*, which presented an improbable but publicly engaging scenario of the effect of climate change on New York City. By the spring of 2005, new levels of public education and awareness were visible. The *New Yorker* published Elizabeth Kolbert's three-part series on global warming, with a dramatic magazine cover showing a cartoonlike drawing of Manhattan under water, with dolphins circling submerged skyscrapers. On June 13 of that year, *USA Today* headlines announced "The debate's over: Globe *is* warming." The article stated:

> Don't look now, but the ground has shifted on global warming. After decades of debate over whether the planet is heating, and if so whose fault it is, divergent groups are joining hands with little fanfare to deal with a problem they say people can no longer avoid.[6]

Even Bush had to acknowledge the new reality, when, at the July 2005 G8 summit in Scotland, he abandoned his strategy of arguing that the science of global warming was inconclusive and instead claimed that voluntary controls would bring sufficient change.

At the state and local levels, an infrastructure supporting renewable energy has begun to be established. In 2004, California passed tougher emissions standards. In 2005, Washington and then other states followed. California has net metering of electricity, and its governor pushed a "million roofs" project to install rooftop solar photovoltaics. The state of Washington passed legislation requiring utility companies to install the technology for net metering. In June 2005, the national Conference of Mayors passed a resolution promising to work on global warming. In addition, more than three hundred cities have made even stronger commitments.

At the same time, signs of stirring appeared even at the national level. Rep. Jay Inslee (D-Wash.) and others introduced legislation to support the New Apollo Project, a massive proposal supported by environmental and labor groups to transform U.S. energy systems to renewable energy and less polluting, more efficient technologies. The energy bill that passed in the summer of 2005—although loaded with subsidies for the oil, coal, and nuclear industries—also included modest provisions for renewable energy and conservation. In a June 22, 2005, column, *New York Times* columnist Thomas Friedman noted that, in this process, "the Senate's top Republican bill negotiator Senator Pete Domenici split from Bush and indicated that he believes the science is clear; climate change is occurring and we need to do something about it."[7] Senator Lamar Alexander (R-Tenn.) noted, "This legislation represents a very significant shift in the consensus in the US toward taking significant steps toward dealing with global warming."[8] Although this bill represented a minor success in movement terms, it was nonetheless a significant indicator of the beginning of changed perceptions in Congress. Fortuitously, a set of converging forces are also playing a significant role in the growing climate movement: the end of the cheap oil era, the war in Iraq, and the coming of age of the renewable energy movement and renewable energy technology.

Between 2004 and 2006, gasoline prices at the pump rose drastically, at some times doubling and reaching more than $3 per gallon. The price of oil has also risen, hovering between $60 and $70 a barrel, up from less than $30 in 2003. In the first six months of 2005, the mainstream press began to cover "peak oil," whose analysts report that world oil production will peak sometime between 2007and 2020 and result in drastically increased prices as demand far outstrips supply. Coupled with increased demand from China and other developing countries, this impending peak in oil production clearly portends the end of the cheap oil era in the very near future. Increases in the price of gasoline at the pump have resulted in the general public asking if the era of cheap oil is over. These changes have sparked an interest in alternative fuels and more fuel efficient vehicles like the hybrid Toyota Prius and Honda's Civic hybrid, and a Seattle company is developing four new biodiesel manufacturing plants in Washington and elsewhere to meet growing demand for biodiesel fuel. One 2007 report indicated that "U.S. biodiesel production more than doubled last year."[9]

The second converging force is the war in Iraq, with its high costs in life, limb, and public treasure. By the fall of 2006, the war had entered a very visible crisis, leading to the rejection of many Republican supporters of the war in the November elections and a Democratic takeover of the U.S. House and Senate. An October 2006 survey conducted by the Democracy Corps, a Democratic Party strategy group, found that "reducing dependence on foreign oil" was the voters' top national security priority and that the public wants higher auto mileage standards and more stringent energy and appliance codes.[10] A significant proportion of the public understands that U.S. dependence on foreign oil is a national security risk.

Finally, on a more positive note, renewable energy technologies, quietly under development since the oil crisis of the 1970s, are available and close to ready for public use, in itself a virtual miracle under the circumstances. Wind farms are already in use, and preparations for expanding them are occurring in rural areas as far apart as Iowa and Washington State. Solar photovoltaics can generate rooftop electricity for homes and businesses. Hybrid cars are here, with plug-in hybrids coming soon. Mark Wilson of the Community Energy Resources in Seattle is proposing a "vehicle-to-grid" project in which plug-in vehicles can send energy back into the grid, resulting in a new source for the renewable generation of electricity.* He is working with municipally owned public utilities to pilot the technology. As Gus Speth details in chapter 2, what is needed is a massive mobilization to scale up the technological experiments already well under way.

So concern about global warming is clearly rising across the public spectrum. The powerholders' long-held argument—that the scientific evidence on whether human activity causes climate change is inconclusive—has been thoroughly discredited. The movement's alternative—transformation to a clean-energy future—is taking concrete shape as Iowa farmers discuss selling wind rights and investors hold conferences on how to invest in renewable energy. State initiatives are already taking this work to a new level, beginning the process of multistate compacts such as the Regional Greenhouse Gas Initiative among nine states in the Northeast. In addition, serious climate legislation was introduced in the Senate in January 2007 by Bernie Sanders (D-Vt.) and Barbara Boxer (D-Calif.), among others.

Stage Four: Take-off (2005–2007)

Movement take-off puts the issue on the public agenda, where it begins to be hotly debated. Movement take-off may be spurred by a major "trigger event": a nonviolent direct action campaign, other forms of movement activity such as the consciousness-raising groups of the early women's movement, or dramatic and publicly visible events that occur independent of movement activity, such as the deployment of new nuclear weapons systems, a new environmental disaster, or an industrial accident.† During take-off, movement groups proliferate, new tactics evolve, and the movement appears to be everywhere. This period is generally short, from six months to two years.

The climate movement in the United States is in the midst of move-

---

* For more detailed information, see the work of Dr. Willett Kempton, senior policy scientist at the Center for Energy and Environmental Policy, University of Delaware, who developed the concept of the electrical vehicle-to-grid project.

† For instance, the deployment of Cruise and Pershing II missiles in Europe served as a trigger event for an antinuclear weapons movement opposing nuclear missile deployment in Europe in the early 1980s. The Three Mile Island nuclear power plant accident in March 1979 served as a retrigger event for the antinuclear power movement.

ment take-off. The converging climate disruptions of the last several years—from melting ice sheets and desperate polar bears to Hurricane Katrina and record forest fires—have caught the public's attention and have served, cumulatively, as a "trigger event" for launching movement take-off. At this point, the take-off process is still in motion, fueled by a wide array of public education efforts. The film *An Inconvenient Truth* has been reaching new audiences, including many who do not think of themselves as environmentalists. In addition, news reports have kept global warming before the public with accounts of "global warming gases seep[ing] out of thawing permafrost,"[11] "melting glaciers . . . vast fires . . . and early season floods" linked to global warming,[12] and a National Academy of Science report that "Earth's temperature . . . is the highest since the last ice age, about 12,000 years ago."[13] California's success in passing climate change legislation in August 2006 is leading the way, showing how state government can make major steps toward climate stabilization, and will help mobilization elsewhere. Nationally based activist work is also rapidly escalating, led by projects such as Step It Up (www.stepitup2007.org), a national day of locally based climate action on April 14, 2007, and Focus the Nation (www.focusthenation.org), a national day of campus-based climate workshops planned for January 31, 2008 (see chapter 11).

Further activist work will undoubtedly be needed to propel the movement to full-scale national take-off. Although it is always difficult to predict how movement take-off will culminate, determined activist efforts can generate the public ferment out of which full-scale movement take-off will come. The major work of movement take-off is to keep the issue before the public as much as possible so that a wide-ranging public demand for change develops. Local political leaders like the signatories of the Mayors' Climate Initiative have committed to major transformations, yet even these reformers will be willing and able to support the necessary drastic changes only when they sense that the public is ready.

What then, might this activist work look like? It will need a proliferation of climate activist groups, working at all levels of society, from neighborhoods to communities to the state and nation. Local grassroots climate action groups or networks, perhaps modeled after the highly successful Massachusetts Climate Action Network and the Chesapeake Climate

Action Network, are one important element. If there is little organizing and public awareness in a local area, however, an action group of five to twenty-five people can be enough to do significant work. Such a group should have as its goal the awakening of the local public. Using existing community networks is a time-tested method for organizing new groups.

These groups, whether large or small, can respond to news reports about climate problems with a call for change. Whether the news is melting tundra in Alaska or changes in the Greenland ice sheet or a drastic increase in forest fires in the West, a local group needs to help the public see such change as a part of the larger climate crisis picture, and—-at the same time—-a reason for local people to take immediate action. Through issuing press releases and other means of gaining public attention, even a small group can become known as the local voice for climate action.

Such a group might have both a protest/political pressure arm and—in Gandhi's terms—a constructive program arm. For the protest work, the group could select a target goal for the local community and make specific demands: to electric utility companies for more wind farms and no new coal plants; to automobile dealers for low emission vehicles; to local transportation officials for new bike paths, bus improvements, or improved train service; to local industries for emission-lowering strategies.

Other demands will also emerge and can be developed. Nonetheless, it is important at the beginning to pick a small number of targets so that the campaigns can be pointed and communicated to the public clearly. As the movement progresses, activists will see other linkages, and new submovements will emerge to address them.*

Local groups may use nonviolent direct action campaign strategies such as vigils, leafleting, and street theater to bring relevant information to the public. In some communities, it may be possible to gain public attention through press conferences, press kits, and public meetings. Because public education is central to this work, speakers' bureaus and house meetings can be important tools.

---

*A submovement may be focused around a particular issue, such as voting rights or hybrid cars, or may be in a particular local community. Submovements are part of the larger movement, but each submovement may travel through the eight stages at its own pace; some will reach success earlier than others.

In addition, for its constructive program work, the group can promote changes individuals can make, such as the installation of rooftop photovoltaics, driving hybrid cars, or switching to public transportation. Guy Dauncey and Patrick Mazza's book, *Stormy Weather: 101 Solutions to Global Climate Change,*[14] is full of suggestions for both individuals and communities and is a great resource for action groups.

In addition to local community organizing, sector-based organizing is also important. Student mobilization, religious community mobilizations, and business community mobilization have already begun in some places, and these efforts need to be nourished and extended. For example, religious and ethical communities could frame the climate crisis as a an issue of responsible stewardship of "God's creation" as well as a moral issue because developed nations are responsible for an oversized share of global warming, but it is the world's poor who will be most severely affected. Information about the effect of rising sea levels on the small island nations, which will likely be inundated, could be particularly compelling. Religious and ethical groups might build alliances with people in those nations.

In this process of awakening the public, presenting a clear vision for a clean-energy future is essential to help people face the immensity of the crisis and mobilizing their own energies for change. Clear paths of action also need to be made visible. As movement take-off occurs in more and more localities, a convergence of sources can ignite a national movement take-off, perhaps because of a major action campaign, a new climate disaster, or both.

In the civil rights movement, it was understood that when a particular community's nonviolent action campaign seemed to be gaining traction, the movement as a whole could gain by bringing in massive movement resources in support. Such was the case in the Selma, Alabama, voting rights campaign after marchers were attacked on the Edmund Pettus Bridge. Climate activists need to be alert to the possibility of a parallel opportunity.

Stage Five: Perception of Failure: a Detour for Some Activists (Future)

After movement take-off, while work is proceeding to stage six in many arenas, some activists may become discouraged and suffer burnout. Those activists who believed that fundamental change would come on the heels of take-off are especially vulnerable. Some respond by withdrawing from the movement, whereas others may call for more "militant" action, which can threaten the movement's nonviolent identity and undermine the growth of public support. Should this discouragement begin to happen to climate activists, others can respond by encouraging them to move on to the work of stage six or perhaps to shift their work to another corner of the climate movement where take-off has not yet occurred.

Stage Six: Building Majority Public Support (2007 onward)

After movement take-off comes the real work of reaching the vast majority of the public. Public education campaigns and developing constructive "next steps" are the key vehicles for this work. It is important to show how the issue affects people from all segments of society. Different framing of the issue may be needed to reach different groups. As public support widens to a majority and some powerholders support movement goals, the movement can work through mainstream institutions such as state legislatures and professional organizations to win important victories. Local direct-action campaigns continue to be important, especially in response to "retrigger events." During stage six, the movement is engaged in a kind of chess game with the powerholders, in which the powerholders' moves must be immediately countered to ensure ongoing progress.

In the climate movement, the work of stage six will build on and further develop the organizing begun earlier, but strategic shifts will also be needed. Outreach needs to extend to even more sectors of the population, and strategies may involve less nonviolent action, more lobbying, and related tactics as mainstream support builds and it becomes possible to move the climate stabilization agenda forward through mainstream institutions. Actions of the powerholders also become more intense as they sense the public tide turning against them, requiring careful monitoring and creative responses from the movement.

Although climate movement strategies for stage six need to be developed by a broad range of climate activists, the MAP model suggests types of strategies that can be particularly useful at this point in the movement's history. These strategies range from public education programs to direct action campaigns.

Public Education Programs

Activists need to continue and further expand massive public education programs by using speakers' bureaus, the media, study guides for groups, Internet sites, and all other communication tools. Particularly important is the development of targeted public education campaigns for specific audiences, framing the issue in appropriate ways for each audience. Examples include discussion guides for religious and ethically based groups on the ethical implications of global warming, conferences for investors on opportunities in renewable energy, seminars on the effects of global warming on marine life for fishermen and fishing communities as well as recreational anglers, and information on new automobile technologies such as plug-in hybrids for automotive publications. The goal is to reach far beyond those who think of themselves as environmentalists (see chapters 4 and 5).

Constructive Program: Personal and Household Change

A wide variety of people should be engaged in making personal and household changes that individuals can make immediately. Examples are installing solar photovoltaics in homes, driving less, buying low-emission cars, growing gardens, eating locally grown food, and conserving electricity.

Strategic Campaigns

The movement needs to identify key demands and create strategic campaigns for each movement issue. These campaigns could include increasing the number of low and no-emission cars, trucks, and buses (and decreasing the number of standard vehicles); switching electricity generation as quickly as possible from fossil fuels to renewable sources and conservation; and shifting government subsidies from oil and gas to renewable sources such as wind and solar.

Other demands and submovements might focus on expanding the passenger rail system, developing local food systems to minimize transport of food, and building bicycle paths to encourage less driving. Groups already working on these issues could be linked to the climate movement. In addition, as public support grows on these issues and victories can be won, it will be possible to work through mainstream institutions such as city councils and state legislatures.

Respond to Retrigger Events and Continue to Wage Campaigns

To keep the issue on society's agenda, the movement needs to be prepared to respond to "retrigger events" such as new evidence of global warming or powerholders' refusals to act on important issues. Responses can include press conferences, nonviolent actions such as vigils and informational picketing, e-mail blitz campaigns, and other activities that highlight powerholders' violations of widely held values and link their refusal to act with the new problem. The movement will need to respond in creative and publicly visible ways to changes in powerholders' strategies or attempts to offer watered-down solutions.

Continue to Build the Movement

Movement building work is especially important in stage six because we can expect a proliferation of new local groups that, in addition to their work in their own communities, must be coordinated into coalitions to mount larger campaigns. There will be work in organizing, strengthening, and supporting local grassroots groups; offering training in democratic participatory group processes to keep groups vital and keep activists engaged when needed; and advising on strategizing and waging nonviolent campaigns. Models for this kind of work can be found in the Highlander Research and Education Center in Tennessee, which has trained southern activists in many campaigns since the earliest days of the civil rights movement, or in nonviolence training offered by groups such as the Fellowship of Reconciliation, War Resister's League, and Philadelphia's Training for Change.

Develop Alternatives and Articulate the Paradigm Shift

The public may see that powerholders' actions are inadequate, but may not yet be ready to support movement alternatives. Therefore, the desirability and viability of these alternatives need to be highlighted.

In the latter phases of stage six, there is general agreement that action is needed, but massive debate about what to do persists. Can biodiesel and ethanol provide adequate fuel? Should we invest in a massive shield in the atmosphere or a new passenger rail system? Will we try to help the poor countries of the world cope with climate refugees, or will we rebuild our

electricity infrastructure? Will "acceptance of wind farms be our generation's way of avowing our love for the next" as energy analyst Charles
Komanoff suggests?[15]

Anticipating these controversies, activists will need to think long and
hard about the desired future. Will we commit to social justice as well as
ecological sustainability, to democracy and community decision making as well as renewable energy, to what Tom Anathasiou and Paul Baer
call a "social justice approach . . . [with] a necessary compromise
between the North and the South,"[16] the rich and the poor nations? Are
we ready for this movement to be a part of a larger movement for social
transformation toward a just and sustainable future, toward "earth community" as David Korten calls it in his book *The Great Turning: from Empire
to Earth Community?*[17] Global warming is clearly part of a much larger
issue: the need to transition to a fully sustainable society. In addition,
paralleling the climate crisis is a rising crisis in social inequality as
incomes sink at the bottom of the socioeconomic scale both in the United
States and globally, the "war on the middle class" takes its toll, and racial
minorities suffer massive rates of incarceration and other tribulations.
Movements are building to address these issues, and finding common
ground with them will be an important challenge (see chapter 9). Leaders in the climate movement need to support activists in seeing these
larger transformative goals while also encouraging continued focus on
the movement's immediate goals.

Indeed, the larger issue of sustainability can provide a frame for thinking about which choices the movement will support. For example, how
will the movement deal with nuclear power as an option? Nuclear power
is controversial among climate change activists, with some, like James
Lovelock, arguing that it is the only thing that can buy us enough time,
and others, like environmental correspondent Mark Hertsgaard claiming
that our money could take us further toward solutions if invested elsewhere
given the immense costs of nuclear power plant construction.[18] Viewed
from the perspective of long-term sustainability, the health and safety risk

---

* For a dramatic proposal suggesting that rich countries take responsibility to take in climate refugees from poor countries, see Sujatha Byravan and Sudhir Chella Rajan, "Before
the Flood." *New York Times*, May 9, 2005, p.A23.)

of nuclear power make it a weak choice. This controversial issue within the movement will need to be addressed.

During stage six, powerholders will increasingly realize that public support for their position is waning and they will change their strategies. These actions can be important signals of the movement's growing strength, indicating new limitations on the powerholders' options, pushing them to fall-back positions that may have higher costs for them. We need to be aware of such changes and be ready both to publicize them as signs of the movement's growing strength and to counter them creatively.

During this stage as public support grows, we can also anticipate powerholders' attempts both to undermine the movement through efforts to co-opt the movement's goals and rhetoric and to disrupt the movement through surveillance, use of agent provocateurs, and attempts to discredit or control the movement. The movement needs to be prepared to minimize the effect of these undermining efforts. During stage six, there will be multiple coalitions around many issues. Some issues will move quickly to success, whereas others will require sustained organizing.

Stage Seven: Success (Future)

Movement successes can be achieved when the movement has broad public support and many powerholders have been persuaded to support the movement's goals, if only for pragmatic reasons. Success may occur through a dramatic showdown and clear victory, such as the passage of the Voting Rights Act of 1965 after the Selma to Montgomery march. Alternatively, success may be reached through a quiet showdown, such as when a "victorious retreat" is announced by the powerholders, or through attrition, in which old plans are simply shelved and the movement's perspective dominates public decision making. For example, many women's movement victories were won through attrition as women made their way into the previously closed doors of medical schools and law schools. Particularly in cases of quiet showdown and attrition endgames, it is important for the movement to claim the victory so as to help activists see the fruits of their work.

The California-based climate movement achieved an important success with its passage of the 2006 Global Warming Solutions Act. There have been other local successes, especially with serious commitments to change being made by college campuses, cities, and other institutions. Other successes will surely follow. The construction of new coal plants might be stopped. Investor interest in renewable energy sources will help propel forward their adoption. With loud enough customer demand, Toyota could bring its plug-in hybrids to the United States shortly. Public utilities could join the vehicle-to-grid pilot project.

Because local governments have expressed a willingness to act and because some of the needed changes can be made via increased consumer demand and new profitable investments, success could be reached fairly quickly on a number of issues if a massive public education effort can be mounted. Changes at the national level will be likely only at the end of long struggle.

Stage Eight: Continuing the Struggle (Future)

After victory is achieved, the movement's work is not over. Some activists must monitor implementation of agreements and guard against backlash. Others can go on to work on another movement goal, share movement energy with new movements, or move toward broader social transformation.

California will give early clues to the unfolding of this work. Activists there will need to support, monitor, and publicize implementation of its wide-ranging 2006 law.

Finally, we need to remember that activism is fundamentally an act of the heart. People need to be in touch with what they love, and when they feel that threatened or in some other way in need of them, they will respond. Ideas and policies are important and can inform that action, but the motivation to act comes from our caring, for our friends, our family, our children, about the earth, and about one another. We must not hesitate to articulate our own caring because it will help other people find theirs.

People are also motivated to act because they want to make a difference, they want to believe that there is meaning to their lives, they want to believe that they can make a meaningful contribution. Taking action to bring change can bring a new sense of dignity. As we organize, we need to make space for people in our communities to claim that sense of meaning and dignity in the work.

We also need to keep our hearts open to all who might join with us. Barbara Deming, a longtime nonviolent activist, poet, and theoretician, urges us to remember the "two hands" of nonviolence: one hand raised, saying no to injustice, and the other hand extended, reaching out to one's opponent, seeking reconciliation and inviting them to join the movement.[19] She reminds us that we are all part of the problem as well as part of the solution and that although we must be strong in our refusal to support injustice, we must also be ready to extend our hand and welcome those who decide to join us further down the line, even those who once opposed us. Our goal is to build a new consensus, a new society, and we need to have faith that even the most recalcitrant can be brought around to join us.

My hopes are that we will find a way to communicate a sense of possibility to the American public and that together we can see in this transformation of our way of life a new richness in our connection to one another and to the natural world upon which all that we know and love depends. It is the climate that surrounds us.

PART II:

Finding Your Voice

4. Irrationality Wants to Be Your Friend

KENTON DE KIRBY

PAMELA MORGAN

TED NORDHAUS

MICHAEL SHELLENBERGER

IN HIS 2005 BEST SELLER, *Collapse*, evolutionary biologist Jared Diamond describes the "irrational motives" behind past ecological collapses. He points to groupthink, crowd psychology, and denial.[1] In a particularly evocative example, Diamond describes the psychology of people who live beneath dams as a kind of metaphor for contemporary attitudes toward today's most pressing ecological crises, such as global warming:

> People living immediately under the dam, the ones most certain to be drowned in a dam burst, profess unconcern. That's because of psychological denial: the only way of preserving one's sanity while looking up every day at the dam is to deny the possibility that it could burst.[2]

For Diamond, the remedy is to present people with more facts about the threat as well as stories of past tragedies.

Imagine for a moment, though, that it was your mother who lived immediately under the dam and refused to move. You've provided her with scientific facts that the dam is likely to explode. You've told her stories of how similar dams have burst in the past, killing everyone in its wake. Still she won't budge.

What do you do? In this chapter, we offer some ideas, both for mothers who won't budge and for those fellow citizens who seem to be sitting around as global warming accelerates. In the spirit of building a movement, we aim to challenge several of your assumptions.

The Nature of Global Warming Denial

Are Americans in denial about global warming? From one perspective, the answer is no: the vast majority of voters accept the facts about climate change. A June 2006 poll conducted by the Pew Research Center for People and the Press found that 70 percent of voters believe that there is "solid evidence" that the earth is warming, and most of that 70 percent believe that the earth is warming due to human activities. Forty-one percent say global warming is "very serious." Only 20 percent of Americans say that the earth is not warming, and another 21 percent say that it is warming but not because of humans.[3] The bottom line? Most Americans are not in denial.

From another perspective, though, the answer is yes, most Americans *are* in denial about the seriousness of the threat. Although 70 percent believe the facts about global warming, only a minority believes that it is "very serious," and strikingly few Americans name global warming as a top national priority. Here's Pew:

> While 41% say global warming is a very serious problem, 33% see it as somewhat serious and roughly a quarter (24%) think it is either not too serious or not a problem at all. Consequently, the issue ranks as a relatively low public priority, well behind education, the economy, and the war in Iraq. . . . Indeed, out of a list of 19 issues, Republicans rank global warming 19th and Democrats and Independents rank it 13th.[4]

By January 2007, global warming's ranking dropped even lower, Pew found, to 21 for Republicans, 17th for Democrats, and 19th for Independents.[5]

That ranking may be misleadingly high because the Pew survey actually offered respondents global warming as an issue to choose from. Other surveys that ask the question in an open-ended way—for example, What is the most important issue facing the country?—find that vanishingly few respondents name global warming. That is why global warming is rarely discussed at election time. Politicians know that there are far more higher-priority issues that influence how people vote. The June 2006 Pew survey was conducted at the height of the publicity around Al Gore's documentary about global warming, *An Inconvenient Truth*. It was then that *Time* magazine published a cover story headlined, "Be Worried, Be Very Worried," and virtually every media outlet, including Fox News, communicated the stark facts about global warming. Yet through it all, Americans mostly yawned.

All that strikes many of us as profoundly illogical. How could so many people continue to believe that gay marriage (fifteenth in the survey for Republicans) or the minimum wage (eighth in the survey for Democrats) is more important than *life on this planet as we know it?* Don't they realize that if global warming continues unchecked, there won't be either gay marriage or a minimum wage *because our civilization will have collapsed?*

From *What* We Think to *How* We Think

Diamond is the author of two books and dozens of articles on how natural selection produced human beings.[6] He knows that the human capacity for reason emerged in very specific evolutionary contexts. He knows that humans have made extraordinary progress over the last 150 years toward understanding human psychology. In *Collapse*, however, he ignores all that out of the faith that more facts about past collapses will overcome allegedly irrational denial.

Collapse, like most environmental advocacy, is premised on a set of Enlightenment-era assumptions about human nature that date back some four hundred years:

1. People are essentially rational.
2. There is but one single rationality. All else is irrational.
3. Rationality is conscious (that is, we choose to be rational or irrational).
4. Rationality is sometimes clouded or eclipsed by fear and other emotions.
5. Rational decisions are better than irrational decisions.
6. Denial is a kind of irrationality.

7. Irrationality, and hence denial, can be overcome by more information: facts, cautionary tales, and so on.

Over the last hundred years, however, a very different scientific consensus has emerged in the *social* sciences.

1. Human capacity for reasoning is adaptive, which means that it was selected for during thousands of years of hominid evolution.
2. There is no single faculty for reasoning. Rather, human reasoning borrows from many different parts of the brain.
3. How humans reason is specific to particular contexts, cultures, and moments in time. There is no single, transcendent Reason, but rather there exist many rationalities.
4. What is perfectly rational in one context may be utterly irrational in another.
5. Most rationalities are "stored" in the unconscious.
6. There is no such thing as emotion-free reasoning. Every rationality is animated by emotion.
7. Every emotion—from fear to anger to hope to determination—is itself a kind of rationality.
8. Rationalities are best understood not as essential "things," but rather as constantly changing processes, narratives, and logics.

As it turns out, the human animal is far more complex than was supposed four hundred years ago.

Why Are People So Dam(n) Irrational?

We tend to curse "irrationality"—our tendency to, say, spend more time thinking about *American Idol* than about the coming eco-apocalypse—but much that we today consider irrational at one point made very good evolutionary sense. Start by recalling that our ancestors, human and nonhuman, were *prey*. Other animals, human and nonhuman, chased and sometimes ate them. Of course, every human on the earth today comes from a long line of ancestors who all survived long enough to reproduce. In short, we exist because our ancestors were "rational" enough to survive a whole range of threats, and not just from predators. Most of our rationalities operate at an *unconscious* level, which should be understood less as a cauldron of Freudian anxieties and more as a vast storage bank of instincts, intuitions, calculations, and motivations that we are only beginning to understand.

Shortly after the release of Gore's *An Inconvenient Truth*, Harvard psychologist Daniel Gilbert wrote an op-ed piece called "If Only Gay Sex Caused Global Warming," making a very similar point:

> We are the progeny of people who hunted and gathered, whose lives were brief and whose greatest threat was a man with a stick. When terrorists attack, we respond with crushing force and firm resolve, just as our ancestors would have. Global warming is a deadly threat precisely because it fails to trip the brain's alarm, leaving us soundly asleep in a burning bed.[7]

Once we understand this point, certain threat-and-response patterns make good sense. For example, we respond most strongly to things that we can form a mental image of, such as the ax murderer we fear will burst through our bedroom window. We respond best to immediate threats, such as when he actually does. We react decisively to threats that involve abrupt changes in our sense perceptions of the world, which is why we find ourselves running away from the man we see swinging an ax long before we ever bother to ask ourselves, Who the heck *is* that guy? In short, that's why we spend so much more time and effort fortifying our homes from virtually nonexistent rampaging ax murderers than we do protesting the invisible climate menace.

Of course, survival for our ancestors demanded more than acute perception and physical agility. It also meant successfully interacting with our fellow humans. These relationships are governed by social rules. Given the importance of these rules governing our interdependence, we tend to respond with great emotional intensity when there is a *social* component to the threat, such as when someone breaks the rules of our society through greed, malice, or other iniquitous motivation (for example, some traitor in our midst was paid to help a whole tribe of ax murderers invade our village). We also respond most intensely when the problem involves something we find morally repugnant (for example, they went after our women and children first).

All these criteria (and many others too numerous to list) determine the ways we prioritize threats. The more criteria a threat fulfills and the greater degree to which it is fulfilled, the more likely we are to turn our attention to that threat (for example, ax murderers, terrorists, or, as Gilbert parodies, gay sex), to the neglect of others (global warming). These criteria are not destiny, but our overwhelming and largely unconscious tendency is to continue to use what worked for us in our evolutionary past.

Taken together, these criteria tell us we're not very likely to put global warming at the top of our list of threats. We cannot form a powerful mental image of global warming. It involves no sudden change in our sense perceptions. It may be happening quickly from a geological perspective, but, alas, global warming is happening quite slowly from an ordinary human perspective.

Lately, some environmentalists have taken to insisting zealously that global warming is a "moral issue." Yet we fear that these jeremiads will mostly fall on deaf ears. Despite the temptation to personify global warming as an evil cartoon character—as *Simpson's* creator Matt Groening did for Gore in *An Inconvenient Truth*—global warming feels about as menacing to most Americans as, well, a cartoon character. As much as we may despise oil executives, very few of us believe that they are the sole or even main cause of global warming. That's why the dominant discourse about global warming, as discussed in chapter 5, is that *we have met the enemy and the enemy is us*. Some causes of global warming—driving to work, making toast for our child's breakfast, and turning up the air conditioner on an unusually hot summer's day—are neither evil nor dangerous nor dramatic. Rather, they are banal, ordinary, and perfectly moral.

None of that is to say there is some "essential human nature" that dooms us to destroy the world and ourselves in it. On the contrary, we humans have many natures and ways of reasoning. To paraphrase Walt Whitman, we contain multitudes. The challenge for the climate change movement is neither to change our natures nor to demand human obedience to some transcendent and singular Reason, but rather to put particular natures and irrationalities in service of overcoming ecological crises.

Seeing the Rational in the Irrational

Beyond understanding how human irrationalities are rooted in our evolutionary history, we must, through a kind of psychological judo, turn the irrational to our advantage. Consider that people tend to *under*estimate the likelihood of an unpleasant event if they believe that they have no control over its occurrence. The more powerless people feel about their ability to deal with a particular problem, the more likely they are to believe that it's not such a big threat. Such is the logic of the person living underneath a dam at risk of exploding: *I can't afford to move; therefore, that dam is not going to explode.* This attitude strikes us as utterly irrational, but there's no advantage to despairing over things outside of our control. In fact, unnecessarily despairing has all sorts of *dis*advantages (like believing there is no way we can possibly outrun that ax murderer).

The implication is fairly dramatic. *The more powerless people feel about global warming, the less likely they are to believe that it is a major problem.*

Now imagine how powerless the dominant eco-tragedy and apocalypse narratives make people feel. Many environmentalists—and liberal movie critics—walked out of *An Inconvenient Truth* feeling excited and happy because they believed that *now Americans are finally going to get it.* Well, we believe that Americans "got it" all right: they got that global warming is so overwhelming that there is little they can do about it. After ninety minutes of overwhelming evidence that global warming has arrived and that it could trigger violent cataclysms, why would anyone believe that buying fluorescent lightbulbs and hybrid cars could ever be enough? Katherine Ellison aptly captured the feelings of many in an op-ed she wrote for the *New York Times* after seeing *An Inconvenient Truth*:

> Well, I for one am very, very worried. As the mother of two
> young boys, I want to do everything I can to protect their
> future. But I feel like a shnook buying fluorescent light bulbs—
> as Environmental Defense recommends—when at last count,
> China, India and the United States were building a total of 850
> new coal-fired power plants.[8]

The bottom line is that most people walked out of *An Inconvenient Truth* feeling disempowered, not empowered, which is why the June

2006 Pew survey found that global warming remains far down the list of the public's priorities.

How can we turn this irrational predisposition—the tendency to underestimate global warming's importance—to our favor? For starters, we can help people feel powerful enough to deal with the cataclysmic effects of global warming. That in itself will require a lot more than better lightbulbs and more efficient appliances.

The Perils of the Blame Game

Nobody likes to be blamed for anything. We are less likely to acknowledge a threat that makes us feel guilty than a threat that does not. Our dislike at acknowledging our responsibility often motivates denial that the threat is real, immediate, or urgent. Even when we do something we know is bad, we *still* don't want to be blamed for it.

In focus groups the four of us conducted in July 2006, we found that resistance to feeling personally responsible is an important factor driving denial about the human causes of global warming. The focus groups were held with moderately conservative voters in St. Louis, about half of who indicated on a form they filled out beforehand that they were skeptical that global warming was either a problem or human caused. (This mixed-gender focus group, middle-aged and up, included a manager, a teacher, a sales representative, a trucker, and a homemaker. The psychographically determined group on the basis of which the members were recruited is characterized as predominantly low-income, poorly educated southerners who are economic populists, aspirational, culturally conservative, and survival oriented and who blend a belief in active government with individual responsibility, and national pride with global consciousness.)

When the moderator introduced global warming in a general way, the participants refused to accept any blame:

> **MAN 4:** And the global warming thing is a bone with me also. Yes, it is warming, but how do we know that it is a man-made thing and not a natural cycle of nature? We haven't had records go back far enough in my estimation to know.

MAN 1: I'd like to agree with him on that because I think, from what I understand about science, the volcanoes cause the hole in the atmosphere, and all the hoo-ha about global warming is kind of blown out of proportion from what is really true.

WOMAN 1: I agree, I don't think my deodorant is doing it. [Laughter]

This problem is compounded even more. When the acknowledgment of a given threat is tied conceptually to actions perceived as unpalatable—such as radically downgrading one's quality of life—we are less likely to admit either that there is a threat or that it is very serious. Yet that's exactly what Gore does in *An Inconvenient Truth*. He emphasizes how unpalatable the change demanded by global warming will be. "The truth about the climate crisis," Gore stresses, "is an inconvenient one that means we are going to have to change the way we live our lives."[9]

These warnings have apparently taken their toll. According to Pew's pollsters, "whereas just 23 percent of voters believe technology can solve global warming, 39 percent reported that 'major sacrifices' would be required."[10]

Don't Be So Certain

The assumption among environmentalists has long been that if the public realized the high degree of certainty scientists have about global warming, they would demand action to curb greenhouse gases. That was the assumption behind the part of *An Inconvenient Truth* where Gore pointed to a review of journal articles that found that not a single scientist disagreed that anthropogenic global warming is under way.

The Gore movie was released on May 24, 2006, and it generated more media coverage of global warming than the issue had ever received in the United States. It was on the covers of *Time*, *Wired*, and *Vanity Fair*, and it received extensive newspaper, television, and radio coverage. Environmentalists excitedly e-mailed each other to crow that *the tipping point is here!* and *the debate is over!* Nobody, environmentalists assured themselves, could any longer continue to deny the facts of global warming.

Of course, denying the facts of global warming was precisely what global warming deniers did. Exxon-funded activists at the Competitive Enterprise Institute produced two ads attacking the science of global warming as uncertain and the consequences of action as severe (one ad showed a man attempting to ride his bicycle in a blizzard). The ads were picked up and parodied in media outlets such as Jon Stewart's *The Daily Show*. These parodies helped communicate that *there is, in fact, still a debate over the science of global warming.* The irony is that there would be no debate if environmentalists stopped insisting that scientific certainty be at the center of their global warming proposals.

The ordinary person's understanding of "scientific certainty" is quite different from a highly educated environmentalist's understanding. Scientists will move forward when there is overwhelming consensus among people with appropriate credentials, even if not everyone in the debate agrees. "Certainty" in the scientific setting is qualified: it equates to "not really subject to *serious* dispute." The layperson's or folk understanding, by contrast, is far more literal. The global warming denier's argument that there's no certainty because there's still debate about the causes of global warming shares the widespread folk concept of certainty—100 percent, absolute, doubt-free agreement—and is therefore able to undermine environmentalists by means of even one dissenter. Given this argument, it's quite understandable that all groups like the Competitive Enterprise Institute have to do to sow doubts is to point to one or two scientists, such as MIT climatologist Richard S. Lindzen. What's less understandable is why environmentalists continue to engage in this endless debate.

In our focus groups, we tried a different tack, one that emphasized not *certainty* but rather *uncertainty* as the basis for action. The moderator introduced weather forecasting as a metaphor, which changed everything.

> **MODERATOR:** It sounds like what you're saying is that, you're not quite sure about exactly how far we should go, but at the very least, people should know what the probability is. They can make their own decision. [If] 3 out of 4 weathermen say it's going to rain, you can decide whether or not to take an umbrella when you go out.

MAN: Exactly. Like Bridget said earlier, weathermen don't always get it right but I still find myself listening to see what they have to say.

The focus group participants became willing to discuss aspects of preparedness such as evacuation routes and property disclosure requirements because they assume a degree of uncertainty is inherent to predicting weather. *Uncertainty in the context of weather and natural disasters is therefore a stimulus rather than a barrier to action.*

Global Warming Preparedness

What kind of a proposal would avoid triggering the psychological barriers described above? Looking over the territory we have just covered, we can infer that it makes sense to define the problem in a particular way:

- It does not make people feel guilty.
- It does not threaten their self-image.
- It involves abrupt changes perceivable by the senses (that is, they are readily distinguishable, discrete events).
- It is immediate.
- It is easy to represent by a mental image.
- It is not perceived as requiring tremendous sacrifices and other unpleasant consequences.
- It does not require absolute certainty.
- It gives people a greater sense of control.

Is such a proposal possible? We believe it is. Our proposal for global warming preparedness recasts global warming in terms of preparation for natural disasters and extreme weather. It fulfills each of the criteria listed above and is the best chance we have for increasing the salience of climate change in the mind of the public.

Natural disasters are something with which we are all familiar and thus can easily imagine. They are dramatic and easily visualized. Most of us no longer believe that anybody is to blame for them. They allow us to respond to well-defined problems and focus on clear and workable solutions. Preparing for them well and responding to them effectively enhances one's self-image rather than threatening it.

Most important is that natural disasters are inherently unpredictable. We prepare for them because they are *uncertain*, not because they are certain. We don't know when, where, how, or even whether they will strike. Their uncertainty effectively short-circuits the endless back-and-forth debates about whether global warming is being caused by humans and whether it will create overwhelming disasters. No longer would a handful of scientists who have doubts about global warming be available as trump cards for front groups like the Competitive Enterprise Institute.

To be sure, some opponents of action on global warming will continue to sanguinely argue that no action is necessary because when the time comes we will simply adapt to the changing climate. Global warming preparedness, however, turns those arguments on their head by positing that *the time to adapt is now* and that *rather than passively "adapting," we should actively "prepare."*

By divorcing the question of human contribution from the reality and immediacy of the threat, one is able to advocate reducing carbon levels in the atmosphere regardless of whether one believes that climate change is 100 percent human caused. In this context, it is far more likely people will believe that if we are contributing to global warming, no matter whether it is in whole or in part, we should do what we can to prevent the problem from worsening.

Irrationality Wants to Be Your Friend

Even if humans had stopped emitting greenhouse gases starting in 1988, when NASA scientist James Hansen first announced to Congress that global warming had arrived, all the changes today resulting from global warming—the melting of Greenland's ice sheet, the collapse of the North Atlantic Gulf Stream, warmer ocean surfaces and more intense hurricanes—would still be under way. That's because there is a roughly two- to three-decade delay between when greenhouse gases reach the atmosphere and when the earth's temperatures rise. So much carbon and other greenhouse gases are in the atmosphere that even if humans stopped emitting new greenhouse gases tomorrow, the planet would continue to heat up for at least several more decades and maybe longer.

For years, environmentalists such as Diamond have believed that denial is a consequence of the public not being scared enough. We believe, however, that what voters need and want are not more frightening facts and cautionary tales, but rather a way to overcome their perfectly rational fears through concrete actions. The public correctly realizes that lightbulbs and hybrid cars are not the solution to hurricanes, droughts, and fires. What the public needs are preparatory solutions to deal with those potential global warming disasters. Once people have accepted that global warming is an immediate threat worth preparing for—an acceptance that global warming preparedness shows great promise in cultivating—the question of wider action can resume, but this time without the baggage of human culpability weighing it down.

This point goes counter to what environmentalists have long held to be true. They have believed that arguments for preparedness are either separate from—or even obstacles to—winning action on global warming. They have imagined human reasoning to be linear, literal, and logical. It is not. When people embrace global warming preparedness, they have made a commitment to one kind of action on global warming. This commitment is the foundation for future action.

Consider what happened at the end of one of the focus groups in St. Louis. After everyone else had left the room, two of the most defensive, outright deniers of global warming lingered behind and collected their things slowly, as though seeking each other out to talk some more. From behind our one-way mirror we watched, dumbfounded, as these two global warming deniers chatted in an animated and nondefensive way about the questionable ethics of owning gas-guzzling SUVs and the relative virtues of more fuel efficient cars. During the two-hour focus group, we had provided them with no "facts" about global warming—about the role played by cars, SUVs, or power plants—and had told no cautionary parables about past civilizational collapses. All we had done was facilitate a conversation about the uncertainty of weather events and natural disasters, the effects of global warming, and the need to prepare for them. All they had done was embrace the need for global warming preparedness.

In embracing global warming preparedness, we make a commitment to supporting action on global warming. It is a commitment that doesn't require people to admit their guilt or responsibility, thus triggering their rejection of the whole thing. Yet it is a commitment nonetheless, one that can, over time, be grown into a much more expansive agenda.

The Meaning of Global Warming

Environmentalists have long imagined that global warming has a single, objective meaning (our greenhouse gas emissions are warming the earth) and an obvious solution (we need to reduce our greenhouse gas emissions). The problem is that there is simply no single meaning of global warming. Rather, global warming contains multitudes. Does global warming mean (a) we'll be growing bigger and sweeter tomatoes in northern California, (b) we're all going to die, (c) we humans will survive but will find ourselves living like prehistoric cave dwellers, (d) we are being punished for our sins against nature, (e) we need better lightbulbs and hybrid cars, (f) we must unite the human race around a vision for a clean energy future, (g) finally we can build those nuclear power plants we always wanted, (h) we need a cap-and-trade system for carbon emissions, (i) we must prepare for the worst and hope for the best, (j) none of the above, or (k) all of the above?

Plainly, global warming has other meanings and other solutions. The question is not, What does global warming mean? Instead, it is, Which of global warming's meanings and solutions should we elevate into a politics to help create the future we want?

Turning the debate away from certainty and prevention to uncertainty and preparedness changes the way people think about global warming itself. Global warming preparedness changes the meaning of global warming. It is necessary, in and of itself, and it is a bridge to wider action. Once people accept that global warming is happening they are on their way to asking, If there is something I can do to cope with the effects of global warming, is there also something I can do to lessen those effects to begin with?

The authors thank the Nathan Cummings Foundation for funding the research that made this work possible.

5. Communication Strategies

SUSANNE MOSER

> There is more than a verbal tie between the words
> common, community, and communication.
>
> John Dewey, *Democracy and Education*, 1916

IMAGINE TRYING TO BUILD A social movement without communication: neither spoken word nor written text, nor pictures worth a thousand words, nor even body language. No leaflets, no e-mails, no campaign ads, no slogans, no clever symbols or taglines, no op-eds in the newspapers, no books or articles in magazines, no TV spots, no megaphones, no nothing. It would be impossible. Successful movements require effective means of communication and, just as important, effective manners of communication. How we speak about an issue, about solutions, and about our goals makes all the difference for building an effective campaign and movement.

That is exactly what John Dewey meant in the quote opening this chapter: that what we share in common, what we treasure in our communities, and how we communicate with others about our hopes and dreams all foster one another. In fact, the word *communicate* comes from a Latin word that means "to impart," "to share," and "to make common." In turn, the word *common* derives from the two roots *com-*, or "together," and *munia*, or "public duties." As Mary Lou Finley details in chapter 3, if building a movement means bringing together the many to take on a public matter of great concern, it is easy to see why communication has to play a critical role. So the message of this chapter is simply that carefully designed communication strategies lay the groundwork for long-term success of the climate movement.

Climate science has grown more confident and compelling over the years, yet far too many people—from public officials to industry leaders to soccer moms—remain unconcerned and disengaged. Why? Over time, I have come to believe ever more firmly that it is a failure of communication.

Communication is absolutely essential to engaging the greatest number of people in solving the climate problem. Global warming challenges society—us—to our deepest core. We must reexamine our relationship to nature and to one another; we must re-create common ground, community, and a common sense of purpose; and we must do so through effective communication: scientists to policy makers and the public, advocates to those not yet engaged, people to people.

First and foremost, communication is the most basic means by which we express a movement's focus. It helps create a lens through which we view matters of concern and understand their deeper causes, implications, and solutions. As such, communication is a critical means by which we set the stage for a movement.

Communication, however, is not only about speaking. It is about being heard. Communication works when it helps us form a connection between speaker and listener. If we speak in ways that scare or annoy listeners so much that they turn away from us or if we speak in a way that confuses or misinforms them, we have missed the opportunity to make that connection, to get attention for an issue, and maybe to create a new advocate in a previously unengaged community.

Maybe more essential is that the way we frame an issue allows us to chart the territory of what is right and what is wrong, providing the moral compass essential to rallying public support. Are we persuasive to only a few or to the many? With what language do we try to encourage and mobilize a still-uninvolved public? Who do we include or exclude by the way we communicate the problem? Can we create, negotiate, and express an engaging vision around which people can unite? Whether at the kitchen table or by word of mouth among neighbors, through community campaigns, or with the help of the media, communication can be an effective and efficient means to connect people across geographic distances and—if successful—social divides.

In this chapter, the importance of framing an issue is discussed, leading to eight communication tasks for building and sustaining the climate movement. Ten somewhat paradoxical strategies for communication that aim to ignite and sustain the climate movement as it emerges are also suggested.

The Importance of Framing

Around the time of the 2004 U.S. presidential election, the importance of "framing," popularized by University of California, Berkeley cognitive scientist George Lakoff, was recognized by many political leaders and social change agents. According to Lakoff, frames—expressed through and triggered by language, images, and even gestures—are "mental structures that shape the way we see the world." They "shape the goals we seek, the plans we make, the way we act, and what counts as good or bad outcome of our actions." Frames are the baskets of associations with certain ideas that we gather over a lifetime and carry unconsciously in our brains. As such, frames can be powerful levers in movement building. So it is critical for movement leaders to identify the most powerful frame(s) to mobilize the actors one wishes to engage—as a movement starts, and as it then builds.[1]

Think of how the leaders of Mothers Against Drunk Driving conceived a highly effective frame when they chose their name. The frame here hinges on "mother" and our cultural archetype of the deeply concerned and caring mother. It is only made more forceful by the group's acronym, which adds the emotional charge that we all can relate to so well. These mothers are not only caring and concerned; they are that and MADDeningly so. Any politician who would dare resist the power of such a frame would probably not fare well with his or her electorate. The decrease in deaths from drunk driving since the 1970s—via tougher state legislation championed by active MADD chapters—owes a lot to the way this successful frame focused the attention of voters and politicians.

It's clear we need a frame that similarly charges us to take action. Global warming for years was framed as the "greenhouse effect" or as a "carbon dioxide problem." Others have tried to reframe it as part of the broader "sustainability" discussion or cast it in terms of "social justice and human rights." So far, none of these frames has been compelling to the majority of Americans. Yet the implications are profound in terms of what we believe the ultimate problem to be about, how serious and urgent we feel it is, how much it should worry us, with whom the issue resonates, and who engages in the search for solutions. By contrast, framing climate change as an "energy security" or even "national security" issue may be more likely to engage military families and leaders of small businesses than a "save the polar bears" frame ever would. As detailed in part III of this book, public health and spiritual stewardship are proving to be two powerful frames for building the climate movement. It may not be the last word on framing the climate problem, but we can learn important lessons about what resonates when and with whom as the climate movement builds. Let's turn to what movement members need to consider as they try to communicate the problem, strategies, and goals.

Eight Core Communication Tasks for the Climate Change Movement

The roles of communication in social movements can be broken into specific tasks, depending on the movement's progress. Over the eight stages of a successful social movement described in chapter 3, the emphases, content, and audiences of these tasks will change. In this section, eight communication tasks that roughly map to each of those stages of a social movement are detailed: normal times, proving the failure of existing institutions, ripening conditions, take-off, perception of failure, building majority support, success, and continuing the struggle.

Problem Framing and Social and Political Agenda Setting

The first communication task of a movement during "normal times" is to establish that there *is* a problem. In some social movements, of course, problems are easily identified by those who are directly affected. That is certainly true of social injustices with a clear victim, such as racial and ethnic discrimination or unjust treatment of women. In the case of climate change, however, scientists first detected and defined the problem before anyone else could clearly see it.

Who initially defines the problem has important implications for the ensuing public discussion. Issue framers—no matter who they are—are affiliated with certain societal subgroups and are thus endowed with a certain public image. Just notice the difference you experience if you're being told about the seriousness of climate change by a scientist versus a clergywoman versus a businessman versus an environmental advocate versus a member of Congress. For the general public, the framer's image may carry varying amounts of credibility, prestige, political influence, and legitimacy. Rosa Parks—a woman, tired, if well prepared for this moment, claiming a seat in the front of a bus, dignified, determined, and civically minded—proved to be an outstanding representative for the American civil rights movement in its earliest stages as she and other leaders framed the problem of institutionalized discrimination against African Americans.

One type of issue framer is not necessarily preferable to another: one who is directly affected by global warming's consequences need not be more effective than a scientist studying them, or vice versa. Climate activists, however, do need to be aware of the influence that different issue framers will have on the importance and relevance of the issue in public circles, on its trajectory, indeed on the shaping of the movement itself. For example, in the 1990s, when the "greenhouse effect" was far and away the dominant climate change frame, global warming discussions were dominated by scientific experts. That marked the issue as "technical" and therefore impenetrable to many (surely one needs a PhD to understand it!). This framing, together with the considerable uncertainties in scientific understanding and the size of the problem, set climate change up as a matter still up for debate. In fact, it was the perfect setup for a "battle between the experts": on one hand, climate scientists with high credibility and demonstrated track records in the peer-reviewed literature; on the other hand, the (typically fossil fuel–industry funded) climate naysayers who could easily drum up an "expert" of their own, usually a PhD-carrying scientist with little or no track record in peer-reviewed climate journals. Such discussions were communicated to the public primarily through the media, for whom "dueling experts" were ideal to maintain objectivity through "balanced reporting." For the public, it was (and still is) hard to discern who's right, providing a good reason to stay on the sidelines before taking sides. The point here is that the framing—through words, images, and messengers—invites some people into a movement while others keep out, and thus who is involved in the conversation shapes what it is and isn't about. Framing thus commits some people to an issue and allows others to disengage, which is why movements have to pay attention to it.

Widening the Circles through Education and Persuasion

The next task is to clearly present the causes and implications of the large-scale societal problem and what it would mean not to act. At this stage, communicators must convey that credible solutions do exist. After all, a problem without a solution, and especially one in which individuals can't see their part in it, is unlikely to attract the masses.

Until recently, this job was particularly challenging in the case of global warming because it was so difficult to see its effects. Signs are emerging now in all corners of the United States, however, and people are beginning to believe that something "odd" may be going on. Certainly the string of hurricanes in 2004 and 2005 got many wondering. Was Hurricane Katrina a sign of things to come? Yet even though public understanding of the matter is improving and opinions are shifting in a variety of ways, the level of concern among Americans is actually just now, after many years of decline, back to where it was in 1989.[2] Others may view a 2006 survey by the Pew Center for People and the Press as encouraging: nearly half (49%) of Americans say it is very to extremely important for the 2008 U.S. presidential candidates to state their plans to deal with global warming.[3] Although it would be an enormously important shift for climate change to become an election issue, the communication challenge doesn't stop there. Because the human causes of global warming are so deeply embedded in the energy, production, and land use systems that make up our modern lives, it can be a tall order to convince any one individual that his or her actions will make a difference in this worldwide, systemic problem. The communication challenge is to convince people that their actions are part of a large-scale, collective effort to developing and implementing clean-energy solutions. Once they believe that, they are much more likely to actually do something.

Demonstrating the Failure of Existing Institutions and the Need for Political Change

Communicators must also demonstrate that those who should be tackling the problem are not doing so, or perhaps they are pretending to do so while not advancing real solutions at all. We must show how existing institutions are failing to meet the challenge before them.

For the climate movement, this task is not easy or clear-cut given the collective nature of the climate crisis. We are all—as individuals and in our businesses, civic organizations, local, state, and national governments—implicated in the problem by our own daily use of fossil fuels. The difficult conclusion actually is that we all are "in charge" and are not doing our part well enough so far. At the same time, we must not let our elected leaders off the hook simply because we are all not doing enough.

In addition, climate change has no quick fix. Building a portfolio of potential solutions will be a daunting task. We must be careful not to adopt "solutions" that don't alleviate the climate problem or that aggravate other environmental or social problems. Moreover, with climate change well under way, mitigating the problem—that is, curbing heat-trapping gas emissions—must be complemented with efforts aimed at adapting to the changing environment. It is quite possible that this complex policy terrain may divide the focus of our collective attention. Therefore, it is critical that in the next few years climate activists not take their eyes off of this ball: the national climate change policies to date have been deeply inadequate, and that must be forcefully communicated to voters, at every turn.

Crossing Boundaries Across Social Divides

Let's face it: if we only talk to like-minded people, we may feel good about having a wonderful circle of friends, but our ideas will have limited reach. A wide range of evidence suggests that even the best technical innovations are not guaranteed to spread across rigid social boundaries. Thus, the task of a social movement is to find ways to reach across the boundaries that separate likely movement members from less likely ones, including those who may have been turned off by the debate to date. As detailed by Jonathan Isham Jr. and Sissel Waage in chapter 1, we must build many bridges to engage the social capital available in all sectors of society effectively.

It is challenging for communicators to cross the divides that separate different ethnic groups, socioeconomic classes, age cohorts, party affiliations, religions, or other associations of social engagement. It requires more than simply the reframing of language; rather, it requires addressing the substance, the very focus of activist struggles. In fact, this challenge has been seen lately within the environmental and progressive movement. The recent hot debate over the "death of environmentalism" between its authors and members of the environmentalist establishment and those on its fringes serves as a good example of this type of struggle. Essentially, Nordhaus and Shellenberger (see also chapter 4) criticized the establishment, "Washington-insider" environmental groups as having become too technocratic and lost in intractable policy debates rather than providing a compelling vision around which to engage the wider movement and the public. The harsh critique spawned a firestorm of defense and counterattacks by members of the environmental community and some scientists.[4] Such struggles—although perhaps uncomfortable and seemingly divisive—are actually part of forming broader coalitions.

To build bridges successfully, climate activists will need cultural and political sensitivity, linguistic vigilance, and strategic creativity. It is encouraging to see many examples of that occurring as the climate movement coalesces. For example, when Bill McKibben, distinguished writer and author of this book's introduction, teamed up in 2001 with some local religious leaders in Massachusetts to launch the "What Would Jesus Drive Campaign" (www.whatwouldjesusdrive.org), it sparked a campaign nationwide. This campaign, which became one of the first manifestations of the growing concern in the evangelical community about the climate crisis, captures the importance of framing and the role that framing can play in uniting communities that have historically had little to say to each other.

Sustaining and Managing the Movement

Another critical task for communicators is to sustain the movement through the inevitable slow times of a long social struggle. Part of the explanation for the inevitable ups and downs can be attributed to the "issue-attention cycle." No one—neither movement members, nor the media, nor politicians—can sustain the focus on one thing alone, however important, for a long time. Interest waxes and wanes.

This communication task may not seem particularly exciting, but its importance cannot be overstated for the climate movement. Global warming—quite different from more localized environmental struggles of earlier times—will be a problem for at least the next few generations. Quite possibly, it will seem to be a worsening problem *even if* the emerging climate movement puts up its best fight, *even if* the United States manages to reduce its heat-trapping gas emissions quickly and significantly, and *even if* the large developing countries such as China and India can be engaged constructively. Momentum of the movement would be hard to maintain *even if* there were no political opposition, and it's clear that this movement will have its entrenched opponents for some time. As communicators, we will need to watch out for these cycles and develop strategies for the uptimes as well as the downtimes.

Building Community and Countering Isolation

As members of all social movements know so well, the opposition is, in some sense, also a movement. It uses its own set of framing, organizing, and political strategies. A tried-and-true tool for any opposition is to create the impression that the movement is an unsavory collection of isolated individuals and marginalized organizations trying to push for unnecessary changes to the status quo. Indeed, divide and conquer is not only a military but also a political strategy. Climate change by its very nature seems to play into such countermovement strategies. It is all too easy as an individual to feel isolated and powerless vis-à-vis this immense problem. Everywhere we turn, we see people driving inefficient vehicles, coal-fired power plants spewing out smoke, cities sprawling farther and farther from their centers, forests being clear-cut.

Therefore, the communication task for climate activists is—over and again—to help overcome the sense of isolation that individuals may experience. As noted throughout this book, we must create communities. Communicators, as suggested by the John Dewey quotation that opens this chapter, can tap into this yearning for community, the moral sense of responsibility that goes beyond one's small self-interest. Through

81

communication, we can creatively illustrate that, collectively, many individual actions will add up to make a difference.

There is maybe no better example of this link between communication and community than in the approach taken by the diverse youth leaders of the climate movement. As they lead the fight against global warming, these climate activists don't simply talk about social justice and clean energy: they also convey, in words and actions, how exciting and how fun it is to be part of this new groundswell. For example, each youth climate gathering—there have been dozens around the nation since the founding in 2004 of Energy Action (www.energyaction.org)—features an infectious song-and-dance routine that features these lyrics: "Shake it to the Left; Shake it to the Right; Shake it to the Left; Shake it all Night; Shake Your Bootie; Shake up the System!" This song and dance has become a regular ritual, one that creates bonds among all those young activists, and helps create bridges with the activists of 1960s vintage who are increasingly joining these young leaders in their movement-building workshops.

Developing an Engaging, Morally Compelling Social Vision

All successful social movements have an unshakable moral foundation. More than any one policy goal, any one slogan, or any one organization, it is this foundation, expressed in actions today and in a compelling vision for the future, that lifts the movement. The climate movement will need to develop a truly compelling vision for the long haul, one that connects with deeply held human aspirations. The struggle to stabilize the climate will be long and difficult and may well seem unachievable at times, especially as the visible effects of global warming get worse in the years ahead. Because movement members will therefore not get quick positive reinforcement for all their efforts, their engagement in the necessary work must be maintained through their personal convictions that they are on the right side of history. The vision will have to be believable, positive, open-ended, able to solve problems, and meaningful. It cannot be simply about avoiding a potential climate crisis. Rather, it has to paint the picture of a better future environmentally, socially, and economically, one that is worth fighting for.

Much of this visioning work has not yet begun, but first examples are beginning to emerge. Watch and listen, for example, to the video that was released on Earth Day 2006 (it can be found at www.climate counts.org).This four-minute clip depicts the United States in 2056, a point in time when the climate crisis is assumed to have been solved. In a clever faux-documentary style (including flashy headlines in familiar newspapers and magazines and a climate-friendly Martha Stewart), it optimistically conveys a clean-energy future that brings good fortune and a sense of having made history to those who took part in the "climate revolution." It echoes and alludes to the success of the antismoking campaign with its lead slogan ("Make climate change history!"). The video also conveys a most-important sense of communal purpose, a sense of community, that counters the prevailing sense of isolation felt by so many: "It took millions, but it *did* happen!"

Establishing and Spreading New Social Norms

Movements are not only about fixing a particular social problem. More fundamentally, they aim to change deeply held beliefs, social norms, and institutions. They can—if successful—achieve paradigm shifts in society. For example, since the Stonewall demonstrations of June 1969, the gay liberation movement has achieved changes that would have seemed impossible then. Even though the gay community still faces stubborn forms of entrenched discrimination, remarkable societal shifts have occurred. Millions of gay Americans now live and work openly in every corner of the country and in every industry; gay men and lesbians now have the right to partner in civil unions in many U.S. states and even legally marry in one (Massachusetts); leading elected officials, from the U.S. Congress to mayors' offices nationwide, are openly gay; and popular television shows and films feature popular, sympathetic gay characters.

In its most visible successes, the climate movement will—through the establishment of federal and state legislation—bring more renewable energy on line, increase vehicle fuel economy standards, change lightbulbs in millions of American households, and push the U.S. government to invest in clean-energy technologies in China, India, and the rest of the developing world. If the movement accomplishes all that, it will be able to celebrate important successes. Yet many in this emerging movement are arguing for deeper change, a rejection of the excessive varieties of individualism and a rediscovery of the communal values of responsibility and justice. Ethicists, philosophers, and spiritual leaders of the movement are asking Americans to reconsider the relationship between humanity and nonhuman nature and to redefine dearly held notions such as progress, growth, and development (see also chapter 8).

Changing values and beliefs is a long-term, intergenerational project. Educational, religious, and other civic institutions will play important roles in this deeper transformation. For communicators, however, it is important to understand how strongly behavior is driven by values and beliefs. For example, repeatedly condemning the pervasive climate-damaging behaviors of individuals or industries ends up confirming—contrary to the intent of advocates—that such behavior is (still) the social norm and hence acceptable. When an environmentalist points an accusatory finger at an SUV driver, the response may well be, "Why should I behave differently if everyone else does the same thing?"

The communicative task is therefore to help bring about new social norms by illustrating them, living them, and communicating them in every possible way so that audiences recognize them as "appropriate" and the new "normal." As these new social norms become widely acknowledged and internalized, people will be motivated not only by external pressures or incentives, but also, and more reliably, by their innermost values and beliefs.

The transformation of our values toward an ethic of responsibility, stewardship, and community feeds the hopeful vision of our future. It is that vision that can and should be at the core of communication strategies for the climate movement.

Ten Paradoxes for the Journey: Communication Strategies to Mobilize the Climate Movement

The success of a social movement depends critically on effective communication. As communicators, we frame the issue of concern, the opposition, and the solutions. We help build a movement, sustain and manage it through challenging times, spread it to unlikely corners, and assist in the deeper societal transformation the movement promotes. The nature of climate change makes these communication tasks particularly challenging. For starters, it's tough to make the prospect of climate change, even runaway climate change, relevant and urgent when so many hard-working Americans worry more about terrorism, how to make ends meet, their job security or their kids' education, and lack of health care or insurance. We therefore need to help Americans make the connection between the climate crisis and the things they care about in their daily lives. In this section, ten communication strategies to deal with these communication challenges are offered.

1. Everyone knows, but not enough care.

To know what needs to be communicated about climate change at this time, it is important to understand where people are in their thinking. Although every audience is different, climate change activists need to start with a general understanding of the awareness and attitudes of the American population.

Research on the American public's thinking about global warming documents that the population is now overwhelmingly aware of the problem. Nine out of ten Americans have heard of it, some know the problem is related to energy and land use, and many Americans can identify some effects of climate change.* In fact, the signs of global warming are becoming apparent even to lay observers: spring arriving earlier, rainfall patterns changing, temperatures rising to uncomfortable levels, glaciers melting, and oceans rising. Although such changes can be frightening harbingers, they are often more persuasive than abstract projections. Only few Americans, however, can explain even the most basic principles of the greenhouse effect. Some researchers argue that such basic knowledge is absolutely essential, whereas others contend that it is not necessary as a precondition for action. The truth, I think, lies somewhere in the middle: fundamentally wrong understandings of the main causes of global warming (such as spray cans that release ozone-depleting chemicals) will lead to a search for misguided solutions. At the same time, knowledge or infor-

---

* The specific figures differ from study to study because researchers have employed different survey questions, varied in the depth of study, and because public opinion varies slightly with time in response to specific events or news coverage. Yet the trends over time in public opinion studies and the general frequency of particular opinions are quite consistent. I provide rough approximations here to indicate general levels of concern or understanding.

mation alone is not sufficient to produce behavior change; indeed, sometimes knowing more about a problem can lead some to believe that they have actually "done" something.

Although a majority of Americans judge climate change to be serious or very serious, only one in three is *personally* concerned or worried. The implications of this opinion research for communicators are clear. Although scientists and environmental advocates have succeeded in raising basic awareness of climate change, they have not yet made it an urgent and personally relevant issue.

Given all that, how can we do better from now on? I suggest using simple metaphors to help drive home the need for action before a full crisis unfolds, and also tapping into people's sense of responsibility and desire to be reasonable. At their best, Americans are bold *and* forward-looking, determined *and* cautious as they go about their daily lives and plan their future. Ideally, we don't wait until we're in a hairpin curve to hit the brakes, we don't wait to save for retirement until the year before we retire, and we don't wait for paying into the college fund until our kids start looking into schools. Building on such metaphors, our message should be, "Let's act on climate change now because being cautious and determined is sensible."

2. It's not about the climate, stupid (it's not even about the environment). Can you imagine building a climate movement without always talking about the climate or even about the environment? This challenge may perplex movement members, most of who probably see it as an extension of the environmental movement. The impression of climate change as an environmental problem goes back to the issue of framing and has deep historical and institutional roots.

Climate change is not just an environmental issue, however, and to some not even primarily so. Its causes are deeply social, economic, technological, and demographic. Its consequences will affect every single place on the planet and every sector of the economy. Its solutions will engage politics, science and technology, education, and all parts of civic society. We will have to address the question of how to manage ecosystems *and* the socioeconomic effects on lives, livelihoods, industries, social relations, human well-being, and health. Ultimately, as argued in many other chapters of this book, climate change will demand deep societal transformation.

This deep reach of climate change into the very fabric of our lives and society can easily become overwhelming. Once aware of that, we communicators should use these linkages to redefine climate change as a deeply social and environmental issue and thus help connect communities struggling for other goals with the emerging climate movement. For example, parents and educators share a deep concern for the education of their children. They want to provide them with the intellectual tools to create a meaningful, enriching, and sustaining future for themselves. That future will—in large part because of climate change—be very different, and quite possibly less predictable, than the present. Thus, the education required to adequately equip the current generation for the tremendous legacy we are leaving them must involve not only learning facts about the past, but also learning a range of critical-thinking skills to deal with an unprecedented future: tolerance for uncertainty, difference, and surprise; the ability to solve problems flexibly and creatively; and the ability to cooperate with others under stress to deal with the challenges that will undoubtedly come. It then makes the fight for good education a preparation for climate change.

The implied communication strategy may be counterintuitive for many climate activists: not every conversation must begin with the global climate. Instead, we can open the door to climate change from a different side of the common house: health concerns, social justice, stewardship of the environment, and spiritual motivations. It will take a little practice to connect climate change to other concerns, but it can be done. In some instances, we may not choose to make the link to climate change explicit at all as long as there is a goal that addresses climate change, too.

3. A good offense is, in fact, the best offense.

The saying goes otherwise, but when it comes to framing the climate debate, following the traditional dictum has not been particularly effective. Many climate scientists and environmental advocates have taken pains to respond to every misinformation and misleading statement by climate contrarians.

There is good reason to do so; misinformation should not be left unchallenged, and opportunities to educate the public should not be missed. Yet this pattern of responding to how the opposition frames the climate issue has left the proenvironmental and scientific side on the defensive.

It is always more powerful to define the frame than respond to someone else's. That is precisely the point Lakoff made with his book title, *Don't Think of an Elephant!* Of course, no one can think of anything but an elephant after hearing this title. The challenge now for the climate movement is to get our own elephants—clean energy, a healthy environment, energy security, vibrant communities, a hopeful future—front and center in every American's mind, thereby putting the opposition on the defensive.

4. Everything is uncertain, but one thing is for sure.

Climate *science* is not the most important thing to communicate to the American public at this point. It certainly should never end there. To the extent we focus on communicating the state of climate science, however, communicators have three key tasks to accomplish so as to strengthen public resolve in the fight against global warming. First, when conveying the state of the science we must rely on the most credible sources, such as assessments of the Intergovernmental Panel on Climate Change and the National Academy of Science, and, especially, communicate how the confidence in the scientific community has grown over time. Second, it is important to convey the nature of science as an activity that will always push back the frontiers of the unknown and in the process stumble upon findings that require revisions of what was previously thought to be known. Third, communicators must never overstate the scientific confidence with which aspects of climate change are known. To retain their credibility, communicators should lead with what is most certain, but never hide or misrepresent uncertainty.

It is an unsubstantiated claim that we need to know everything for sure before we can act. We make decisions in the face of uncertainty all the time. Uncertainty does not stop us from dealing in the stock market; we just diversify our portfolios. Uncertainty and risk don't stop us from buying a house or driving a car, but they make us buy insurance. What's for sure is that uncertainty must not be a showstopper.

5. The future is scary, so be very, very careful with alarmist messages.
A common tactic that advocates use when trying to convince others of the seriousness of an issue is to focus on what's most scary and sometimes make it sound scarier than it actually is. The impulse—especially around climate change—is understandable, but the success of this approach is far from guaranteed and the price to pay potentially tremendous.

It's one thing to be written off by political opponents as "alarmists"; it's another for communicators to gamble with their credibility. Climate change may turn out to have truly scary implications, maybe even more so than we now know, but it may also be less serious than anticipated. It is not yet clear. What should really give a communicator pause in using this tactic, however, is that alarmist messages may produce not only denial and inaction, but responses that could make things worse.

People respond to fear with attempts to reduce the external danger or contain the internal anxiety. Alarmist messages are intended to mobilize people to reduce the external danger (for example, reduce emissions and thus global warming). Often what they achieve, though, is people simply turning down the internal anxiety. They block out more news on the topic or distract themselves from feeling the fear. They hang on to the tiniest threads of uncertainty to tell themselves (and others) that the problem isn't so bad after all, or—if they decide to take action at all—they might actually increase their own risk or that of others through the actions they take. For example, after the terrorist attacks of September 11, 2001, people feared flying, so they drove instead, an action that raised their personal risk of death or injury by orders of magnitude compared with flying.

Thus, a communication strategy that does not—very quickly—tell people that there are feasible solutions with which they can begin to address the problem, that they have the skill and power to take these actions, and what exactly are the appropriate actions they can take is more likely to hinder than help the mobilization effort.

6. Words are everything, except . . . meaning matters even more.
Over the years, environmental advocates have tried giving climate change different names to increase the perceived urgency and

resonance with the public: global warming, climate disruption, climate crisis, climate catastrophe, and so on. These terms have all circulated along with the more scientific and neutral term, climate change. Some have tried to tie climate change to larger concerns such as sustainability. Opponents of climate action have tried to diffuse any sense of urgency by calling it climate variability (technically, the term scientists use to refer to shorter-term changes due to natural causes). Given these deliberate efforts to find words that match campaign goals, it is obvious that words matter a lot.

Words are signifiers that trigger deeper meaning. Words carry history, institutional baggage, and culturally and thus temporally specific meanings. That's why communicators, especially when they aim to bridge social and cultural divides, require such enormous sensitivity and vigilance. Words can build trust and even more quickly break it. Words can heal or be weapons. Words acquire this power from all the meaning that comes with them. The highly ambiguous advice that emerges from this recognition is that the name of this new movement is important and that the naming should be conscious and strategic. Most important, however, is not the name, but how people relate to what the movement stands for.* If a movement clearly stands for communal values, for a positive future, for efforts to ensure a livable world and a just and meaningful life, it could be called almost anything.

7. To build a movement, don't try to persuade everyone, only the critical few.
In *The Tipping Point*, a popular science best seller, Malcolm Gladwell described how small ideas can become prevalent social phenomena, spreading like wildfire across a nation or through a culture.[5] Among the key ingredients in making such small ideas cross the tipping point threshold and beyond, where they seem to proliferate on their own, are three types of people. The first, which Gladwell called *connectors*, are people who seem to know everyone; they are well-connected individuals with enormous contacts and, especially, the ability to cross social divides. The

---

* The naming—and renaming—of movements is not peculiar to the climate or environmental movement. Similar struggles are under way, for example, in the feminist/gender equality movement.

second group of people, called *mavens*, are individuals with a seemingly unlimited repertoire of knowledge and resources to find out whatever they may not know. The third type are the *salespeople*, those who know how to make just about anything attractive and relevant to you, and make you come along for the ride.

It's not hard to see why these types of people would be essential in spreading a new idea. Movement organizers often include or are connected to these types of people. To help the climate movement take off, those already in it would do well to identify connectors, mavens, and salespeople within each new community they want to spread to. This method promises to be more effective and efficient than trying to persuade masses of random individuals one by one.

8. People like us, and those who are everything but, are important.

Most people associate and bond with others who are like them: our work places us in the context of people who share similar expertise and responsibilities, we choose faith communities in which people hold similar beliefs and values to our own, our friends frequently have similar political leanings. Of course, in a diverse society, these social separations are not absolute, but for sociohistorical, institutional, and psychological reasons, divisions are common and hard to overcome. "People like us" (or PLUs, as Julian Agyeman has called them) are important for our personal comfort, identity, and group-internal norms and cohesion. Often, PLUs (especially if we know them personally) have greater credibility and legitimacy than those who do not know our circumstances as well.

PLUs are very important from a communications perspective. Sometimes information can only be heard and taken in as relevant and important if it is conveyed by PLUs. In other words, the climate movement must choose its messengers carefully and strategically if it wants to approach a heretofore uninvolved group. Is there a connector who could link to the yet-uninvolved group or a respected PLU within that group? PLUs are not always necessary (for example, scientists tend to have considerable credibility with a wide cross section of Americans), but they may be all the more critical depending on how socially cohesive and impenetrable the yet-uninvolved group is.

9. We can't ever give up, even though no one alive today will ever "win."
The climate movement may become known as one of the most altruistic of all social movements ever. Most movement members alive today are unlikely to see greenhouse gas concentrations in the atmosphere return to preindustrial levels, or even to 2005 levels. Short of a dramatic shift of the climate system to an unforeseeable new state, people born today will live in a far warmer world no matter how successful the climate movement is. This statement is not meant to be discouraging, but rather realistic about the time lags built into our society and the climate system. It requires the movement to think hard about what "success" or "winning" would look like both in the short- and in the long-term, an important element of its communication strategy.

Human nature will demand encouragement and some indications that all the work and struggle are worth doing. Those taking on difficult changes will want rewards and public recognition. The vision that the movement will define thus must include measures of progress, indicators of movement in the right direction. Communicators must convey these indicators of forward achievement just as much—and maybe even more—than what is wrong or not yet happening. They must acknowledge and appreciate those who act in exemplary ways, thus portraying and spreading the social norms of the future.

10. It may get nasty, so be kind!
Social movements fight oppositions. They feed on having "enemies," too. Having something or someone to fight against is an easily visible and strategically useful target. Now imagine this quite possible scenario: as climate change accelerates and its effects become more widespread and severe, the urgency to find solutions will be felt by more people and sectors of the economy. The demands to reduce emissions from fossil fuels will become louder. If (or when) such demands are met, resources to implement cleaner technologies will have to be shared more widely. Meanwhile, the need to deal with the consequences of climate change will also grow. Different sectors of society, different communities within countries and nations across the globe, will fight for limited resources to address their increasingly pressing concerns. For some, these fights

will be matters of life or death; for others, they will be over historical status, power, and entitlements.

Society doesn't have a particularly good track record of dealing with these kinds of situations peacefully, which is all the more reason to tackle them sooner rather than later. Yet there is an implication for communication in this scenario as well, one that astronauts have been telling us ever since that first trip to the moon: we here on this planet are all in this together. Climate change—maybe more than any other problem—brings home that we are an Earth community. Indeed, those who today may be the movement's opponents will still share this one planet tomorrow; they, too, are part of our community.

Global warming will not be solved by a few, but through cooperation among the many, through building coalitions and communities that grow larger and larger until they encompass us all. It is in the hands of each movement member to make this cooperation a little easier through basic decency and kindness in the way we communicate. It simply comes back to John Dewey: there are more than verbal ties between our common future, communal struggle, and communication.

6. Coming Home to Roost

BILL SHUTKIN

A journey of a thousand miles
begins with a single step.

Lao Tsu

I'M A PLACE GUY. PLACE IS what happens when people inhabit space and make it their own. It's the sum of their feelings, beliefs, practices, and policies, embedded and expressed in the built, the natural, and everything in between. Place is where the feedback loops are tightest, where what happens anywhere in the world comes home to roost, on your front doorstep, on Main Street, on the local ridgeline. Place is the proverbial backyard.

The vagaries of climate change discourse—the policy-speak, the models and charts, the grand pronouncements of doom—have never moved me. On the contrary, I've grown inured to them, I get lost in them. That's what happens when you're a place guy. Climate change is space, it's macro; place is micro.

It's the homely farmsteads that dot Lake Champlain's eastern shore in Vermont, some of which have recently taken to calling themselves vineyards. As it turns out, winemaking in cooler regions like Vermont has gotten easier in recent years as temperatures around the globe have increased, about one degree Fahrenheit on average since 1900 and more in the higher latitudes. Warm air causes sugar inside grapes to be released, which in turn leads to ripeness and wine.

In Vermont, the moderating effect of Lake Champlain, around which most of the state's vineyards are located, has clearly helped local winemakers. Yet stories from other winemaking regions like Oregon, Italy, and Germany that have linked dramatic improvements in their wines to sharply warmer temperatures suggest that global climate change is a factor.[1]

Now as much as I like a beefy Barolo or fine chardonnay, I like trees better. So if winemakers are benefiting from higher temperatures, what does that mean for my local woodlands in southern Vermont's Green Mountains? Take the region's signature species, the sugar maple, for example. The delicate chemistry that regulates sap flows in sugar maples will likely be disrupted by warmer winter days and nights, reducing the amount and quality of sap produced. In addition, sugar maples and other broadleaf trees in the North Woods stand to be harmed by rising temperatures as severe ice storms, like 1998's, become more common. That, in turn, will affect not only the wood products industry, but also the forest's very look and feel.

I like the North Woods just the way they are, remembering that it's the region's colder climate, among other key factors, that best distinguishes these forest ecosystems from their more temperate cousins to the south. It's what makes the North Woods the North Woods, a unique, singular place.

Sugar maples versus chardonnay, syrup versus syrah. Climate change as place, as micro.

That is why place-based, grassroots approaches—what I'll call "microenvironmentalism"—to addressing the climate crisis are so compelling. They resonate with my sensibility and ground me in a particular place, a particular moment, a particular group, and a particular set of change strategies.

Take the dozens of socially concerned artists in Boston, for instance, who decorated the windshields of hundreds of SUVs with mock traffic tickets, citations of shame for the drivers of what has become the premier symbol of Americans' in-your-face flouting of environmental responsibility. Or, consider the stealthy citizens of northern California who rove shopping mall parking lots affixing anti-SUV bumper stickers ("Ask Me How

I'm Contributing to Climate Change") to offending vehicles in a slightly more permanent variation on the mock tickets.[2]

These creative, if light-hearted, actions, undertaken voluntarily and without great fanfare, are being deployed in countless communities across the United States, revealing not only the frustration many Americans feel over the nation's inability to get over the infatuation with fossil fuels, but perhaps more importantly an emerging trend in environmentalism away from traditional, inside-the-Beltway approaches and toward more creative, more localized actions.

The turn toward the microenvironmentalism of parking tickets and bumper stickers is the result of two primary factors. First, these efforts are a response to the failure of the U.S. environmental protection system to significantly change the way Americans—whether governments, firms, or individuals—use and consume natural resources. Consider, for example, the George W. Bush administration's energy plan, enacted into law in 2005. Its unabashed call for full-scale development of fossil fuels, from coal to oil to natural gas, harkens back to the nineteenth century and the birth of the petroleum age. It's as if our modern environmental laws, born of the oil spills, mining disasters, and soot-belching smoke stacks of the 1960s, didn't even exist.

The second factor has to do with the character of the modern environmental movement itself. Defined by high-powered national groups headquartered in Washington, D.C., San Francisco, and New York City and staffed by lawyers, scientists, and policy researchers, environmentalism has been committed to the notion that reform begins in the nation's capital and spreads out from there. The problem, as the Bush administration's policies have made all too clear, is that not all reform is necessarily good for the environment. Put another way, what one election cycle may give, another can just as easily take away.

Yet notwithstanding these shortcomings, U.S. foundations, for decades the cornerstone and key underwriters of public interest environmentalism, have overwhelmingly supported the national groups at the expense of local, grassroots efforts. Of the roughly half-billion dollars given by foundations each year to environmental organizations, 70 percent goes to fewer than fifty national groups and the remaining 30 percent is divided among more than twenty thousand local, largely volunteer efforts, notoriously under-resourced and understaffed.[3] This disparity has created a substantial rift between the national organizations and the grassroots groups, which tend to view each other not so much as allies but competitors or worse, adversaries, insiders versus outsiders, haves versus have-nots.

Consider an alternative. If the funding ratio were tilted even slightly in favor of the grassroots groups, local initiatives would be given a chance to flourish, to shift from voluntary to full-time staff, develop more sophisticated and long-term strategies, and build alliances with regional and national organizations. Meanwhile, the national environmental groups would be forced to reprioritize their efforts, invent more creative approaches to advocacy and litigation, and embrace partnerships with the now better leveraged grassroots environmentalists. Thousands of communities would be empowered to fight against the oil drilling, coal mining, and power plant construction the Bush plan has unleashed[4] in a kind of nation-wide "not in my backyard" campaign. Working together, from the bottom up and top down, these local efforts could dramatically shift national energy policy, forcing a reconsideration of conservation measures and alternative technologies as energy priorities.

In New England, the New England Grassroots Environment Fund exemplifies this approach. This organization has alone distributed small grants of up to $2,500 to well over three hundred local groups.[5] Across the six New England states, in rural towns, suburbs, and urban neighborhoods, the fund is supporting citizens engaged in place-based efforts to clean up polluted land, shut down dirty power plants, and stop hazardous mining operations, among other projects. With time, and more money, these efforts could well coalesce into a New England–wide environmental constituency, changing the policies and practices of not only local governments and businesses but also of states and the region as a whole.

If the Bush administration offers environmentalists anything, it is the lesson that so many years and billions of dollars spent doing battle in Washington, D.C., have yet to pay significant dividends or substantially alter the terms of the debate. With more attention and more philanthropic dollars, directed to local and regional efforts, the situation can change.

It's changing already. As documented throughout this book, citizens are joining the fray in their own communities in search of ways to act directly and creatively on their sense of environmental responsibility. Ad hoc and episodic, their efforts are cause for hope in an otherwise uncertain situation. The Bush administration's weak environmental leadership is, in part, a reflection of the American environmental movement's own frailties: its inability to galvanize a strong nationwide constituency; its traditional reluctance to join with labor, civil rights, housing, and other social movements; its narrow strategic focus on legal and policy fixes. Local and decentralized, the grassroots climate movement is making up for these shortcomings and, in the process, defining a new kind of environmentalism.

There's a striking paradox here. Global climate change—the transcendent, metaenvironmental issue, what Bill McKibben has called "the mother of all environmental challenges"[6], is triggering an avalanche of bottom-up, localized activity. The title of the conference "Stopping Global Warming from the Ground Up: Igniting a Thousand Points of Clean Light" captures this creative tension between the local and global. Countless gatherings, trainings, and other similar offerings are popping up across the United States and beyond to empower the emergent grassroots global climate movement in the ways of community organizing, outreach, and communications. Something's in the air.

But back to place, to the micro that, for me at least, animates the climate change issue.

There's a plant that goes by the name Japanese knotweed. I thought I had left this insidious herb behind when my family and I moved from the city to Vermont in 2004. I was mistaken.

Known euphemistically as New England bamboo, knotweed is a roadside plant that, like so many invasive species, was introduced from Europe via the Far East. With its alternate leaves and arching stalks, it looks at first glance like the gentle hobblebush, an understory shrub of Vermont's mountain forest. Anything but gentle, knotweed is spreading across the state, from downtown lots to remote wilderness paths, at a rapid clip.

After we installed a new septic system at our house recently, I was horrified to find that within days, small red stems with oblong leaves began to sprout. The gravel used to backfill the leach field must have carried with it knotweed. I immediately began pulling out the young plants and burning them.

Unfortunately, thanks to its thick underground stem and endless supply of carbohydrates, every single fiber and cell of the plant has to be stripped out of the earth or it will regenerate. That's no small labor considering its root stem can grow quickly to tens of feet.

That knotweed is outcompeting native plants is bad enough, but what's really troublesome is its effect on my sense of place. I remember hiking down a section of the Catamount trail in Weston, Vermont, many summers ago. About two miles from the nearest road, I came across a large stand of knotweed stretching approximately forty feet along the trail. In an instant, I was no longer in the Green Mountain National Forest. Instead, I felt as if I could have been in any urbanized setting, any city where invasive species like knotweed are so common thanks to their high tolerance for blight. It was disorienting.

Observing the spread of invasive plants like knotweed, writer David Quammen warns that we're heading toward a "planet of weeds," a place where crows, kudzu, and cockroaches dominate, where superspecies whose ability to thrive in the most extreme environments has given them a competitive edge in a world where the line between the pristine and developed is no longer so clear.[7]

Maybe I'm too much of a purist in believing that certain plants simply don't belong in certain places, that the spread of knotweed is an unqualified threat. After all, we live on a dynamic planet; change, not equilibrium, is the norm. Yet what is place if it isn't something defined, in part, by those things indigenous to it? And what's the fate of Vermont's distinctive understory plants in the face of knotweed's homogenizing effect?

Isn't that the way of climate change? It's not that knotweed's spread, or that of any other invasive plant, is necessarily the result of a changing climate, but the effects are essentially the same. Human habitats, human places, are being transformed before our very eyes and in ways I find disturbing, at least when it comes to invasive species. Change, it seems, is happening *to* us; our hands have been loosed from the controls.

With the same impulse that inspired the Boston artists and other grass-roots climate change activists, I asked my kids last summer to join me in a knotweed patrol, to stand guard against the invader along our roadside and fields, to take control. I might not be able to save the planet from knotweed, I thought, but I can sure do something about my own backyard.

It's my small step in the long march toward a healthier planet, a new pathway to a better climate. Microenvironmentalism, it seems, has come home to roost.

PART III:

Finding Your Allies

7. Focus on Health

BOB MUSIL

> If you want to learn about the health of a population,
> look at the air they breathe, the water they drink,
> and the places where they live.
>
> Hippocrates

I WAS IN KYOTO, JAPAN, IN December 1997 for what I thought would be the start of a global—and, in the United States, a national—commitment to addressing the dangers of climate change. At the time, concerned, activist leaders of the American medical and public health community had little doubt about the validity of the science linking climate change to human activity. My own organization, Physicians for Social Responsibility (PSR), had helped craft a national statement by more than twelve hundred physicians and health professionals, published as an ad in the *New York Times*, that stated the threat to human health from disrupted climate systems and called for a strong international treaty.

Each day, the scene outside the Kyoto Convention Center could not have been more picturesque or pleasant. Brilliant, sunny, late autumn skies meshed with cool temperatures. A small lake nestled behind the center with pine trees, birches, and chickadees; it was a scene, but for strolling Japanese families, that might have been from *On Golden Pond*. In front of the entrance to the sprawling concrete modern center stood, amusingly, ice sculptures of penguins gently melting throughout the negotiations inside. Those of us who were not official delegates spent our time on a huge convention floor with perhaps four thousand members of the international media, NGOs from around the world, and assorted lobbyists. None of us could avoid the lobbyists and spinners from the Global Climate Coalition, an Orwellian-named collection of about a hundred of the leading oil, coal, and gas corporations.

When the Kyoto Protocol was announced, we were elated. We had pushed for deeper cuts, but were still happy that it called for 7 percent reductions in U.S. carbon emissions below 1990 levels by 2012. What I remember about that moment is the exhausted exhilaration of American environmentalists, friends and colleagues from the Sierra Club, Environmental Defense, Natural Resources Defense Council, National Environmental Trust (NET), World Wildlife Fund, Union of Concerned Scientists, Greenpeace, and more. I can still see the defeated, slumped, and frustrated postures of the slick and once mighty representatives of the Global Climate Coalition as they stumbled out into the cool fall Kyoto air, past the penguins, and onto buses, cars, and taxis that carried them off, back to the United States, in ignominious defeat.

Kyoto seemed to be a sweet victory of the first order. As we returned home from Japan, we thought that the environmental movement was about to have its greatest triumph.

It was a Pyrrhic victory, though. As those of us who had triumphed at Kyoto returned to home, the backlash had begun. The carbon lobby regrouped and began a grassroots lobbying campaign against the Kyoto treaty. Soon, conservative commentators, right-wing Senators, and climate doubters seemed to jam the airwaves. Their take on Kyoto—that tree-hugging liberal elites had negotiated a treaty that would harm American workers—soon held sway. Before we knew it, the media and powerful political circles were dominated by such questions as, Was the treaty really fair to the United States? and Wouldn't the agreed-upon cuts in emissions hurt American workers? The subtext was clear: this treaty is the work of a gaggle of elitist international scientists, bureaucrats, and environmentalists in league with Al Gore (Ozone Man) and Bill and Hillary Clinton. Soon, the support in the United States for the Kyoto Protocol was on the ropes and, later, totally abandoned by President George W. Bush in 2001 soon after his inauguration.

How did a movement that had come so far then fail so quickly? I believe that those of us who were so committed to the goal of an international treaty had not prepared the ground for it. Yes, we had effectively monitored and lobbied the complex international negotiation sessions and scientific debates that preceded Kyoto. We had pushed our friends inside the Clinton administration. Yet we hadn't noticed that few other Americans seemed to share our passion. That was the essence of our miscalculation: we did not build a case, for the millions of Americans working towards a more hopeful future, that showed that greenhouse gas reduction would improve their communities, their lives, and the lives of those they loved. Because we had not made this case, the environmental movement could not mobilize enough resources nor harness political opportunities to get the Kyoto agreement ratified or to pass serious climate change legislation.

Believe me, we've all learned from that battle. Now, as radiates throughout the pages of this book, the new climate movement is under way. In networks that include climate-friendly business leaders and forward-thinking politicians, environmentalists are building strategic new pathways for communicating, organizing, and changing the political landscape. One promising set of pathways comes from the growing involvement in the movement of medical and public health professionals and their framework of caring for human health. Stopping global warming, as many of us in the health professions understand it, is not an airy, environmental cause for liberal elites. Rather, it is about taking responsible, ethical action to protect human life and about creating healthy homes and communities. Examining global climate change through the lens of public health and prevention not only offers a potentially powerful and respected new set of messengers, but it also allows Americans to see the sometimes numbingly complex, arcane, and abstract subject of global climate change as something important to their immediate lives, their communities, family, and friends.

Framing Global Warming as a Health Issue

Activists and scholars alike are increasingly using the term *framing* to describe the process of choosing how we present and communicate our ideas. Our minds use preexisting frames, wiring, metaphors, pictures, stereotypes if you will, to speed insights and sort out the irrelevant. As scholar George Lakoff has famously put it, if you ask people not to think about an elephant, they will (see chapter 5). In political and policy discourse, these preexisting notions can be tapped and used, manipulated through advertising and repetition. Political framing is exactly the approach that the carbon lobby used so successfully after Kyoto. They framed the debate around environmentalists, whom they portrayed as elitist backpackers, more concerned with natural vistas and vacations than with you or your job.

These stereotypes are, of course, false. Yet to some degree they flow inexorably, like runoff to the Chesapeake, from the way environmentalists have objectified the environment as things in nature: landscape, species other than humans that exist outside of and apart from us to be observed, measured, and protected. When global warming is posed as strictly an environmental problem, it is harder, given such a standpoint, to put people back into the picture.

Don't get me wrong. Cactus and vermillion flycatchers, coyotes in the United States, and caribou in the Arctic are all are worth caring about. The permafrost in the Arctic is also quite real, even if it is now slipping out from beneath buildings thanks to global warming that has increased average temperatures at the top of the globe.

The environment, however, is also *inside* us. It *is* us. For instance, human health studies of the Inuit living in the Arctic circumpolar region reveal that their bodies contain accumulations of PCBs, mercury, and dioxin, minute quantities of toxins whose molecules have traveled thousands of miles to get inside those Inuits' bodies. Now we know that these molecules, carried by wind and deposited in water, enter the ecosystem and move up the food chain into fish and seals and whales and are then eaten by the Inuit. The result can be disruption of the endocrine system, learning and developmental disorders, low birth weights, and cancer.

These findings are relatively new insights about what happens to us as what we call "the environment" moves freely into, throughout, and out of our bodies. Such new understandings depend on rapid advancements in microbiology and biomedical engineering along with countless epidemiological studies of populations of animals all over the map: alligators, herring gulls, beluga whales, human beings. Our ability to see and understand how the dumping of an electrical lubricant into a landfill in Texas can be found in and affect the cellular function, the health, of a child in the Faroe Islands is a revolution in our thinking as profound as the photographs from space that first allowed us to see ourselves as simply a part of one fragile, finite planet, a global ecosystem.

The lesson here for the new climate movement is that this "the environment is us" perspective can be a powerful way to effect social change. To illustrate, we need only look at the environmental health movement that continues to grow in size and influence (see, for example, the Center for Health, Environment and Justice at www.chej.org). Our recent ability to observe and measure *inside* our bodies the effects of say, mercury, a potent neurotoxin increasingly found in the environment, has launched this movement. The blurring of distinctions between the outside environment and the inner environment of the human body has allowed the frame for this new movement to shift from cormorants, whose bills become malformed and twisted from endocrine disruption, to the health and well-being of people. It allows activists to offer concern and ultimately hope for healthy homes and communities, families with disabilities, workers in farms and factories, women who may become pregnant, urban joggers and cyclists, and more.

Another similar example of framing that offers lessons for the new climate movement comes from Cold War history. When President John F. Kennedy announced an end to open-air nuclear testing on June 10, 1962, it followed years of widespread education and protest from the antinuclear movement, the world's first truly global environmental health and human rights campaign. Kennedy declared: "We all love our children. We all breathe the same air. We are all mortal." In his words, one can hear how a focus of human health helped bring the abstract threat of global nuclear war and radiation poisoning down to ordinary citizens in the United States and around the world. The combination ultimately vastly reduced nuclear weapons and the threat of nuclear war, achieved a global nuclear test ban and nonproliferation treaty, and won compensation for those Americans exposed to radiation as nuclear weapons were being built and tested. Over time, positive, practical solutions promoted by the global antinuclear movement led to détente and the beginning of the end of the Cold War. Such can be the power of seeing global climate change in similar terms of healing for humanity.

Reframing the Climate Crisis after Kyoto

When it became clear that the push for the Kyoto treaty unwittingly created a mental framework that failed to move or motivate most Americans, PSR, like many other U.S. environmental groups, went back to basics in public education and grassroots organizing. In the subsequent years, putting climate work in terms of health has changed the approach to climate and organizing by PSR and national-level groups such as the Natural Resources Defense Council, Union of Concerned Scientists, and Environmental Defense. As detailed in this book, there's a lot to learn from this process.

At PSR, we began, with help from a number of leading foundations, by carrying out state-by-state reports and grassroots organizing campaigns in eighteen states over the years 1998 to 2001. Called *Death by Degrees* (and later changed to *Degrees of Danger* out of respect and sensitivity after the September 11, 2001, terrorists attacks), the reports were the first to link climate change and human health effects to a domestic, American audience in local settings.

Why the emphasis on local settings? Yes, the global health effects of unchecked climate change will be devastating. According to Sir John Houghton, chair of the International Panel on Climate Change Scientific Working Group, some 45 to 60 percent of the world's population could live in malaria-endemic zones by the latter half of the twenty-first century. Most recently, in sum, the World Health Organization (WHO) has estimated that global climate disruption is already causing an estimated 150,000 deaths worldwide each year.[1] These mind-numbing consequences of the climate crisis are too often far from the average American's concern. Therefore, as we built a growing network in the United States of concerned physicians and other health professionals and their citizen allies, our organizing around the *Death by Degrees* series was designed to localize the effects of climate. Our work also drew on the political premise that even though the worst effects of global climate change were likely to occur outside the United States, progress on the global front would necessarily involve changing American attitudes and policy about climate change at home. Our strategic and interrelated use of framing, resource mobilization, and political mobilization was deliberate and an important part of our approach.

We began in New Hampshire during the presidential primary season of 2000. PSR created and mobilized local advisory committees of doctors, nurses, health scientists, and other experts and released its reports at media events at state capitols. We coordinated with the Sierra Club, Ozone Action, and various local groups. Together, we aimed at state legislatures and the anti-Kyoto efforts of the U.S. Chamber of Commerce and others as well as the general public. These kickoff events were followed by educational events and lectures at medical schools and grand rounds, hospitals, universities, and civic gatherings. The focus for this effort was twofold. Climate change, with some state and regional variations, will create serious negative effects from sea level rise, flooding, wetland destruction, and the spread of waterborne and vectorborne diseases. In addition, almost all areas of the United States will suffer from increased heat.

For example, we developed materials based on a study we did with Ozone Action that showed that the number of heat stress days around the country had doubled since 1950 and the number of four-day heat waves had tripled. The predicted result was a doubling of U.S. deaths from heat by 2050 when, according to the National Center for Health Statistics, heat deaths already count for more deaths annually than any other natural disasters, including hurricanes, tornadoes, and flooding combined.[2] We taught our colleagues in the field that increased particulate air pollution (soot) from sulfur dioxide and ozone (smog) from volatile organic compounds are closely related to rising temperatures. Death and disease from dirty air, which is directly related to and exacerbated by global warming, currently account for more than fifty thousand deaths annually in the United States, with the bulk coming from vehicles and power plants. It is this connection between global climate change, dirty air, and death and illness in the United States that has proved the most powerful and effective link in organizing, especially when trying to involve more and more health professionals and American constituencies other than pure environmentalists.

Here's an example of how this frame, via resource mobilization, led to political success. During the Clinton administration, the Environmental Protection Agency (EPA) proposed new, tougher national ambient air quality standards (NAAQS) that were based on up-to-date health studies and analysis required by the Clean Air Act. Quickly, energy producers and their congressional allies began to mobilize against these standards. Faced with yet another huge, conservative backlash against standards that would save fifteen thousand lives a year, PSR was central to a huge political battle.

We joined with NET, the American Lung Association, and others in a classic grassroots campaign to save the NAAQS standards from being overturned by Congress. Featuring a fifteen-foot high, theatrical-size tombstone resembling Ebenezer Scrooge's worst nightmare, NET and PSR traveled to key districts, joined with local coalitions, asthma sufferers, pulmonologists, and moms, and gained massive publicity and effect on legislators *at the grassroots level.* A defining moment of this effort came when a new medical study indicated a correlation between sudden infant death syndrome (SIDS) and particulate air pollution. A hastily called national press conference with environmentalists, physicians, and organized mothers who had lost babies to the mysterious and dreaded SIDS was perhaps the final blow. Congress backed off trying to repeal the new NAAQS standards, and many American lives were saved.

Pathways Forward for the New Climate Movement

There is a limit to a movement that would confine its concerns primarily to the physical environment outside of humans, its main messages to environmentalists. A new and stronger climate movement should use frames and messages that reach, engage, and empower more Americans.

How can climate activists put this strategy into action? Take the environmental campaign against the Bush administration's mercury rule as an example. On the surface, it seems small, arcane, legislative, incremental: one more battle inside Washington, and it doesn't even address climate change. Well, that's not quite right. Yes, the mercury rule proposed in December 2003 by the EPA to control toxic mercury emissions from coal-fired utilities was indeed weak and obscure, but it must be seen in a larger context: as an assault on environmental progress related to human health, progress that must include addressing global climate change.

In part, it was the years of renewed grassroots organizing, media work, and campaigns by environmental groups that gave rise to a massive outcry against such an obscure rule. After PSR revealed that the

EPA had ignored its own expert panel on mercury and after a letter to then EPA administrator Mike Leavitt stating that the proposed rule "does not adequately protect children" was leaked, all hell broke loose. PSR further made the inadequacy of the rule clear by reviewing and touting carefully buried EPA pronouncements revealing that more than 630,000 newborn infants per year (far higher than generally supposed) were exposed in the womb to unsafe levels of mercury. Environmentalists, public health groups, parents, disability activists, and consumers were now fully banded together. More than 600,000 individual public comments were drafted and sent in on the EPA's proposed rule. More than 12,000 of them were from the medical community, as well as from forty-five U.S. senators, ten state attorneys general, and numerous state and local officials.

National press events in March 2004 held by a coalition of medical, nursing, public health, labor, learning disability, and faith groups excoriated the proposal. These press events also linked the mercury rule to practical advice in the form of clinician and consumer guides to fish consumption and how to limit exposure. This critical step allowed new messengers to penetrate health websites and magazines, food and women's magazines, and, with a video press release featuring Dr. Erica Frank of the Emory School of Medicine's Department of Preventive Medicine, to get television coverage in eighty-five media markets with 162 stories reaching 10.5 million viewers. Such campaigns begin to indicate the potential power of putting traditional environmental issues, and climate change in particular, within a human health framework.

More recently, starting with the primary season leading up to the 2004 presidential election, PSR has sought to incorporate an additional framing lesson into the public health approach to climate change: solutions. As we organized across the United States, both medical professionals and citizens began to say they had been convinced that climate change was indeed real and that the effects of such serious disruption of climate systems would be harmful to human health, their families, their livelihoods, and the nation. They wanted to know what PSR and other environmental and public health groups had to offer as solutions, both in policy and in their personal lives.

This frequent request coincided with a framing exercise carried out for the Green Group of environmental organizations concerned with climate by the Frameworks Institute. The findings, put simply, were that environmental organizations should explain the science of climate change in simple, human terms and, most importantly, offer practical solutions to such an overwhelming problem. What was being suggested was a positive, practical appeal: leave behind the familiar framework of fear, gloom, and doom that often leads to despair and disempowerment and eschew wonky, scientific, and policy jargon. (It is advice that would have helped in the aftermath of Kyoto when I cajoled my wife, a sympathetic, professional woman and feminist, to watch a C-SPAN panel of four environmental friends who had just returned from Kyoto explain that the treaty, although not sufficient to stop climate disruption, was an important first step. They went on to extol, in impenetrable acronyms, the virtues of JI, carbon sequestration, and sinks, the position of the JUSCAN countries, the financial mechanisms of the GEF, and more. I still recall the teasing, yet telling, glance from my wife before she channel-surfed away from C-SPAN and my pro-Kyoto pals. "Bob, is *this* what you do for a living?" she asked.)

That is not the response I and others now get from campaigns based around human health and new energy solutions to both climate change and the adverse health effects of our outdated and dangerous fossil fuel economy. Energy independence and solutions emerged as major issues, after the war in Iraq, in the 2006 national elections. Environmental websites now bristle with health effects, energy plans, and more and emphasize local effects, actions, and solutions, as in the Apollo Alliance's *New Energy for Cities: Energy-Saving and Job Creation Policies for Local Governments*. PSR's grassroots campaign, called *A Breath of Fresh Air*, developed new state-based reports and organized to reword the climate issue. How can Americans build a new, vibrant, and sustainable economy for the future? How can we end the outmoded and unhealthy fossil fuel age that is causing global climate change and hazardous air pollution while taking direct action to protect our families, friends, and community?

In Pennsylvania, for example, the *Breath of Fresh Air* report, released in September 2004, was endorsed and used by PennFutures, a statewide coalition and lobbying group concerned with energy efficiency and renewable energy, as well as by the Pennsylvania Council of Churches and local environmental groups. As was the case with *Death by Degrees* reports, this newer report has engaged a statewide network of medical and public health experts and health officials, medical schools, hospitals, and universities. Its approach combines the passion and vision of the Hippocratic oath and the stewardship concerns of the faith community (see chapter 8) into an overarching vision of human health and wholeness. In addition, of course, it offers hope and action to protect our children and the future. Within such a frame, the health effects of Pennsylvania's aging coal-fired utilities, the production of mercury, the need for fish and health advisories and for policy advice on global climate change legislation, as well as business and individual choices and investments in solar, wind, and energy efficiency, cohere in a single, powerful approach.

In such a context, anglers, academics, the American Baptist Church, the American Heart Association, or the American Federation of State, County and Municipal Employees, for example, can all be involved. Framing the issue in terms of human health and community concerns for a safe, clean, and prosperous future makes sense of and links together for all Pennsylvanians some simple and startling statistics. In Pennsylvania, fine-particle pollution from power plants alone is responsible each year for 35,405 asthma attacks, 3,329 heart attacks, 194 lung cancer deaths, and 200,100 lost workdays.[3]

As we in the public health community, along with environmentalists, have begun to frame climate change in terms of energy solutions and human health, two new emerging and promising trends remain to be explored and further developed. The first is the huge, but exciting, prospect of redesigning the entire U.S. infrastructure or built environment (and that of other developed nations as well) in terms of a new, clean-energy future that moves away from fossil fuels and protects human health. The campus-based youth movement (as documented in this book's afterword) has successfully mobilized around this vision. The other new approach is what is coming to be called energy security. This focus suggests the need to enhance U.S. national security and protect American lives and families by reducing dependence on oil and gasoline. This has led to military and foreign policy strategies designed to secure access to those resources through U.S. involvement, intervention, deployment, and military bases in places like Uzbekistan, Iraq, Saudi Arabia, and Venezuela. This approach is very promising for integrating the concerns of many traditional conservatives. For example, at a Capitol Hill briefing in the U.S. Senate in 2005, James Woolsey, former director of the Central Intelligence Agency, a self-proclaimed "cheap hawk," talked about the need to move away from fossil fuels and toward renewable energy sources and efficiency as quickly as possible, both to protect U.S. security and to prevent global climate change. From this perspective, Republicans and Democrats, hawks and doves, energy specialists and environmentalists can find a common vision and common ground.

One way to measure achievements and outcomes is by immediate reductions in carbon emissions or by legislative victories, both of which are sorely needed. We can also, however, measure progress by steady growth in grassroots support and in a wider circle of allies, from physicians and health professionals to business, labor, academics, disability activists, and reproductive health and women's rights groups. Through these messengers and framing the issue in terms like energy security, we can take the climate movement beyond environmentalists, without excluding them.

There is no silver bullet to preventing global climate change, but putting people and their health, safety, and well-being first helps. Reframing environmental questions in terms of human health has the benefit of involving everyone across boundaries of neighborhood, class, and ethnic group (see chapter 9), while adding a powerful set of respected messengers—health professionals—to environmental debates.

The Americans we must talk to are not blank computers to give input to or to urge on to worry more about whales if they are worried about their families. Often, they will "frame" our work for us, if we will but listen. Not long ago, I found myself sitting in the office of a major developer in Maine, seeking funds for PSR's work. I had been brought to that office by Dr. Peter Wilk, PSR's past president and head of the organization's Maine chapter. The conversation rambled through programs and priorities until I asked about our potential donor's children. I was taken aback at the sudden pride and passion as Wilk's friend talked about his asthmatic son: how deeply he cared about him and how outrageous it was that their home was near an EPA monitoring station that steadily revealed hazardous levels of ozone. He knew, thanks to PSR and environmentalists, that ozone is a cause of and exacerbates asthma attacks and that things are even worse with increasing heat and, ultimately, global warming. "If you can do something, anything, serious about that, I will give you more money than you are talking about now and I will engage others," he said.

The environment is not only outside us, although it surely is. It is also inside us. It *is* us. Unless we act, the environment can harm the health of a child. We all love our children. We all breathe the same air. We are all mortal. Human health brings a powerful frame, a powerful message, messengers, and motivation that can build and is expanding the new climate movement.

8. Binding Life
to Values

REBECCA KNEALE GOULD

IN THE LATE SUMMER OF 2005, when Hurricane Katrina obliterated sections of Louisiana, Alabama, and Mississippi, I found myself driving back and forth to work (there is scant public transportation in Vermont), shaking my head and listening to the news with tears streaming down my cheeks. For so many of us, this hurricane knocked down the levees of our hearts. Yet the discussion about the hurricane also troubled my head. As a scholar working jointly in the fields of religious studies and environmental studies, I could not help but note the explanatory language people used to make sense of the crisis. It was an "act of God," some claimed, thus putting themselves in the age-old position of having to wrestle with theodicy (the problem of evil): Why would an ostensibly good God cause such terrible things to happen? Others said, "It was a freak of nature," and some (with more of a penchant for personification) declared, "Nature was exacting its revenge." In his presidential speeches, George W. Bush gave the hurricane an especially vivid personality; it was whimsical, "cruel and wasteful."

For myself, the hurricane was caused neither by an act of God nor by the doings of a feminized vengeful force called nature. It was, scientifically speaking, an outlier weather event of considerable magnitude, evolving from the simultaneous alignment of favorable circumstances, favorable, that is, if you are a hurricane. Yet I seldom view the world *only* scientifically; I also see it morally and often symbolically. In this sense, the hurricane took on another form: it resembled the God-as-whirlwind of the Hebrew Bible, a divine reminder that when idolatry (which, in our time, includes consumerism, greed, social injustice, and addiction to oil) trumps reverence for life, there is hell to pay. And that hell is on earth.

The root of the word *religion* means "to bind" or "to bind back." At its worst, the binding power of religion can lead to tribalism, exceptionalism, crusader mentalities, and war. At its best, however—and what is true for many of us—religious and spiritual life calls us to bind ourselves back to the source of life. That "source" may be the God of the Abrahamic religions; the many divine forms found in Hindu, Jain, and Sikh traditions; the varied sacredness of plants, animals, and landforms acknowledged by indigenous peoples; or the principles of interdependence found in Buddhist worldviews. Alternatively, the source may be nature itself, with its wondrous ecological and evolutionary magic. What we experience as the source may be quite different depending on our birth countries and families and on whether we choose to call ourselves "religious," "spiritual, but not religious," or simply, as is said in Buddhist circles, "awake." In contrast, the path that takes us away from this source no doubt includes the many "isms" that have led us to our current global climate crisis: materialism, consumerism, individualism without community, blind adherence to technological progress, and the headlong pursuit of wealth and status over meaning and purpose.

The evidence is rich that Americans today, from all walks of life, are seeking purpose and meaning with a particular zeal. Having lost ourselves in other imagined goals, we have difficulty finding our way out of the maze we have constructed. Within the maze, our options may seem limited. Are we forced to accept the moral relativism and secular cynicism of the broader American culture that Eban Goodstein, founder of Focus the Nation, sees as a hindrance to speaking from the heart on climate change? Or, does it seem that religious values are only synonymous with the black-and-white biblicism and antipluralistic approach of *some* of the Christian right? What does religion have to say about the global climate crisis, and what do religious responses tell us about hope for the future?

We've Done it Again: From the Garden of Eden to the Tower of Babel

I have long been interested in religion as it is wrestled with, expressed, and practiced not only by elite thinkers and writers, but by everyday people—like you and me—dealing with the messiness of encountering religion and spirituality in our daily lives and not always knowing what to do with it. While doing doctoral work at Harvard University, I became increasingly interested in the study of *lived religion* in American history.[1] It was there that I also brought my longstanding interest in eco-theology into a new context. At Harvard, and later at Middlebury College, I began teaching and writing about how people bring together their religious identities and their environmental concerns. These interests have blossomed into a full-fledged study of the burgeoning (and interfaith) environmentalism of religious organizations, clergy, and laypeople.

Through doing this work, I have become utterly convinced that there is room in the maze to which I earlier referred—the maze of meaning making—for spiritual language (and spiritual practice) in the face of global climate change. Indeed, for us not to succumb to complete despair in the face of this challenge, there *must be* room for spiritual language and practice. Moreover, it is the *diversity* of religious opinions and practices that will give us the tools we need to face the crisis of values that is at the heart of the global climate crisis.

Religious environmentalism is a kind of religious pluralism, and it is the unexpected interreligious cooperation, as much as the environmentalism, that has particularly interested the media and, more importantly, has the greatest potential for creating social change. Countless times in my research I have seen clergy and laypeople set aside differences of belief and practice and agree not to talk about abortion or gay marriage so that they can roll up their sleeves and get to work on protecting our collective future. We do not have to agree theologically on all matters, to agree that global climate change is—in addition to being a scientific, technological, and political challenge—a challenge of the greatest moral urgency. It is *the* spiritual challenge of our times, a challenge of apocalyptic proportions.

Some of us identify as religious, some as spiritual, but not religious. Many of us feel connected to the spiritual traditions of our ancestors on one day and deeply cynical about religion in general on the next. Yet one need not be religious in any formal sense to find hope in the slowly emerging eco-religious voices that are singing, praying, and speaking out in synagogues, temples, churches, full moon circles, and mosques around the country. Even those who are confirmed atheists and secular humanists can take heart in what is emerging right now. The new intra- and interfaith work on global climate change is doing precisely what some have called for (see chapter 4): it is moving beyond science, technological tinkering, and policy strategizing alone. It is reaching deep into our hearts to ask, What are the values we hold most dear?

Asking deep questions of ourselves, taking these questions seriously, and transforming them into action is what the new grassroots work on climate change is all about, and it can have fascinating and lasting effects within religious contexts. For instance, if Jesus is at the center of our spiritual lives and we guide our lives by asking, What would Jesus do?" we must also ask, What would Jesus drive? It may sound like a clever one-liner to some, but the question—circulated by e-mail, ad campaigns, and bumper stickers—has been taken very seriously in Christian, and especially evangelical, communities. Jesus would probably walk, take the bus, or at least carpool with a Toyota Prius, some speculate. That very speculation has led to serious grassroots action.

Most prominently, a November 2002 Detroit-based protest of the automotive industry made it into the headlines in part because the interreligious story was irresistible. During that protest, nuns drove rabbis around in hybrid cars, and Jews, Catholics, and evangelical Christians together visited automobile companies and dropped interfaith calls for new emissions standards on the desks of corporate executives. For these Protestants, Catholics, and Jews, global climate change was not a matter of "environmentalism" in the old sense; indeed, many of them would hesitate to identify themselves as environmentalists. When asked to consider what it means to be an American Christian or Jew at this moment in history, however, they responded by attending to one of the most urgent moral problems of our time.

How else are deep questions about values expressing themselves in religious communities? If the practice of Shabbat (or Sunday Sabbath) is at the center of our spiritual lives, we might ask, What can Shabbat—a day of rest and no labor—mean today? Perhaps today, more than ever, Sabbath observance stresses *being*. Some aspects of work might not get done for those who take one day a week for contemplation and gratitude, but the practice itself recharges the body, mind, and soul. It rejects consumption and overwork (both of which contribute to environmental degradation) and asks us to pay attention to the uniqueness of creation and all its creatures. Today, the practice of Shabbat is being reinterpreted by various forward-thinking rabbis as the ultimate spiritual, environmental practice, the one day a week when we exercise no effect on or control over nature. (The emphasis on Shabbat as a form of resistance to the most negative consequences of modernity—unchecked consumption, a rushed pace of life, emphasis on work over life—began with the writings of Rabbi Abraham Joshua Heschel. Today, others have led the way in understanding Shabbat as an environmental practice, a time once a week when nature is appreciated, but not transformed, by humans.) In addition, the question of how to define what is kosher has led to the rise of an "eco-kosher" movement, a movement that takes old dietary prohibitions into a new era and asks whether it is moral, in our time, to eat genetically modified food, to buy products that are nonlocal or nonorganic, or even to drive SUVs. The idea of eco-kosher both draws on and contributes to organic, slow food, and "localvore" movements, but it grounds these ideas in an ancient tradition that has always understood eating to be a sacred act that must support the principles of the flourishing of life and the establishment of justice. When Jewish New Yorkers refuse to buy food from California that has a large "carbon price tag" attached, they are acting against climate change, while also understanding themselves to be participating in new forms of an ancient religious tradition, a tradition that tells them, "Justice, justice shall you pursue."

Religious orientations—whether we accept them as our own or simply choose to learn from them—are essential because they exhibit compassion for humanity while maintaining a sense of the big picture in which the more-than-human world is also cared for and recognized. Our varied traditions teach us that we humans are *not* the center of the universe, even if—in the twentieth century especially—we had been acting as if we were.

They teach us that unchecked power and human hubris can lead to dire consequences (as originally narrated in the story of the expulsion from Eden). Today, through our greed, through our hunger for as many "apples" (televisions, cars, air conditioners) as we can consume, we are kicking ourselves out of the earthly Eden into which we were born. Our childhood Edens were imperfect worlds, to be sure, but they were more healthy and sustainable than what we have at present.

What I am talking about here are matters of interpretation, matters of *framing*, ways of knowing, understanding, and communicating to others that all the writers of this book see as crucial to building a sustainable future or to having any future at all. To face the climate crisis in all its force, we have to go beyond scientific understanding (the crucial starting point) or activist mobilization (the essential next steps). We have to meet the climate crisis where it meets us: in the guts, in the heart, in the soul.

The climate crisis is a crisis of science, of politics, and of culture. At its deepest, however, it is a moral crisis, a crisis of psyche and spirit. In our moments of honesty with ourselves and with the world—what I call the two o'clock in the morning moments—we ask ourselves, How is it that we have let our hubris go this far? That we have begun to control *our own weather*? That we have taken the fate of the planet *into our own hands*? That we are creating conditions in the United States that will wreck the lives of our cousins in the Pacific Islands and in the Arctic? It is the Tower of Babel revisited. We have stretched beyond our human limits, and now we are beginning to feel the consequences, be they flood, fire, or both.

For as long as I can remember, I have been deeply interested in questions of meaning. For an equally long time, I have turned to the natural world, sometimes to answer those questions, more often to quiet them down. The woods and mountains and urban garden plots that I hold dear have always been a hedge against those crises of the spirit that we all, at times, experience. Lately, I have wondered what happens when the very places we have always gone to for spiritual solace or spiritual guidance become degraded or disappear. The climate crisis is a spiritual crisis in this sense, too. It not only threatens the resources on which humanity depends for food, shelter, and a livelihood; it also threatens our sacred lands, our sources of spiritual renewal, our touchstones of childhood memory.

Religious Environmentalism

In 2002, *E-Magazine* devoted its cover to religion and the environment. In 2006, *Time*, *Newsweek*, and Bill Moyers all focused on evangelical Christians involved in "creation care" at both regional and national levels. These stories represent a kind of coming-out party for religious environmentalism, although the historical roots of this appearance go back decades. In academic and political circles, the term *religious environmentalism* may seem like an oxymoron. Michael Shellenberger and Ted Nordhaus claim (often rightly) that environmentalism is dead, in part because it prioritizes technological solutions and policy-wonking over a call to values.[2] By contrast, however, religious environmentalism stands out because it is very much alive and speaks directly and eloquently to the question of values.

Beginning in the mid-1980s and reaching a high point in the spring of 2006 with the rise to prominence of climate change activist Rev. Richard Cizik, vice president of governmental affairs for the National Association of Evangelicals, religious leaders, national organizations, regional interfaith groups, and countless clergy and lay leaders of all denominational stripes have gathered forces to speak out on global climate change from a position of faith. As Cizik told *Newsweek* in February of 2006, "This is not a Red state issue or a Blue state issue or a green issue. It's a spiritual issue."[3] In spiritual and religious contexts, environmentalism may not be dead as much as born again.

In the late 1990s, I teamed up with my old friend and colleague, Professor Laurel Kearns, to reenergize our mutual interests in religiously based environmental activism. Kearns had long studied the environmental work of Quaker communities, as well as the mainline Protestant organization, the Eco-Justice Working Group (EWG) of the National Council of Churches. The EWG was a leader in national, religious environmental work and early on had aptly cast contemporary environmental problems as being also, always, social problems. Alongside nonreligious environmental justice movements and scholarship, the EWG acknowledged and sought to educate others about the disproportionate environmental burdens that had to be borne by poor and minority communities. The EWG was soon joined by three other groups—the United Catholic Conference, the Evangelical Environmental Network, and, the Coalition on the Environment and Jewish Life (COEJL)—all united under the institutional umbrella of the National Religious Partnership for the Environment (NRPE). As the global climate crisis has heightened and as religious groups, in keeping with the general public, have become more aware of the climate change threat, our research on religious environmentalism has, correspondingly, focused increasingly on global climate change. Our findings have inspired us with success stories in Michigan, Washington, New Jersey, California, Massachusetts, Vermont, and, indeed, almost every state in the country. We have encountered daring national initiatives and creative local projects (such as shrinking planned church parking lots in favor of organic gardens behind the sanctuary and blessing compost piles and recycling bins on Rogation Sunday). We have interviewed countless courageous and tireless individuals working in the trenches and have discovered that, when asked, these individuals often tell poignant stories of longstanding spiritual connections with nature, of profound childhood experiences with particular mountains, rivers, backyards, and trees. Many have felt the profound grief of seeing backyards flooded, mountains eroded, city parks developed, and favorite trees cut down.

For so many of the individuals we have interviewed, significant spiritual experiences in nature were seldom addressed in the religious contexts of their youth. Now, however, as creation care movements are emerging, as the concept of eco-kosher is being debated, as the environmental as well as spiritual purity of communion bread and wine is being discussed, these individuals are finding that it is finally possible for their spiritual lives in nature to be reinscribed into their more traditional religious identities and communities. It is no longer religion *or* nature, but religion *and* nature as a new kind of spiritual and ecological direction.

In our research, Kearns and I have found that religious environmentalism belongs to no one congregation, no one denomination, nor even to any one particular faith. It has also become clear to us that this engagement is *not* of the "add religion and stir" variety, but rather has come from a deep place of integrity and authenticity. In 2002, for instance, when the Sierra Club and the National Council of Churches joined together to sponsor a television advertising campaign against drilling for oil in the Alaska National Wildlife Refuge, some religious environmentalists took pains to make important distinctions. "Our teachings are not those of secular environmentalism," Paul Gorman, executive director of the NRPE, told the *Christian Science Monitor* in February 2002, "and these can't be bridged in sound bites. Our call is to be distinctly ourselves and for the long term."[4] In March of the same year, John Carr, secretary of social development for the U.S. Catholic Council of Bishops, gave a similar caveat to the *Wall Street Journal*: "We're not the Sierra Club at prayer. We're the Catholic community trying to take our responsibilities seriously."[5] Conservative strongholds such as the ExxonMobil-funded Acton Institute have lambasted the NRPE, calling it a "radical" environmental organization, expressing "pagan" tendencies," but religious groups, including evangelical Christians who take a conservative position on other social issues, have responded by emphasizing their moral obligations to the planet, to the people who inhabit it, and to the future generations who will inherit the environmental legacies of our current behaviors.

Through their growing work, religious environmental organizations have made significant progress, much of it attracting increasing media attention. Significantly, the work of environmentally oriented religious groups has even reached the Bush administration. On March 6, 2001, Christine Todd Whitman, then head of the EPA, drafted a letter to the president pressing him to consider the seriousness of global warming as a public policy issue. Her memo contained several key observations, but the central focus of the letter had to do with a significant shift in the way environmental concerns were being expressed. "For the first time," Whitman wrote, "the world's religious communities have started to engage in the issue. Their solutions vary widely, but the fervor of the focus was clear."[7]

Whitman's memo may not have been effective on a policy level, but as a primary text of a moment in recent American religious history, it is telling. Here a senior federal administrator acknowledges what we have since understood to be a change in framing. It was not a change in tactics, but a change in participants and therefore a change in *how* environmental threats were being framed, understood, and addressed. Whitman heard a new and forceful voice on environmental issues, the voice of mainstream religious organizations. These new environmental voices are often being raised across preexisting theological and religious differences, differences that once divided Christians and Jews internally and from one another.

Revelations: The Emergence of Religion on the Ground

Let us tour through two examples of what I call "religion on the ground," a concept that has several different dimensions. First, it is on the ground as opposed to "in the air." In other words, I am not talking about lofty intellectual arguments, theological hair-splitting, or long philosophical discourses on the nature and existence of the divine. Actually, as a scholar, I love all that in the air kind of thinking and am deeply indebted to it. Where would we, or our traditions, be without Plato, Augustine, Maimonides, or Kant? The reality, however, is that most people do not make daily decisions with reference to what Kant or Plato might have said. Instead, we muddle through, and depending on our heritage, our families, our place in the world, and our freedoms—or lack thereof—to shape our lives, we make decisions based on some mix of gut feeling, rational choice, opinions of friends and families, and pragmatics. When we can, and when we are aware enough to do so, we think about where our values come from, what values are most important to us, and how we might act more in line with our values. When we do so, we tend to experience vitality, integration, and a deep sense of psychological and spiritual satisfaction. When we can't—or won't—align action with values, we often feel profound unease. Attention to religion on the ground—to religion (or philosophy and spirituality) as it is lived—is attention to religious life as it is worked out in the real world. The study of religion on the ground is the study of our attempts at "binding back" in the context of our full, fallible humanity and in the midst of cultural pressures to do otherwise.

Second, religion on the ground refers to the foundation on which we all stand, the earth, our planetary home, spinning in space as part of a vast universe of planets. The phrase suggests that if religion is to have integrity and authenticity, the religious traditions we inherit and continue to create must recognize that ground. We must start by acknowledging that we humans, *homo religiosus*, owe our very lives to the ground.

The Hebrew Bible (Christian Old Testament) reminds us of this debt of gratitude in the opening story of Genesis, where Adam (*adam*) is clearly synonymous with *adamah*, arable soil (also translated as "earth" or "clay"). Adam is *adamah*, with divine breath breathed into its nostrils, the same breath a birthing mother might breathe into the airways of her newly born infant.

Indeed, some translators, in attempting to capture the wordplay of the original Hebrew, have retold the Adam story as the creation of "earthling from earth" or "human from humus." Religion on the ground, then, is religion that acknowledges the earth as the ground of our very being. It recognizes and honors the divine, but it does not place the divine or humanity only "up there." It reminds us that we are all birthed from, dependent on, and called to be protectors of the earth and its creatures. It is no surprise, then, that the individuals and groups who are part of this religion on the ground are those who see current patterns of consumption, individualism, and greed—all causal factors in climate change—as versions of idolatry or sin.

In the face of global climate change (as well as wilderness shrinkage, forest destruction, species extinction, and the ongoing pollution of air, ground, and water), what are religious organizations doing, how are people coping, and what on-the-ground action is emerging? One story takes place in a small evangelical church in a low-income neighborhood in Seattle. Both the church and the neighborhood are located far from the ecological beauties we often equate with the Seattle bioregion. The neighborhood is situated next to Boeing Field and close to a Superfund site. Noise, air pollution, and water pollution are daily challenges, and compared with those of well-heeled congregations, community members have few resources to face them. Drug addiction, employment, and putting food on the table all could easily take precedence over the seeming luxury of environmental issues. Pastor Leroy Hedman, however, has recognized that all these problems (from drugs to air pollution) are connected and, correspondingly, that the solutions (garden growing, antipollution lobbying, building self-esteem among congregants) are also bound together.

At Georgetown Gospel Church, Hedman has transformed his otherwise typical evangelical church into a center of Christian ecological action and education. He has recovered much of the land outside the church (a relatively small lot) into gardens that simultaneously memorialize the dead, beautify the church, and feed (for free) the community. He has installed water barrels to capture rainfall and keep runoff from flowing into Puget Sound and has replaced every lightbulb in the church with compact fluorescent lightbulbs, thus saving the church 75 percent of its energy costs. In the basement of the church, where Kearns and I met with

Hedman one spring morning in 2004, we sifted through piles of brochures, white papers, and pamphlets on composting, gardening, energy efficiency, fuel conservation, and public transportation. These pamphlets were filed in magazine racks side by side with other pamphlets on Christian missions, care for the poor, biblical interpretation, and pastoral counseling. For the pastor, the environment is not a special interest for those who have the luxury to care about whales and wolves. He exhibits in his very being that the "special interests of elites" stereotype of environmentalists is simply that, a stereotype. In the context of Georgetown Gospel Church, care for the earth, water, and air is deeply intertwined with care for poverty, neighbors, and the soul. Worshipping Jesus Christ and being a master gardener are two expressions of the same commitment.

A different example of religion on the ground can be found in the work of the previously mentioned Coalition on the Environment and Jewish Life, or COEJL. This organization is one of the four arms of the NRPE and, like the other three arms, operates quite independently while remaining in active communication with the other groups. Often, as in the case of the 2002 Detroit protest described above, COEJL has teamed up with partner organizations to launch interreligious environmental initiatives. COEJL has also worked closely with the EQG of the National Council of Churches to launch the Interfaith Climate Change Network, an interreligious climate change initiative that has launched statewide campaigns in eighteen states.

Even without the environmental focus of its mission, COEJL would be a unique Jewish organization by anyone's calculus. On one hand, it reaches outward, partnering with evangelical and mainline Christians in ways that would have been unheard of even in the recent past and in ways that defy popular conceptions of the United States as becoming increasingly religiously divisive. On the other hand, from an *intra*religious perspective, COEJL also has been astonishingly successful in building bridges in very unlikely places. Rabbi Larry Troster, an active leader in COEJL, commented on COEJL's unique stance one afternoon in May 2006:

> This is an issue which can transcend any differences. Everybody can find their way in this because it's an issue we can all agree on! I first saw this when I started attending the COEJL institutes

. . . and *every* kind of Jew was there, from Orthodox to secular to whatever. It was the most diverse group I had *ever* been involved with. . . . The energy level was *fabulous* because we were all there concerned about the same thing and we could all go to our communities and work in our own way and use our own language, but there was no *conflict* on this! And I still see this as one of the *finest* issues to pull together Jews from all different groups. Even more than Israel because Israel—there's big fights about Israel. But this, everybody agrees there's a problem. So if the Orthodox want to handle it *this* way, that's fine, and if the Reconstructionists want to handle it *that* way—that's great.[8]

Troster's enthusiasm for COEJL's approach is not unique. Year after year at the annual Mark and Sharon Bloome Leadership Training Institutes, new participants praised the open spirit on display when mostly "secular" environmental Jews sat side by side with Orthodox Jews and chanted the traditional Shabbat blessings together. Although such ritual "togetherness" was not without its occasional tensions, the quest to unite around a common concern for the planetary future kept such tensions at bay.

COEJL not only bridges denominational gaps, but also other kinds of identity fissures. As one institute participant said:

In my usual life, I'm an environmental lawyer during the week and a Jew on Shabbat. I live in two worlds, a professional one and a spiritual one. But at COEJL I have come to feel like I can finally integrate the two. Environmentalism is an extension of my Judaism. And in some ways it's the essence of my Judaism. Judaism is about *tikkun olam* [the repair of the world], and it's environmentally where our world needs the most repair right now.[9]

COEJL and other eco-Jewish movements are evidence of the power of reframing. Just as evangelicals are reaching out to some unlikely bedfellows to form creation care alliances, so too are Jews reimagining Judaism as being less about "what *kind* of American Jew are you" and more about "how do you plan to do *tikkun olam* work at this time and in this place." In addition, because COEJL clearly "speaks to the unaffiliated and the young," as one college student put it to me, it is having the unexpected effect of drawing Jews back into Judaism. COEJL's own self-study document observed: "In particular, among those under 40 were many who began to 'rediscover'; and reconnect with Judaism through the environment. . . . Five years of discovery resulted in a palpable sense of the potential of 'Jewish environmentalism' both to be *a source of freshness and vitality for Jewish renewal* and to help address environmental challenges."[10] What we hear in this COEJL report is not only that religion may be good for environmentalism, but also that environmentalism may be good for religion.[11]

From Reframing to Re-acting

Like religion, environmentalism reminds us that we are not at the center of it all, that there is a wider world out there than our particular (sometimes out of control) needs and wants. Environmentalism, in its best sense, in its least "ismy" dimensions, can help keep religion honest. It can remind us that religion is not about tribalism, denominational schisms, and debates about who is a "real Jew" or who is a "real Christian." In the religious-environmental worlds I have inhabited, these questions of identity and difference tend to be put on hold for wider concerns: What is my place in the world? What is my responsibility to my human and nonhuman neighbors? What does it mean to be a keeper of the garden? What does it mean to be humble before the whirlwind? These existential questions take us to new places.

Until very recently, the climate crises has been discussed and debated in primarily scientific terms, leading many to either dismiss or "tune out" of the conversation. In contrast, the people I have studied (both theist and otherwise) are experiencing the climate crisis as the deep moral crisis that it is. They, like me, sometimes cry when they listen to the news. Yet our connection with the source (God, or nature, or the interdependence of all things) provides us with a moral language, sometimes halting in its despair, sometimes vaunting in its hopeful vision of a new future.

Lakoff has argued that "new framing" is vital for social movements to be able to respond to the values experienced and articulated by the broader public. A new language, a new vision, indeed, a new dream, are necessary for the public to recognize that care for the earth is not only about wilderness and is not simply an "interest" of white, liberal elites who like to climb mountains. Religious forms of environmental concern bring us back to the essential questions: of social justice, of care for our neighbors, of love for our children, of honoring life in its myriad forms.

Ultimately, religion leads us past reframing and is far more than a tactic. Religion is about ideas, certainly, but it is lived in practices, in rituals, and in daily attempts at repairing the world. Reframing, then, is just a beginning (and in religious groups, it is less reframing than getting back to the original frame that reminds us that humans are not at the center of it all). From reframing we move to re-acting, to acting anew.

The act of binding back is always about second chances, returning again to what is essential. In the Jewish tradition, a song is often sung as the sun sets and the day moves from Shabbat to the dawn of the week of work: "Return again. Return again. Return to the land of your soul." There is much work to be done. Reframing is the start. Then there is re-acting and returning to the work of the world, to soul work that renews us within while repairing without. The climate change crisis reveals our brokenness in so many senses, but, like many fissures, it lets in the light of a new world of opportunity and hope, a world to which "religion on the ground" has much to contribute.

9. Climate Justice

JULIAN AGYEMAN

HARRIET BULKELEY

ADITYA NOCHUR

> Where US energy policy is concerned, African
> Americans are proverbial canaries in the mineshaft.
> Congressional Black Caucus Foundation, 2004

MEDIA IMAGES OF POOR AFRICAN Americans stranded on rooftops in the wake of Hurricane Katrina in 2005 shocked all Americans. Indeed, Katrina suggested a disturbing picture of who will be most vulnerable in a world in which climate change continues unabated. Since the early 1980s, the U.S. environmental justice movement has addressed the unjust reality that poor people and people of color are disproportionately affected by environmental "bads," such as toxic facilities, poor transit, and increased air pollution, and have restricted access to environmental "goods," such as quality green and open spaces. As a result, scholars and activists have developed specific Principles of Environmental Justice* and redefined the "environment" as "where we live, where we work, and where we play." As the climate movement grows, environmental justice groups are increasingly grappling with the issue of climate change. They recognize that extreme

---

*The Principles of Environmental Justice were developed at the First People of Color Environmental Leadership Summit in Washington, D.C., in October 1991 to provide a guiding vision for the U.S. environmental justice movement. For the complete text of the principles, see www.ejrc.cau.edu/princej.html.

weather events, rising sea levels, food insecurity, worsening air quality, and heat and tropical disease will also visit disproportionate consequences on low-income people, people of color, and indigenous communities.

To be truly powerful and effective, the climate movement must mobilize all Americans, including and engaging people of all colors and income brackets. In this chapter, we illustrate how mainstream climate change advocates and environmental justice organizers can work on the ground to achieve their common goals. Articulating key connections and exploring common goals is not only crucial to the process of building a unified climate movement in the United States; it will also help climate activists to create strategies and tactics that work.

Given these issues, we three believe that it is necessary to examine the historical links between climate change and justice and the ways in which environmental justice movements are addressing climate change. Our collaboration on these issues began during the fall of 2005 when author Nochur, then a student at Tufts University, engaged in some preliminary research for author Agyeman's environmental justice class. Bulkeley, a colleague of Agyeman whose work has focused on climate change politics, joined the conversation shortly thereafter. In this chapter, we argue for climate justice as a central organizing principle for the climate movement. By engaging issues of climate justice, it is our belief that the climate movement can create a sense of urgency to mobilize activists, communities, and policy makers alike toward truly just and sustainable solutions.

The International Climate Justice Movement

Just as mass protests against globalization took place on the streets of Seattle and Genoa, the concept of environmental justice has spread and become interlaced with broader sets of visions and demands, and a global movement for climate justice has emerged. This movement can be seen in the work of many groups:

- Think tanks such as India's Centre for Science and the Environment
- Activist organizations such as Rising Tide, an international network of groups in Europe, Australia, and North America

- Faith-based initiatives such as the European Christian Environment Network around international equity issues
- U.S.-based policy groups such as EcoEquity
- Indigenous groups such as the U.S.-based Indigenous Environment Network
- Indigenous peoples such as the Inuit who are spearheading arguments that those in the global south, although responsible for few emissions of greenhouse gases, would feel the effects of climate change disproportionately

International climate change negotiations have always included discussions of equity issues with regard to the extent of responsibility for emissions reductions as well as the distribution of effects and the possibilities for compensation. The United Nations Framework Convention on Climate Change (UNFCCC), recognizing the high levels of emissions produced to date by North America and Europe, has acknowledged the need for "common but differentiated responsibilities and respective capabilities" between the developed and developing worlds, as well as the requirement that the "developed country Parties should take the lead in combating climate change."[1] The issue of how vulnerable geographies, such as small island states, should be compensated for climate change impacts has proven more contentious. By the end of the 1990s, many in the global community believed that the international negotiations had turned toward predominantly technical and economic agendas at the expense of justice- and equity-related concerns.

As a result, a climate justice summit was held as a parallel alternative to the Sixth Conference of the Parties (COP-6) to the UNFCCC in The Hague, Netherlands, in November 2000. Organized by CorpWatch and the international Rising Tide climate justice network, the summit marked "the first time that such a diverse group of grassroots activists from around the world gathered to focus on climate change."[2] As official government delegates met on the other side of town, summit attendees spoke about the impact of fossil fuel corporations on communities and the need to build a global grassroots movement to combat climate change.

Such climate justice advocates recast the issue away from technical and scientific aspects and toward thinking in terms of justice and human rights. They also highlight the importance of adaptation measures for communities already threatened by climate change. At the same time, they challenge the role of market mechanisms in climate policy. Under the Kyoto Protocol, these mechanisms include carbon trading, which allows countries that are not meeting their emissions reduction targets to purchase emissions credits from countries that are exceeding their targets, and the clean development mechanism (CDM), which allows developed nations to invest in sustainable development projects in developing countries in lieu of reducing their emissions domestically.

Many climate justice activists see such measures as means by which developed countries can evade equal per capita emissions rights and continue to emit a vastly disproportionate share of global carbon emissions, thereby transferring the burden of emissions reductions to the developing world and further entrenching global economic inequity. Advocates see the CDM as especially contentious, arguing that CDM projects such as large-scale tree plantations created as carbon sinks can cause social disruption by appropriating the natural resources and lands that support the livelihoods of local communities. Such views are expressed in the Durban Declaration on Carbon Trading, which was signed by international environmental justice organizations in Durban, South Africa, in October 2004.

Climate justice activists contend that the only way to address the climate crisis is through actual emissions reductions on the part of the developed world. They emphasize the need for the participation of vulnerable communities in developing policies that incorporate social and environmental justice concerns, such as equal per capita emissions rights. They also call upon mainstream environmental organizations to develop climate justice analyses and to not settle for policies that merely make incremental progress. These values are reflected in the *Bali Principles of Climate Justice*,[3] which were developed by an international environmental justice coalition using the original Principles of Environmental Justice as a template.

The *Bali Principles of Climate Justice* were released at the U.N. World Summit on Sustainable Development in Johannesburg, South Africa, in August 2002. They provide a guiding vision for the growing global climate justice movement, articulating the connection between the localized effects of the fossil fuel cycle and the global effects of climate change and arguing that marginalized communities are vulnerable to both. The Bali Principles make it clear that a wide range of peoples—Pacific Island nations threatened by rising sea levels, indigenous tribes in the Arctic threatened by melting ice sheets, communities of color affected by oil refineries in Louisiana, Nigerian communities devastated by oil extraction—all have a direct stake in working to end fossil fuel extraction and to stop climate change. Affected peoples all over the world are building transnational networks and pursuing legal, diplomatic, policy, and community-level strategies to achieve these goals. One example is that of the Arctic Inuit people, who are seeking "a ruling from the Inter-American Commission on Human Rights that the United States, by contributing substantially to global warming, is threatening their existence."[4] In the United States, the Environmental Justice and Climate Change Initiative spearheads many climate justice initiatives, and we turn our attention to them in the next section.

The Environmental Justice and Climate Change Initiative and Domestic Climate Justice

Building on the international climate justice perspective and the conclusions of domestic reports,[5] U.S. environmental justice leaders who had attended COP-6 at The Hague recognized the need to address climate justice on a domestic level.[6] As a result, the Environmental Justice and Climate Change (EJCC) Initiative was founded in April 2001 as a project of Redefining Progress, a think tank in Oakland, California. The EJCC brings together twenty-eight U.S. environmental justice, climate justice, religious, policy, and advocacy groups to achieve its mission "to educate and activate the peoples of North America to drive the creation and implementation of just climate policies," with a focus on protecting and empowering vulnerable communities on a national rather than international level.[7]

Guided by the developing global context and movement for climate justice, the EJCC focuses on two areas: grassroots training and policy analysis. Every summer, the organization offers a ten-week-long training and internship program for young people called the Climate Justice Corps. In addition, the EJCC also offers a series of trainings targeted at communities affected by climate change. Former EJCC director Ansje Miller argues that "information about climate change issues hasn't really penetrated to low-income communities and communities of color in the United States."[8] To bridge these gaps, the EJCC has developed a curriculum to discuss with community residents the basics of climate change and climate justice as well as offer guidance in grassroots organizing. The EJCC plans to create an extensive network of trainers who will go into their own communities and teach people about climate change issues. Through this train-the-trainers program, the organization hopes to engage more than seven hundred people all over the United States, thus building a vibrant grassroots movement for climate justice.

In addition to building capacity at the community level, the EJCC also addresses broader issues of climate policy on both the domestic and international levels. By releasing press statements and research reports while also participating in international climate negotiations, the EJCC seeks to place social and environmental justice at the heart of the climate policy agenda. Reflecting these concerns, at the 2002 World Summit on Sustainable Development in Johannesburg, the organization released a series of *10 Principles for Just Climate Change Policies in the U.S.*[9]

1. Stop cooking the planet.
2. Protect and empower vulnerable individuals and communities.
3. Ensure just transition for workers and communities.
4. Require community participation.
5. Global problems need global solutions.
6. The United States must lead.
7. Stop exploration for fossil fuels.
8. Monitor domestic and international carbon markets.
9. Use caution in the face of uncertainty.
10. Protect future generations.

The EJCC has used its ten principles to evaluate the effects and implications of various federal climate and environmental policies. It is also now using them to also analyze state-level climate policies, particularly in the Northeast and California where climate activism and climate justice activism are growing. As former EJCC program coordinator Jihan Gearon argues, "It is not enough to take action on climate change—we also have to focus on doing it in the right way."[10]

An important policy principle that the EJCC and its international counterparts advocate for is the notion of "just transition." Specifically, just transition recognizes that many workers and communities will face adverse economic effects as the world moves from an economy based on fossil fuels to one based on renewable energy. The EJCC calls for measures to ensure that these groups be compensated for their losses and are able to sustain their livelihoods. It is not enough that workers and communities are protected from the adverse affects of climate change; they must also have the means to participate in the new economic order that results from adapting to climate change. According to Miller, the ideas of just transition and adaptation are increasingly filtering into mainstream environmental organizations working on climate change. Much as the original environmental justice movement challenged mainstream environmental organizations' ideas of the environment as only natural areas and wilderness, the climate justice movement is making mainstream climate activists consider issues of social, economic, and environmental justice more broadly.

The EJCC sees a great deal of promise as many of its members and other organizations as well as communities of color and low-income communities in the United States increasingly work on climate-focused initiatives. For example:

- The South Dakota–based Intertribal Council on Utility Policy has been working with mayors and Native American tribes on renewable energy issues.
- West Harlem Environmental Action is working with the City of New York on climate policy.
- Environmental justice groups in California are participating in advocacy and public hearings around climate-related legislation. Most notably, they were heavily involved in debates around carbon trading in the implementation of the 2006 California Global Warming Solutions Act.
- At the September 2006 National Latino Congreso, the largest gathering of Latino political leaders in the United States since 1970, an entire day was dedicated to environmental and climate change issues. At this event, Roger Riviera of the

National Hispanic Environmental Council exhorted the crowd
to "take control of our environmental destiny."[11]

Given that the United States has not ratified the Kyoto Protocol and
that it contributes 25 percent of global carbon emissions despite representing less than 5 percent of the world's population, the need for such
domestic mobilization around climate change is crucial. As Miller suggests,
"We're in the belly of the beast [in the United States]."[12] In the absence
of federal action on climate change, the EJCC is playing a key role in the
struggle to ensure climate justice for all.

The Promise of Climate Justice

Upon reviewing the international context for climate justice movements
and the domestic activities of the EJCC, it is clear that a groundswell of
grassroots climate activism led by low-income people and people of color
is taking place. The growing climate movement must include these constituencies to realize its full potential to effect policy change. Several challenges, however, lie ahead in the efforts to build a truly unified climate
movement. Civil rights advocate Van Jones points out that recent climate-
focused issues of *Elle*, *Vanity Fair*, and *Wired* magazines barely featured any
people of color and did not mention any initiatives led by people of color.
He further argues that such media portrayals might lead people of color
to believe that they do not have a stake in the climate movement.[13] Along
with Van Jones, we know that could not be further from the truth.

When climate change is framed as an injustice that will disproportionately affect an ethnic group (or many different ethnic and low-income
groups), the case for action among affected groups becomes greater. The
destruction of New Orleans provides a shocking glimpse of what will
become a more frequent scenario worldwide if carbon emissions continue
unabated. The vivid images of an iconic U.S. city flooded emphasize the
need to address climate change as a fundamental issue of human security to ensure public welfare now and into the future. To create public
impetus for action on climate change, the growing movement must forcefully articulate these connections and make clear that climate change is

not a future abstract issue; rather, it is already causing severe human costs that will only get worse if nothing is done.

If the climate movement is truly to succeed, it must also speak to the needs and aspirations of marginalized peoples facing pressing social and economic challenges. To this end, the notion of climate justice has transformative potential to reframe current policy debates and mobilize people by engaging in issues of housing and transport and in the challenges of ensuring a just transition to alternative, less carbon-intensive ways of living. There is significant potential for addressing issues of social and environmental justice—concerning, for example, access to mobility, decent housing, and energy—through policies for climate mitigation. The introduction of codes for sustainable buildings, the renewal of public transportation infrastructure, and retrofitting energy conservation measures in affordable and social housing all have the potential to address "traditional" environmental and economic justice issues, such as poor health from air pollution and fuel poverty (a situation in which a household has to spend more than 10 percent of its income to maintain a basic level of warmth in a house), while simultaneously meeting the wider justice objectives of climate protection.

Along these lines, the development of renewable, carbon-free energy sources such as wind power can also alleviate the pollution and environmental justice issues associated with fossil fuel generation. Such initiatives also have the potential to revitalize economically distressed communities, like Native American reservations, in a sustainable way. Similarly, groups such as Van Jones's Ella Baker Center for Human Rights in Oakland, California, see immense potential for green economic development and job creation in a renewable energy economy. These examples further exemplify how poor people and people of color stand to benefit from a well-executed, just transition away from fossil fuels. The climate movement must discuss these issues if it wants to broaden its core constituency.

Just as environmental justice groups challenged the mainstream environmental movement to consider environmental justice issues in the early 1990s, the climate movement today must develop a climate justice analysis. There is immense potential to support the work of and build coalitions with groups working on climate justice issues, and we need to start having conversations about how to go about this work in a spirit of mutual respect and trust. Communities that are most affected by climate change have the most critical stake in mitigating the problem. Because these groups tend to be excluded from policy debates, we must take additional steps to ensure that their voices are heard.

We must demand that policy solutions to climate change address issues of social and environmental justice and protect vulnerable communities; as we have seen, policy mechanisms like the Kyoto Protocol's CDM can actually create and exacerbate social and economic inequity. Similarly, in line with the principle of just transition, we must advocate for climate change mitigation and adaptation policies that will not create an undue economic burden on the poor. Finally, we must challenge the disproportionately high consumption rates of the developed nations and recognize who bears historical responsibility for the climate change problem. If we are serious about achieving climate justice, we must work toward these goals as a climate movement.

Given the current state of climate policy, it is clear that we have our work cut out for us. Although equity- and justice-related principles are present in international climate policy, little attention has been paid to the environmental justice implications of climate change on the municipal, state, and national levels, despite the increasing currency of environmental justice as a policy principle (particularly in the United States and the United Kingdom). For example, the Climate Protection Plan for Massachusetts makes numerous references to sustainability and sustainable development, but no mention of environmental justice or the state's environmental justice policy. Climate justice teaches us that advocacy around climate change must bridge such disconnects and address issues of sustainable development and environmental justice *together*. To this end, we could learn from the example of Scotland, where the Scottish Parliament has accepted the principle of environmental justice and the campaign group Friends of the Earth is using the discourse of climate justice to mobilize action around climate change policy and fuel poverty.

Perhaps most important is that climate justice challenges us to envision a world free of environmental injustice, where just and sustainable communities are the norm and meaningful participation in a renewable energy economy affirms our human dignity. It is up to us to create that world, and now is the time to start, for the benefit of present and future generations alike.

PART IV:

Getting Mobilized

10. The Tidewater

JULIA WEST

BEN GORE

WE STAND NOW AT THE TIDEWATER where the river and ocean mingle. It is a turbulent place as the rushing water tries to find a path forward. Climate activists are being forced to rethink environmentalism. The issue is not the classic questions of conservation or toxics. It is not about how to best use land or how to keep from sickening ourselves. Rather, the question we now face is how to live well without undermining the forces that support that life.

From where we stand, looking into the next era of human history, the postoil future of our middle age, we see boundless possibilities for both civilization and our natural environment to flourish. It is up to us to use this moment to our advantage.

The History of Opportunity

It is not the first time the United States has stood in such a moment. The nation was itself created out of a rift over freedom and self-determination. It was held together, and strengthened, following the Civil War by its struggle to address the issue of freedom. More recently, we have witnessed the ability of the country to repeatedly adapt and thrive during a century of rapid technological and social progress. We need to learn from this past, but also recognize that we are in era unlike any other.

The civil rights movement—one of the most successful movements in recent history—is an important example. The movement was exactly that: the inexorable motion of millions of people demanding social change. It was not only the Southern Christian Leadership Conference and the Student Nonviolent Coordinating Committee. It was an idea that had reached unbearable potency: equal opportunity, freedom, for all. The movement created the great leaders and organizations, not the other way around.

It is difficult to imagine how, in our speed-obsessed world, an action as aggressive and bold as the Montgomery bus boycott of 1955 to 1956 could be undertaken, but it is humbling to imagine the effect such an action could have. The boycott was made possible by the support of a massive, united movement. Effective action for the climate needs a similar mass of support.

Although we certainly do not need to start boycotting buses today— in fact, we need many more people to start riding them —we may need to leverage our consumer power in other ways, and the Montgomery bus boycott shows that such things can be done. Similarly, the overarching banners of justice and equality, and the moral nature of the fight for our future, could be applied to the climate movement as they were to the civil rights movement.

Much has changed in the world since the civil rights movement. Although organizing is still simply "talking to one person, then another and then another," as Cesar Chavez said, the technology with which to "talk" has changed dramatically, and the civil rights movement alone cannot be used as an exact template for the climate movement.

The global justice movement (which was called "antiglobalization" by outside observers) and movements against the war in Iraq, the two most recent large-scale movements, can give us insight into the climate movement as well. They were both concerned with creating a sustainable, just structure for human society to live in, much as the climate movement is. To oversimplify, the global justice movement hoped to globalize a set of sustainable, egalitarian values, whereas the antiwar movement aimed to prevent an unsustainable approach to furthering development by dissuading the United States from beginning a war defined by oil.

One early manifestation of the global justice movement emerged in the southern Mexican state of Chiapas. The Ernesto Zapata National

Liberation Army staged an attack on New Year's Day of 1994, the day the North American Free Trade Agreement went into effect, seizing San Cristóbal de las Casas and other towns. The *Zapatistas* fled from or lost every encounter they had with the Mexican army, and many of them died. Through their use of the Internet and the interest of the international media, however, the charismatic fighters brought worldwide attention to their cause, which they named *zapatismo*. *Zapatismo* is a unique philosophy of decentralization, localism, personal autonomy, respect for the rights of minorities and women, and the establishment of a proper place for humans in the environment, equally a mix of indigenous and postcolonial philosophy. The *Zapatistas'* uprising was, in essence, an elaborate and very tragic act of theater. But it was one that had a profound effect on its worldwide audience.

The spirit of *zapatismo* was seen in the streets of Seattle in 1999 when the World Trade Organization (WTO) held its ministerial meeting there. The tech bubble was still inflating hotly, the United States was more or less at peace, and the country was outwardly optimistic. The Washington consensus—the suite of free-market reforms also known as neoliberalism— was completely unchallenged in polite circles. Yet *something* was amiss, and the WTO became associated with it. Organizers began uniting disparate advocacy groups to ask publicly, in the face of conventional wisdom, what values society should be globalizing. The labor and environmental movements, long at odds, recognized common ground and finally began cooperating. A small group had a radical idea, taken straight from the *Zapatista* playbook: they would use nonviolent civil disobedience to blockade the Seattle Convention Center, thereby preventing the meeting from taking place. If citizens had no power in the WTO, then the WTO would have no power in the city. The idea initially seemed preposterous and inflammatory, not one to be taken seriously.

On November 29, 1999, the Monday before the meeting, there were some small preliminary marches and the assembled world leaders breathed a sigh of relief. Tuesday morning, however, when the delegates left their hotels, they found their path cordoned off by twenty thousand people peacefully blockading the roads. The meeting's opening was delayed a few hours as the police violently dispersed protesters. Later in the day, seventy thousand people marched through the city. Such dramatic tension had not been seen in U.S. streets since the 1970s, and as the meeting and protests dragged on all week, the event became front-page news the world over. The official talks collapsed as the inherent conflicts of interest among countries were exacerbated by the chaos in the street.

Mass mobilization became the calling card of the movement. Over the next several years, there were mobilizations in Washington, D.C., Genoa, Quebec City, Philadelphia, and Los Angeles. The mass mobilizations petered out, for a variety of reasons, after the devastation of September 11, 2001, but by then the Washington consensus lay in tatters. Representatives and senators were voting against agreements they would have sponsored ten years earlier. Latin America shifted even further and was electing left-wing leaders even as anarchist workers in Argentina locked out their bosses. The new conventional wisdom was that globalization must be done right.

The antiglobalization movement should be recognized as a confluence of interest, a braided river punctuated by deep pools where all strands united. There were lobbying organizations, unions, direct action collectives, and service organizations. All were doing their own work, on their own campaigns, related to creating a just economy, but periodically coming together for massive demonstrations. The mobilizations served as a nexus for educating and radicalizing activists, developing new networks, and generating widespread media coverage and debate. Their unique, photogenic combination of impassioned young people, riot police, tear gas, and giant works of public art drew attention that was then harnessed by the various participating groups. The largest demonstration, in Genoa, attracted at most one hundred thousand people, but the effect of these thousands was immense and global.

The organizing principal was "a diversity of tactics." Rather than creating a unified strategy, the goal of organizing was to create space and opportunity for groups whose goals were similar in spirit but very different in specifics to advocate for their own causes in their own ways. This strategy was a very conscious contrast to how international trade negotiations were run. The organizing model was meant to embody the values of the movement: egalitarianism and diversity.

With the terrorist attacks of September 11, 2001, the people who had organized the mass mobilizations mourned along with everyone, but they did not disappear. In the following year, as the George W. Bush administration became more bellicose, a demonstration was called to protest the impending war with Iraq. The names of the organizations were different, but many of the faces were familiar. On little more than two months' notice (the Seattle demonstrations had a year of lead time), one hundred thousand people marched in Washington, D.C. Over the January 2003 Martin Luther King weekend, again in Washington, two hundred and fifty thousand people marched. Then, as the war hysteria reached a fever pitch, an unprecedented event took place. Simultaneous marches, with more than twenty million participants, took place on February 15, 2003. New York saw half a million people clog First, Second, and Third avenues near the United Nations. San Francisco was flooded with people. London reported one million marchers; Rome, two million. Unfazed by the most rapid mass mobilization of political forces in history, though, the U.S. government went ahead with the invasion of Iraq in March.

What happened? The demonstrations lacked the spectacle, drama, and edge of the global justice movement and therefore got proportionally less news coverage and were less able to puncture the conventional wisdom of the time. Perhaps more important, the public was still unsettled by the terror attacks. People were looking for both comfort and action from their leaders and were less willing to give voice to disbelief or doubt.

Yet despite the eventual ineffectualness of the movement, it was a brilliant success at getting people into the streets. A couple of new things were also learned. One was that millions of people felt uneasy about what was happening in the world. The other was that the Internet had changed.

Whereas the early Internet was an extremely inexpensive printing press, the new Internet is a virtual meeting. Social networking software allows users to create their own content and establish useful connections. Webmasters have become *facilitators* rather than publishers. It is beguilingly simple. Now, rather than needing to be canvassed by an organizer, people in Houston, Texas, can log on and search for activities nearby. If there are none, they can post a request for one and receive materials on how to carry it out. Then, if other Houstonians go searching for an event, they find it, reply, invite their friends, and find rides all in the same place. Many of the thousands of peace vigils before the war in Iraq were self-organized in this fashion, and the mass mobilizations could not have occurred without it; the organizations simply did not have the resources. The grassroots organizing community now has a virtual analogue, one that is a powerful tool for creating more effective action in the real world.

Learning to Surf the Big Waves

Now, as the climate movement accelerates, we must learn from previous social upheavals. Many of the organizers who will make the world-shaking marches of next year and the year after cut their organizing teeth by bringing their friends to antiwar marches. The technology of the interactive Internet is maturing, and more people than ever know how to use it. The climate movement contains actors more diverse than even the global justice movement, and the lessons of creating cooperative structures that allow for different groups to work productively towards similar goals will be imperative. There is no better example of this than Step It Up, the National Day of Climate Action scheduled for April 14, 2007. The insight of the leaders of Step It Up (Bill McKibben and several recent graduates of Middlebury College) was that the 'March on Washington' model was passé. Their collective mobilization has been decentralized, with their website, www.stepitup2007.org, acting as an organizing hub for a range of diverse groups—including environmentalists in the Adirondacks and the women of the Alpha Phi Sorority at the University of Texas.

We would do well to note, too, which was more effective, the antiglobalization movement or the antiwar movement. Because of its multifront approach and its willingness to be truly disruptive, the global justice movement shattered a monumental piece of conventional wisdom. The antiwar movement, which dismissed disruption in a bid to attract a broad swath of the middle class, was brushed aside politically even as it made history. Of course, circumstances such as the national mood should be taken into account, but the contrast is certainly informative.

The immediate lesson is that disruptive militancy has a very straightforward, pragmatic role. In a situation such as we face with climate change, where severe consequences are potentially only decades away, we must make those in power uncomfortable enough so that they act now; we must create consequences in the present. Disruptive protests, when situated in a rich, constructive framework of other organizing, have the capacity to do that.

The deeper lesson, though, is that when we talk about "diverse actors," we must truly embrace diverse activities. A direct action collective will not see eye to eye with a green investment house, but we must set up a framework, such as nonhiearchal councils of speakers, that allows communication and cooperation as much as possible. In addition to its own direct effect on the situation, radicalism in the streets brings attention to the ideas of moderate intellectuals and makes lobbying groups look more reasonable. Climate rebels can enhance the work of climate reformers, and vice versa.

These recent movements are the kindling of a coming fire. The embers of experience, technology, and passion are smoldering, waiting for the right conditions. Movements, like fires, rarely have a defined structure or shape. The growing climate movement has little hierarchy, little superimposed structure, and few set boundaries. Although it has been seeded by previous movements, it is still very new and largely undefined. Although we talk of social movement theory and although it may be applicable, there is no guarantee that this emerging movement will follow any pattern or rules that it, in theory, should. It could surprise us all.

A snapshot of the current climate movement shows many promising things. It shows a young, vibrant set of actors with seemingly boundless energy. Clean energy is the buzzword on college and university campuses across the country and around the world. The problem and solutions are being studied, taught, debated, and addressed at many institutions, and many more are recognizing that now is the time to jump into the melee. The Campus Climate Challenge, which advocates a carbon neutral stance for all educational institutions, is active on more than four hundred campuses nationwide. The group is a framework, providing organizing materials and other resources for diverse student groups, bringing them into the national dialogue. Already one school, the College of the Atlantic in Bar Harbor, Maine, has taken the plunge into carbon neutrality, and great strides are being made at institutions with great intellectual clout. Students, the vanguard of any social change, are moving. The same snapshot also shows a diverse set of actors, although not necessarily in a racial or cultural sense. The diversity seen in the climate movement is a diversity of backgrounds, politics, and ideas as well as gender and age. There are scientists, environmentalists, economists, and students, of course, but also parents, politicians, pastors, business leaders, and even insurance companies asking the same questions and signing some of the same documents. These networks are not yet linked, though, and we have yet to see a coordinated national action of any import. Some strides are being made by umbrella groups such as Energy Action, a collaboration of more than thirty student environmental networks, and the environmentally and labor-backed Apollo Alliance. A national mobilization such as the Seattle WTO protests or the February 15, 2003, antiwar marches would be a powerful catalyst for widespread communication and cooperation and could leave in its wake a more fully realized climate movement.

Not everyone in this movement is ready to shut down a city, but everyone is increasingly concerned about the effects of uncontained climate change and increasingly willing to work together. This movement is not a single-issue group, and its concerns are not distant; if anything, they are too close to home. The fundamental nature of the problem means that everyone has a stake in its successful solution. This mutual interest is a large part of why the climate movement has a good chance of succeeding.

It appears as though the climate movement will continue to grow most visibly at the local level, with more campuses, businesses, and communities reconfiguring their energy systems and developing new energy sources. Although localism is a rational response to this ultimate crisis of globalization, many of the systems in which we are enmeshed are national and global in scale. As challenging as it may be, we must leverage local action into national and international power.

In the end, a movement may not be an appropriate way of describing the form our response to climate change will, or could, take. Movements, like fires or floods, can sweep through an area, superficially altering the prevailing feeling for a time but leaving the roots of the problem intact and allowing the problem to regrow over time. Climate change is not a problem we want our children and grandchildren to have to tackle.

We need a climate movement whose goal is not only to enact a set of policies, but also to enable a new way of seeing our place in the world. Even more than we need carbon trading, we need to create a paradigm shift in which sustainability is the fundamental variable in the calculus of our everyday lives. We—the people of the United States and all people of the world—need to fully understand and accept the limits we face as a species that relies on a finite, physical world.

11. Your Mission:
Focus the Nation

EBAN GOODSTEIN

LIKE MOST PROGRESSIVES OF MY generation, I grew up under the mythic shadow of the civil rights movement. My version? In 1954, my New York City–raised parents left graduate school at Cornell, packed their old green Ford, and headed south, to the Cumberland plateau and the town of Sewanee, Tennessee, population fifteen hundred. As they climbed the two-lane road to the top of the mountain, they came to a viewpoint, or, actually, two adjacent viewpoints, each providing a sweeping vista across the deep, shaggy coves spreading down to the flat farmlands in the valley below. A sign at the first viewpoint said "White View." The sign at the other said "Colored View." My dad had been offered a job teaching at a college that, although small, bore a grandiose name and tradition: *The University of the South.*

Ten miles down the road from Sewanee was a place called the Highlander Folk School. Founded in 1932 by Miles Horton, a southern labor organizer who had studied with Reinhold Niehbur at the Union Theological Seminary in New York, Highlander's original mission was to educate "rural and industrial leaders for a new social order." The school quickly became a major organizing center for the labor and later the civil rights movements, providing training, sharing information, and developing networks. During the late 1950s, virtually every major civil rights activist, from Rosa Parks to Dr. Martin Luther King Jr., attended Highlander workshops.

Civil rights was in the air as my parents, with three other white families and four black families, brought suit to integrate our local public schools. My mother, along with the local NAACP chapter president, sat down for coffee at the town restaurant and broke the color bar there. The State of Tennessee brought trumped-up charges against Highlander; my father testified at the county courthouse in its defense. The school was shut down, forced to relocate to east Tennessee. Pete Seeger slept in our family room while on tour. My parents listened to records by Joan Baez and Miriam Makeeba. We sang *We Shall Overcome*. And the signs came down. The South changed.

Here is the lesson I took from it all. In the United States, political change happens in this way: people adopt a moral cause (abolition, women's suffrage, labor rights, civil rights, antiwar, environmental, antinuclear) and build a movement to educate the public. They demonstrate in courageous ways the depth of their conviction. They build a tide of moral sentiment that eventually converts even the *existing* political establishment. Then the movement's demands are codified in national legislation.

Fast forward to 1999. With my kids growing older and my career established, I decided to apply the political lessons I had learned to the central challenge of our time: global warming. Human-induced climate destabilization, if unchecked, will kill and impoverish more people, destroy more natural ecosystems, and drive more animals, plants, and creatures into extinction than has any other industrial pollutant in human history. I believed that deep concern for the well-being of our children, grandchildren and the other species of the earth could form the heart of a new and powerful grassroots movement demanding an end to the fossil fuel era and a future of clean energy.

Some wonderful colleagues and I founded a nonprofit organization called the Green House Network. The core idea was to multiply leadership supporting the clean-energy revolution that we need to stop global warming, to be the Highlander of a burgeoning grassroots citizen's movement. As the school did during the labor and civil rights movements, we have brought together citizen activists and educators and provided information, networking, tools, and organizing models. These leaders return home to engage in action and education—giving talks, organizing conferences, holding media events, meeting with political and opinion leaders—all helping to stop global warming.

Since 1999, in partnership with many regional organizations—Clean Air–Cool Planet in New England, Massachusetts Climate Action Network, Blue Water Network and Redefining Progress in California, Grand Canyon Trust in the Southwest, Environmental Law and Policy Center in the Midwest, and Climate Solutions in the Pacific Northwest, among others—the Green House Network has held sixteen intensive weekend training workshops. Through this series of workshops—in Oregon, California, Massachusetts, Colorado, Arizona, and Wisconsin—a network of hundreds of volunteer climate change activists has been established. Collectively, Green House Network speakers—ranging from engineers to artists, from students to nurses to college professors—have now talked directly to tens of thousands of people about the need for urgent action to reduce global warming pollution. Many have done much more: Green House Network grads have gone on to found regional climate groups, work with cities and corporations on emission reduction campaigns, write newspaper editorials, lobby their legislators, organize media events, bring Green House Network training to new parts of the country, and even run for office as clean-energy candidates.

In February 2006, the Green House Network launched an ambitious national educational initiative called Focus the Nation: Global Warming Solutions for America. This project is being led by coordinating teams of faculty, students, and staff at what will be more than a thousand colleges, universities, high schools, and other educational institutions in the United States. Beyond this base, Focus the Nation is also involving religious, civic, and business organizations. Focus the Nation will culminate on January 31, 2008, in the form of one-day, national symposia held simultaneously on campuses and other venues across the country. Because the event will occur early in the political primary season, it will provide an opportunity to engage political candidates from across the country and at all levels of government in nonpartisan, campus-based discussions of climate solutions. The goal is for Focus the Nation to become a catalyzing event that shifts the national conversation about global warming from a paralyzing fatalism to determination to face the challenge of our generation.

In late fall of 2006, my colleague Chungin Chung and I began to spread the word about Focus the Nation, and the reception as we traveled across the country—from Columbia University to Central Florida to Boise State

University and many points in between—has been amazing. Already more than four hundred institutions—elementary schools, community colleges, research universities—have planted green flags on the Google Earth map on our website (www.focusthenation.org). It looks like Focus the Nation has hit the country at just the right time. Until the one-day national symposium, Focus the Nation will provide a place for the growing national concern about global warming, and growing public excitement about clean energy solutions, to coalesce into a unified national voice for action.

If you are reading this chapter before January 2008, you have, we hope, already heard all about Focus the Nation. Perhaps you are, or soon will be, deeply involved in organizing your own Focus the Nation event, at your school, place of worship, in your civic organization or business.

If you are reading this chapter after that, you are, we hope, part of a new politics: a bipartisan politics, reminiscent of America's Progressive Era, that is electing and holding accountable a new generation of political leaders committed to a clean-energy future. This chapter is about the genesis and mission of Focus the Nation and how this project can help build the new climate movement. In this context, perhaps you can reflect back on chapter 3 in this volume and ask yourself, How can I act as a citizen, a rebel, a social change agent, or a reformer?

Echoes of a Previous Era of Social Change

Focus the Nation was initially sparked by a 2006 interview with Dr. James Hansen, the top U.S. government climate scientist and director of the NASA Goddard Space Center at Columbia University:

> How far can it go? The last time the world was three degrees [C, or 6 degrees F] warmer than today—which is what we expect later this century—sea levels were 25m higher. So that is what we can look forward to if we don't act soon. . . . How long have we got? We have to stabilize emissions of carbon dioxide *within a decade*, or temperatures will warm by more than one degree. That will be warmer than it has been for half a million years, and many things could become unstoppable. If we are to stop

that, we cannot wait for new technologies like capturing emissions from burning coal. We have to act with what we have.
This decade, that means focusing on energy efficiency and
renewable sources of energy that do not burn carbon. *We don't
have much time left.*[1]

Americans really don't know this. We need to talk about this. Critical
policy decisions will be made over the next decade that have irreversible
consequences for the future. As we considered the implications of Hansen's
words, it became clear that we owe our young people at least one day of
national, focused, nonpartisan discussion of the decisions to be made in
these next critical years, decisions that will profoundly affect their future,
indeed the future of all human generations to follow. It is to this idea that
Focus the Nation is dedicated.

The Green House Network took its inspiration from the civil rights
movement, and the national network that has evolved has provided a strong
foundation for Focus the Nation. As we build this new project, however, we
look to another model of social change: the Progressive movement in America at beginning of the twentieth century. Just over a hundred years ago,
Progressive Era reformers took the country by storm. They created, for the
first time in U.S. history, a major regulatory role for an active government:
breaking up monopolies, regulating workplace and consumer health and
safety, and, under state management, establishing the country's unparal-
leled system of national forests and national parks. Progressives also democ-
ratized the political system, advocating for and eventually passing reforms
that included women's suffrage, direct election of senators, and the replace-
ment of party caucuses with the primary system.

To do so, Progressives first had to overcome a deeply entrenched laissez-faire ideology that argued against any government involvement in the
economy. They also faced down the dominance of government by the giant
trusts and monopolies of the day, and by corrupt politicians at both the
state and federal levels. Progressives achieved all that through electoral
politics. The movement elected state legislators, governors, and presidents—Theodore Roosevelt and Woodrow Wilson—from both the Republican and Democratic parties.

The clean-energy agenda is the new Progressive agenda. Clean energy can unite a powerful political coalition, including moms, patriots, unions, rural and religious voters, and environmentalists. Rewiring the world with safe, clean energy would address the asthma crisis in our cities, deprive Middle East terrorists of their source of funding, create millions of new jobs, provide new sources of farm income, stop oil drilling in sensitive habitat, and begin to stabilize the global climate.

One version of this vision is fleshed out in more detail in the Apollo Alliance (www.apolloalliance.org). Proposed by a coalition of environmental and labor groups, the project demands a federal commitment to clean-energy initiatives similar to President John F. Kennedy's launching of the Apollo moon expedition. This new Apollo Project could mobilize blue-collar workers behind the goal of stabilizing the climate by generating good manufacturing jobs. The proposed ten-year, $300 billion program would help build more-efficient cars, appliances, industrial motors, and public transit. It would develop renewable sources of electricity, with wind power and biofuels providing new sources of income for farmers in rural America. Apollo would create an estimated three million new jobs in the process.

Can the clean energy agenda be truly bipartisan? The Republican Party has a long and honorable tradition of environmental stewardship, with progressive roots stretching back to Teddy Roosevelt and extending forward to George H. W. Bush, who oversaw passage of the 1990 acid rain cleanup legislation. Today, in the Northeast and California, moderate Republican governors such as George Pataki and Arnold Schwarzenegger have carried the party's traditional torch and used government authority to protect the environment. The most powerful climate stabilization legislation yet is the California Global Warming Solutions Act of 2006, which places a cap on that states' global warming pollution. At the national level, a few Republicans, such as Sen. John McCain (R-Ariz.) and Sen. Lindsey Graham (R-S.C.), understand how serious global warming actually is. Some Republican senators from farm states, such as Oregon's Gordon Smith and Nebraska's Chuck Hagel, are attracted to the potential for rural development from clean energy (while continuing to oppose global warming legislation).

As is well known, however, the Republican Party in recent decades has seen the rise to prominence of a "government is the problem" ideology. Reminiscent of the 1890s laissez-faire world view, so-called free-market conservatives are deeply opposed to a progressive role for government. As a result, at the national level, Republican moderates who believe in strong environmental standards have largely been voted out of office. For "government is the problem" politicians, global warming is a very difficult issue. Holding global warming to the low end will require very active, very smart government action in the next few years. So there is a strong, and perhaps irreconcilable, tension between "government is the problem" politicians and a clean-energy agenda.

Given all that, the Republican Party, particularly after the November 2006 elections, now faces a major internal battle that will soon come to a head over global warming. On one side will be traditional moderates (with a base in the northeastern and western states), farm state representatives who understand the economic potential of clean energy, and procreation evangelical Christians. Against them will be small government true-believers and folks on the ultraconservative side of the culture wars. A clean-energy agenda can and must take deep root in the Republican Party, but it will always be fighting a rearguard action against party members who simply do not believe that government should cap global warming pollution or take a leadership role in driving new technologies.

Just as the Progressive movement won converts in the Republican Party, the climate movement needs to support a new generation of pragmatic Republicans. The movement also has to hold Democrats accountable. National figures are talking a good game, but the Democratic Party has in recent years too often lost its nerve. Al Gore wrote *Earth in the Balance* in 1990, but the Clinton-Gore team got little done on global warming. Kennedy family members have generally been leaders in clean energy, but they have worked to defeat a plan to put a large wind farm off Cape Cod. In 2006, citizen Gore returned to his roots with a vengeance through the release of his film, *An Inconvenient Truth*, and clean-energy rhetoric is politically fashionable. With their new but still narrow base of power in the U.S. House and Senate, will the Democrats have the nerve to face down the oil and coal industries and well-heeled donors, as well as the right-wing noise machine, and lead this country into a serious response to global heating?

Stopping global warming is not a partisan issue, but it is clearly a political one. Global warming will not be solved by individual consumers changing their lightbulbs or buying hybrid cars, desirable as these actions may be. What is required is a fundamental change in the way the United States does business, and for that kind of transformation to happen, converts from both parties need to support sweeping federal action.

In the same way the Progressive movement crystallized reform ideas that were reverberating throughout the country, Focus the Nation will provide an avenue for growing national concern about global warming and growing public enthusiasm for clean-energy solutions, helping to create a unified national voice for action. If humans seek to hold global warming to the low end, the U.S. government must do two things during the next decade. First, because Americans are only 4 percent of the world's population but account for more than 23 percent of the world's global-warming pollution, the United States must stabilize its own emissions of global-warming pollution. Second, we must invest tens of billions of dollars annually in basic research and development and the commercialization of a whole suite of clean-energy technologies. Because these technologies will take twenty to thirty years to mature, the investments must begin now. Americans certainly have the know-how, the markets, and the wealth to drive the costs down for these technologies and create the foundation for a sustainable and prosperous future.

How Focus the Nation Will Work

To move us toward this future, Focus the Nation is asking each participating campus to begin a deliberative process about policy options facing the nation in the coming decade. The goal is to get more than a thousand campuses involved. Educational institutions are a natural foundation for this national conversation: faculty and students organize symposia frequently, one-day events are quite simple to organize, and most educational institutions already have substantial faculty expertise available. Once a campus has committed to organizing its own event, it can focus on getting groups at similar institutions as well as business and community leaders to do the same. The Focus the Nation organizing committee, at the national level, will then help tie these individual campus and community-based discussions together. On the Focus the Nation day itself, each campus will endorse online a list of their top three priorities for national action in the next decade. This information can later be used to keep these issues in front of the nation's top policy makers.

Meeting these goals will mean involving approximately five thousand to ten thousand students and faculty as symposia organizers and another twenty thousand faculty, students, alums, and community members as symposia presenters, all engaging several million college and K–12 school students in day-long discussions of the climate agenda for the next decade. Each Focus the Nation site will be encouraged to end its event in the same way: by holding a nonpartisan roundtable with political leaders, elected officials, and political candidates. Imagine all one hundred U.S. senators in the country receiving invitations to come talk about clean-energy solutions to global warming at dozens of different schools in their states on the same day! Beyond campuses, faith, business, and civic organizations are also participating. The potential for this event is huge: it could catalyze the climate movement, playing the same kind of role as the original Earth Day in 1970.

What will a Focus the Nation event look like? In the summer of 2006, a couple dozen faculty, students, and staff at my school, Lewis and Clark College, hammered out one vision with three goals. First, do justice to the complexity of the subject of global warming solutions; nothing is off the table for debate. Second, involve every academic department on campus as educators. This issue is not an environmental issue; it is a civilizational challenge. Faculty—from religious studies to theater and from computer science to anthropology—all have important insights to offer as we grapple with solutions. Finally, involve students, alums, and community members in discussion.

The Focus the Nation day will start the evening of January 30, 2008, with a national podcast keynote speech by a prominent climate scientist. Throughout the next day, concurrent with classes, will be interdisciplinary plenary sessions in our school's largest venue: the gym. We are looking for serious engagement on the part of the entire campus. At many schools, presidents, faculty senates, and student governments will have endorsed the Focus the Nation resolution:

Global warming presents a serious challenge to the well-being of both people and natural systems across the planet. Public and private policy decisions to be made in the next decade regarding global warming pollution and technology investments will have impacts lasting for generations. Therefore, on or about January 31, 2008, [institution], in conjunction with colleges and universities across the country, will hold a symposium focusing on "Global Warming Solutions for America." On that day, faculty are strongly encouraged either to incorporate a focus on climate change into their classes, or else travel with their class to attend symposia programming related to their discipline. The symposium program committee will work with interested faculty to develop appropriate material for their classes, and to insure that throughout the day, diverse disciplines are represented in symposium panels and workshops.[2]

Focus the Nation is not calling for classes to be canceled and faculty will face no mandate to participate. Yet we anticipate broad and exciting involvement as teachers across the curriculum bring leading scholarship from their field into the classroom. At Lewis and Clark, we are hopeful that the entire body of students, faculty, and staff will attend some of, if not all, the day's events. The final event at Lewis and Clark, as all over the country, will be a nonpartisan roundtable (not a debate) including students and local, state, and national political leaders. Focus the Nation will engage thousands of the politicians at all levels in serious campus dialogue about global warming and the future that young people face.

But Focus the Nation won't stop there. At our Lewis and Clark planning meeting, we realized that Portland State, University of Portland, Northwest School of Law, Reed College, and Pacific University as well as Rock Creek, Sylvania, and Portland community colleges would be participating. So would a dozen high schools and two dozen mosques, temples, synagogues, and churches. Civic organizations and businesses would also be holding events. Someone suggested that we reserve a large basketball arena and get a top-notch band to play. After the band warms up the crowd, let's have Oregon's two U.S. senators, Gordon Smith and Ron Wyden—one a

Republican, the other a Democrat—take center stage with half a dozen students—two Republicans, two Democrats, and two Independents—and have an open conversation about U.S. solutions to global warming.

As Chungin and I have spoken at colleges across the country, this same conversation, and this same broad vision for Focus the Nation, keeps getting replicated. Focus the Nation will start out, and be rooted in, serious, academic, campus-based discussions about the critical policy choices the nation faces in the next decade, but we are increasingly excited by the prospect that it will become much more than that. Across the country, we believe that Focus the Nation events will spill out from campuses, and places of worship, and businesses, and civic clubs, to culminate in regional town meetings. American concern about global warming is growing, and America's engagement with clean-energy solutions is growing. Focus the Nation can be the moment at which this rising awareness coalesces into a unified national voice for action. It can be the beginning of the clean-energy era, which, like the Progressive Era, fundamentally transforms the politics of the United States, creates the tools needed to rewire the entire planet with clean energy, and lays the economic foundation for a century of American prosperity.

Or not. Time will tell and may have already told. This chapter catches me in the enthusiasm of a vision for the future, a vision that prevents vast human suffering and the mass extinction of many of the beautiful creatures with which we share the planet, a vision that offers a way out of a trajectory toward a hot planet.

Eyes on the Prize

I have been writing and speaking about global warming now for almost a decade. Before Focus the Nation, I never really knew what to tell people when they asked, What can one person do to stop global warming? How could I reply? Change your lightbulbs? Recycle? Write to your senator? No answer I could provide measured up to the scale of crisis.

Today I have confidence in my response, at least for now: organize a Focus the Nation event at your school, faith or civic organization, or business. As a reader of this book, you have the opportunity to work with others in your region to make Focus the Nation so big that it dominates the political discussion in the presidential election of 2008. I believe that together we can build a moment in which millions of Americans squarely face the future and shift the national conversation about global warming from fatalism and toward determination.

No social challenge short of mobilization for war has ever demanded the kind of rapid, global action the climate stabilization challenge now presents. It bears repeating: we have only a few critical years to act decisively if we are to keep global warming pollution below dangerous levels. To hold warming at the low end, the United States needs, very soon, to stabilize that pollution and invest the kind of money needed to drive a clean-energy revolution. The obstacles to taking these two steps are neither technical nor economic: the obstacle is a lack of political will.

If Focus the Nation is succeeding (or has succeeded) just as we are dreaming now, I know why. It is because thousands of Americans stopped thinking that someone else was going to solve this problem, because thousands of Americans recognized the historic importance of the moment in which we are living, and because thousands of Americans enlisted thousands more, in the service of a shared vision of a sustainable and prosperous future.

12. Practical Steps to Create Change in Your Organization

BOB DOPPELT

The difficulty lies not in the new ideas,
but in escaping the old ones, which ramify
for those brought up as most of us have been,
into every corner of our minds.

John Maynard Keynes

IN THE LAST FEW YEARS, I have been lucky enough to work with leaders of many different types of organizations—large, small, private, nonprofit, public—as they try to make the transition to a clean-energy economy, and here, in a nutshell, is what I've learned. Organizations that prosper over the long haul are those that first pay homage to the visions, values, and priorities that helped them respond successfully to past conditions. In response to new challenges, their leaders explicitly choose to retain some of those beliefs while modifying or jettisoning others. After a creative process of consulting, listening, and responding, they arrive at a new set of visions, values, and priorities that are better suited for contemporary and future circumstances.

The experience of Interface, Inc., the world's largest manufacturer of commercial floor coverings, illustrates the response to climate change I have witnessed: the right kind of organizational strategies can accelerate the transition to a clean-energy future. Several years ago, Interface adopted a seven-part strategy for becoming a sustainable enterprise, including the reduction of its carbon footprint. One part of the strategy focused on eliminating air emissions and effluent components; another focused on renewable energy, which meant slowly shifting to solar and other forms of renewable energy.

As the leaders of Interface began to design this new strategy, two previous unsuccessful attempts to become more sustainable were still fresh on their minds. Several years before, the company had promoted a climate-friendly floor-covering product called selenium that never took off. A few years after that, when senior executives started to talk about producing a "Cool Carpet" line of products, employees balked. According to Buddy Hay, vice president for sustainable operations at Interface, many folks at the company believed that "it had been tried before, and it had failed."[1]

In response, leaders at Interface began to envision ways to reorient their employees' thinking about what they produce and why they produce it. They began by conducting "life cycle" assessments to determine carbon dioxide emissions throughout the entire value chain: in carpet production, use, and end uses. With feedback from a wide range of employees, the product concept was then changed; for example, carbon offsets were offered as an optional sales benefit. Most important, according to Hay, is that a "big sales job internally" was then instituted to help employees and salespeople understand the need and benefits of the Cool Carpet product.[2] With the establishment of this organizational buy-in, the product became an essential part of Interface's new strategy.

This example underscores the most important questions organizations face: How do people change? How do organizations change? A related question takes us to the heart of building the climate movement: how do we mobilize resources *within* our organizations so that they become leaders in our push for a clean-energy future?

Organizations and the Power of Systems Thinking

When you strip away corporate logos and physical structures, it becomes obvious that organizations are nothing more than groups of people working together. Because they involve people, organizations are complex social systems. In my work on organizations, I regularly use "systems thinking," which can help us diagnose the nature of our organizations and their cultures. This diagnosis, in turn, can help us transform our organizations into clean-energy leaders.

A system is a whole consisting of two or more parts interacting and inter-relating with a specific purpose. Airplanes, washing machines, and automobiles are examples of mechanical systems: each has numerous parts that work together to produce a specific outcome. Organizations are social systems: they involve two or more people interacting to achieve specific purposes. The purpose of a social system—the production of a product, the delivery of a service, or the growth of profits for shareholders—shapes the way people design the "structures" of their system. These structures can include tangible or measurable components such as policies, capital investments, or the number and skill levels of employees; they can also include "soft" or difficult-to-measure components such as the quality of relationships, unspoken but accepted procedures, communication styles, and accepted thinking, values, and behaviors.

To change the performance of an organization, you have to alter the way this type of social system is structured. You also have to address the organization's culture, its dominant thinking, beliefs, and behavior patterns that shape its values and norms. Transforming an organization into a clean-energy leader requires more than just new technologies or practices; it also requires that climate-friendly thinking, beliefs, and behaviors become standard practice.

Why, though, is this transformation so often slow in coming? A basic premise of systems thinking is that social systems tend to have feedback mechanisms that help them maintain the status quo. Put another way, social systems are structured to resist change.

Now some resistance is not a bad thing: without it, chaos would reign whenever new input was received. Too much resistance, however, can lead over time to what I call "cultural sclerosis," when the beliefs, ways of thinking, and cultural norms that drove success in the past prevent new ones from emerging and becoming accepted. Under cultural sclerosis, organizational structures—including policies, capital investments, communication styles, and spoken and unspoken rules of behavior—are created that reaffirm the existing views of people within the organization. Over time, these structures create rigid, closed feedback mechanisms that make it difficult for people to keep an eye on the changing external conditions and new trends that may be critical to future success.

Unless an organization takes corrective action, cultural sclerosis will lead to "systems blindness," when people submissively and often automatically fall into patterns and get stuck there. In my work, I've frequently come across two types of this phenomenon: under *spatial* systems blindness, people see the parts but not the whole; under *temporal* systems blindness, people see the present without seeing the past or future. Systems blindness of either type always leads to big time trouble.[3]

This systems perspective can help explain the relative inaction on climate change since the 1980s. Too many of our organizations have been in a state of cultural sclerosis. In fact, at the root of the climate crisis is both spatial and temporal systems blindness with regard to our energy use: the inability of humans to see how our current behavior affects the atmosphere (we see the parts but not the whole) and the inability to see how our current behavior affects the future (we see the present but not the past or its affects on the future). Consequently, despite the imminent risks posed by climate change, the majority of people in most organizations have been blind to their organization's contribution to these risks, which makes it impossible for them to begin to envision potential solutions.

To succeed, strategies of the climate movement must be meshed with efforts to change the culture of our organizations. In the face of the immense challenges that confront us as we try to spark a clean-energy revolution, the starting point for overcoming our cultural sclerosis and systems blindness will be the willingness to honestly examine the utility of current visions, values, beliefs, and strategies. Which of them make sense to maintain, which must be altered, and which must be abandoned altogether for ones better suited to respond to the challenges of the climate crisis?

This process will not easy, nor will it be linear. It will generate discomfort and turmoil, at least in the short term. Nonetheless, if we are to overcome our collective cultural sclerosis and systems blindness, we must make a commitment to lead our organizations in this process. By altering our organizational cultures, we can choose our own future, not simply respond to events.

Culture Change and Governance

With an understanding that organizations are social systems often characterized by cultural sclerosis and systems blindness, how can we then become agents of change? The first step is identifying the greatest levers for organizational change, the points in a system at which a small modification in one thing will eventually generate big changes elsewhere. Finding the most powerful levers for change, however, is harder than it may sound; because such levers are difficult to find, managers can focus on the wrong things and push the wrong levers.

For example, many businesses and nonprofit organizations have leaders who believe that incremental improvements in energy efficiency will stimulate big changes toward climate protection. When energy efficiency is identified as a key lever, these organizations then go on to purchase costly and time-consuming software programs and install sophisticated energy monitors to reduce energy use per unit of product or service. Although these actions can be important if they are viewed as initial steps, they often make people believe that the problem is somehow solved. In the worst cases, the organizational culture may develop a feedback loop that sends the signal, "We're doing our part!" every time, say, an employee installs a new compact fluorescent lightbulb. Unless this status quo is altered, it is likely to divert attention and money from actions that could lead to substantial reductions in energy use or even a shift to renewable energy sources such as redesigning processes and products.

What are the key levers? My research suggests that changes in organizational governance provide great potential to unleash the most important types of organizational change. That does not simply mean a change in how the board of directors does its business: this view of governance is too narrow. Rather, I mean adjustments to governance systems, which determine how information is gathered and shared, decisions are made and enforced, and resources and wealth are distributed throughout an organization (figure 12.1). Because organizations are social systems, each of these three factors of governance influences the others. For example, the information an individual or group can access about the organization's greenhouse gas emissions shapes its ability to make informed decisions about climate protection. The roles

Figure 12.1: Governance systems, a three-part interactive process. Each factor influences power and authority.

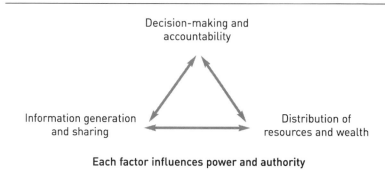

Decision-making and
accountability

Information generation
and sharing

Distribution of
resources and wealth

Each factor influences power and authority

and responsibilities people have in climate-related decision making influence the type of information they desire and the way resources may be allocated to address climate protection. The way resources and wealth are distributed often determines the levels of commitment people have to the organization and affects the type of information they want and the role they are willing to play in decision making. In short, each factor influences how power and authority are distributed within an organization that is trying to become a clean-energy leader.

Ineffective governance systems may persist because of cultural sclerosis. Long after an organization's founders have established its governance system, variations of this system may still be in place because of inertia or the power of vested interests, even though the organization's purposes or external environment may have changed substantially over time.

For example, organizations founded in the United States in the 1940s and 1950s often adopted tightly controlled hierarchical governance systems. The top-down autocratic model was common at the time: the country had just come out of a major war in which top-down centralized control won the day, most people were not well educated and therefore needed strong direction, and the management of large organizations was relatively new. Today, though, external conditions have changed significantly; for example, people are better educated than ever before and thus want a say in what they do and how they are treated. All too often, however, renditions of old governance systems have remained in place; as the country tries to transition to a clean-energy future, these tightly controlled hierarchical organizations may depress the capacity of people to create and innovate in response to new challenges such as carbon constraints.

The Wheel of Change Toward Sustainability

As the climate movement grows, successful organizational change will require clarity on two questions: What are we striving to achieve? and What is our theory of success?

Change agents are often not clear about what they want to achieve. Is the goal to simply improve energy efficiency, or is it to redesign processes, products, or services and dramatically reduce and eliminate greenhouse gases? An old saying summarizes this dilemma: "Any path will get you there if you don't know where you are going." Without clarity of purpose, organizational members often get confused and invest time, money, and resources on dead ends or counterproductive paths.

Similarly, a theory of success is vital to determining how to achieve the purpose. A theory of success allows change agents to plan, monitor, and assess progress. Organizations that struggle when engaging in major change usually do not have a theory of success, or, if one exists, it is based on fundamental misperceptions about how their social systems function. Without clarity of purpose and a coherent theory of success, organizations often end up pursuing a scattered array of disconnected activities and projects that produce little meaningful change and often frustrate or depress members.

In this section, a set of interconnected interventions that can foster fundamental organizational transformation is presented. With an understanding of this wheel of change, leaders of the climate movement can accelerate the transition to a clean-energy economy. Although these interventions are described step by step, it is critical that you understand that organizational change is not linear. It's messy. In chapter 3, Mary Lou Finley cautioned that the climate movement will involve fits and starts, progress and reversals. The same will be true for the organizational change that will be required within this movement.

Figure 12.2: The wheel of change toward sustainability.

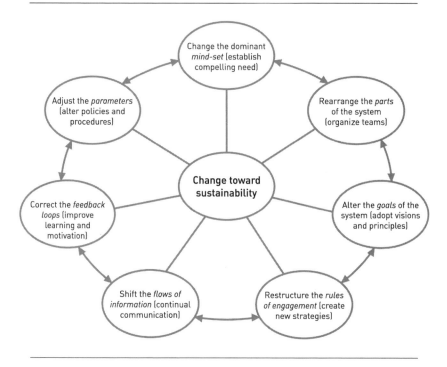

It is possible to start the change process anywhere on the wheel of change (figure 12.2). For example, leaders of a university may begin by increasing the inflow and dissemination of information about the likely socioeconomic and environmental effects of climate change. Once students, staff, and faculty have become educated about the global dimensions of the problem and risks to the organization, teams may then be formed to craft a vision of success and develop a climate protection strategy. At a Fortune 500 company, change efforts may begin with senior executives announcing their intent for their organization to become climate friendly and then instituting most of the interventions in sequence. No matter where change begins, however, eventually each of the seven interventions must be sufficiently addressed for the wheel of change to roll forward successfully. Any especially weak intervention will produce a flat spot on the wheel and cause the change effort to, say, go off the road.

Intervention 1: Change the dominant organizational
mind-set through the imperative of becoming climate friendly.

As the Interface, Inc., example points out, the greatest leverage point for transforming a social system is to change the dominant controlling thinking, beliefs, and assumptions or mental mind-set that created and supports the current fossil-fuel–dependent system. Disrupting an organization's controlling mental paradigm is the most important step toward operating in a climate-friendly manner. Little meaningful change will occur if this step is unsuccessful.

If you can alter the dominant mental paradigm of an organization, you can change the entire way the organization is governed and operates. How do you change the controlling mind-set? You must acknowledge the benefits that traditional thinking and beliefs historically have provided. You can point out the risks that the old mental paradigm now poses to the organization and workers, and clearly and repeatedly describe how new, climate-friendly thinking and beliefs are better for everyone.

An enlightened leader in a small organization can sometimes alter the controlling mind-set by simply talking with other senior executives, employees, and stakeholders. Most organizations, however, seem to require a major top-to-bottom effort led by senior executives or a major crisis to spur action. In the vast majority of cases, a relentless and compelling message is required to make the case that safety from the financial consequences of carbon caps, social protest, financial losses, customer defection, or environmental crisis can be achieved only by adopting new climate-friendly thinking, behaviors, and practices.

Intervention 2: Rearrange the parts by organizing
climate protection teams.

Once business-as-usual thinking has been shattered, the next step is to rearrange the parts of the current system. Recall that the way the parts of a system are arranged shapes how it functions. If you can reconstitute some of the core elements of an organization, you can change how it operates. Rearranging the parts means involving individuals representing the whole system of the organization in climate protection planning and implementation.

Because planners and decision makers often surround themselves with like-minded people and consequently handle problems in the same way time after time, involving people from every function, department, and level of the organization—and possibly even key external stakeholders—in clean-energy planning and implementation is important. Changing the composition of decision-making groups elicits new ideas and fresh perspectives. Different people often identify problems and generate solutions one group could not see because it was unconstrained by the norms and values of the old team.

The organization of climate protection transition teams is one of the most effective ways to rearrange the parts and get the whole system involved. These teams can be charged with crafting the vision, goals, strategies, and implementation plans for the shift to climate protection. Over time, as clean-energy planning becomes part of the everyday fabric of the organization, the makeup and purpose of the teams are likely to shift. The most important step each team must take is to get clear about what it is striving to achieve, about the role each team members will play, and about the rules to follow in accomplishing the mission.

Interface, Inc., involved many people from throughout the company in its process of designing its Cool Carpet program. This move was critical to the company's success, according to Interface's Hay, who led the effort.[4]

Intervention 3: Change goals by crafting an ideal vision and guiding principles of climate protection.

The next leverage point for transforming an organization into a climate-friendly entity is to alter its goals. If you change the goals, different types of decisions and outcomes will result. Goals that ignore or give minimal attention to the need for clean energy will lead to thinking and decisions that generate harmful outcomes, whereas goals aimed at reducing the emissions of greenhouse gases will lead to responsible choices and governance patterns.

How do you change the goals? You establish the unambiguous purpose of reducing greenhouse gases to specific levels and becoming climate friendly at a specific time in the future. One of the best ways for transition teams to develop new goals is to use "ends planning," or "backward thinking." This strategy involves envisioning how an organization will look and function as a climate-friendly entity in five, ten, or twenty years. The climate-friendly vision becomes the new goal. Because compelling visions are felt in the heart and understood in the mind, it is best to describe the vision in a way that engages people emotionally as well as intellectually.

Once the vision is crafted, organizations can adopt first-order principles that support the vision and provide a road map for decision making. For example, a principle can be adopted stating that renewable energy will be the first choice for any new energy or transportation decisions whenever feasible.

Intervention 4: Restructure the rules of engagement by adopting source-based, climate-friendly strategies.

After a compelling case for change has been made, people are sufficiently motivated to participate on transition teams meaningfully, and the teams have adopted clear purposes and guiding principles, the next greatest intervention for change is altering the rules that determine how work gets done. Power over how work gets done is real power. If you change the rules that determine how the various units of an organization interact to achieve their purpose and how information is produced and shared, decisions made and enforced, and resources are distributed to support the new workflow, very different types of outcomes will result. How do you change the rules of engagement? You have transition teams develop new operational and governance strategies, tactics, and implementation plans.

To do so, four questions must be answered.

1. *How do we affect the climate now?* To respond, baseline data describing where and how the organization's processes, products, or services currently affect the atmosphere are needed.
2. *How do we want to affect the climate in the future?* The answer to this question involves adopting clear goals and targets that clarify when and how the organization expects to achieve climate-friendly milestones.
3. *How do we get there?* This step requires the adoption of new operational and governance strategies and tactics for achieving the goals and targets.
4. *How do we measure progress?* Credible indicators and measurement systems are needed to assess progress toward the goals so that adjustments can be made as needed.

Interface, Inc., used life cycle assessment software to calculate the total carbon dioxide emissions from its carpet, including the extraction and processing of the raw materials, internal manufacturing and transportation, sales and administration functions, product installation and maintenance, and ultimate return and reuse. The emission reduction credits used for the Cool Carpet program were then secured from a variety of sources. Some come from its supply-chain partners, others come from companies that sell carbon credits. Through continuous improvements in energy efficiency and increased use of renewable energy resources such as solar, wind, and biomass power, Interface has reduced its total greenhouse gas emissions by 29 percent since 1996.

Intervention 5: Shift information flows by tirelessly communicating the need, vision, and strategies for achieving climate protection.

The information that is available to people shapes their understanding and their ability to make good decisions. Even when all other interventions have been successful, progress will stall without consistent exchange of clear information about what global warming is, how it may affect an organization and workers, what the organization can do to reduce its risks, and the benefits of making the transition to clean energy. The more that climate-related information becomes dominant throughout an organization, the more likely people are to grasp its meaning and commit to change.

Therefore, the next greatest leverage point for change is a constant exchange of information about the need for the climate protection initiative and its purpose, strategies, and benefits. How do you change the information flows? You tirelessly communicate the need, purpose, strategies, and benefits of climate protection internally with employees and externally among stakeholders.

Focus groups and other research completed on climate change communication suggest that many people do not understand the problem or what can be done about it. Systems blindness is part of the problem. The mental framework many people hold makes it hard to grasp the lag time between the emission of greenhouse gases and its effects. The lack of scientific certainty about how climate change will play out is another issue, which has been made more problematic by vested interests that use scientific uncertainty to confuse people into doubting the science of global warming. To overcome these issues, it is important to clearly and constantly describe what global warming is, to repeat that by working together the problem can be solved, and to simultaneously provide concrete examples of what the organization as a whole, and employees and stakeholders personally, can do to address the problem. (For more guidance in this process, see chapter 5.)

Intervention 6: Correct feedback loops by encouraging and rewarding climate protection learning and innovation.

Even with compelling visions of a climate-friendly organization, sound guiding principles, and excellent strategies and communication, obstacles to greenhouse gas reductions and the adoption of clean energy will surface. To overcome the barriers to change, the organization must alter its learning mechanisms and feedback systems so that employees and stakeholders are continually expanding their skills, knowledge, and understanding of climate change and protection. Constant learning and feedback allow people to understand the effects of their choices and actions and to make appropriate adjustments. The lack of consistent and credible learning and feedback systems leads to poor understanding and thus to flawed decisions.

How do you change feedback and learning mechanisms? The key is to foster and reward continual individual, team, and organizational learning. The adoption of new learning mechanisms leads to wholesale changes of traditional feedback systems that are oriented toward maintaining the status quo.

Intervention 7: Adjust organizational parameters by aligning systems and structures with climate protection.

Once a climate protection change initiative has progressed and new ways of thinking, beliefs, and behaviors have emerged, the approach must become embedded in the parameters of organization. In the organizational context, changing the parameters means aligning key systems and structures with climate protection. For example, performance on climate protection must become a core element of employee performance evaluations, hiring, promotion, succession planning processes, incentive and internal measurement systems, and other mechanisms that influence the behavior of employees and stakeholders. A set of consistent and mutually

reinforcing signals must continually bombard employees and stakeholders until it is impossible not to think or behave in ways that are consistent
with a clean-energy future.

Although many organizations start change efforts by altering internal policies, by itself that is the least effective intervention. If the old ways
of thinking and belief systems remain intact, changing internal policies
will have very little effect on decision making or behavior. People will find
a way around. When linked with the other six interventions, however,
adjusting the parameters can help embed climate protection in the organization's standard operating procedures and culture.

Changing policies is generally the last step in the change process.
Change, though, should never actually end at this stage. Becoming a climate-friendly organization is a long-term iterative process. The wheel of
change must continually roll forward. As new knowledge is generated
and employees gain increased know-how and skills, new ways of thinking and acting will need to be incorporated in the way the organization
thinks and does business.

Organizational change is difficult under most conditions. The climate crisis poses a special challenge because resolving it will require a major paradigm shift that will involve everything from the type and amount of energy
we use to our transportation patterns, use of plastics and products based
on fossil fuels, agriculture, forestry, other natural resource practices, and
waste-disposal methods.

After years of studying organizations, I have come to believe that people and organizations move in the directions of their thoughts. Our images
of the future guide our actions and achievements. Therefore, keep focused
on what you want your organizations to achieve, not on the obstacles. By
focusing on your goals, you and your organization will achieve success.

PART V:

Getting Results

13. The Sound of
Birds Not Singing

WILLIAM CHALOUPKA

AS I BEGAN TO STUDY the making of environmental policy, my graduate work often focused on the odd political discrepancies between the New Left and various countercultures. Since then, I've kept it up. For twenty years, I lived in western Montana and watched the environmental movement blossom, at the same time that a proud two-party tradition very nearly died amid the resentful conservatism of the rural West. Now nestled in Colorado—and more than a little pleased by the political change in the rural West evidenced by the 2006 midterm election results—I'm also still convinced that the best strategic course for environmental politics is neither obvious nor yet in place. Some of that work is intellectual work. As much as our urgency counsels us to act, our history should remind us of the risks inherent in large-scale interventions in complex systems. That is a founding wisdom of the environmental movement. Try to kill the bugs and you end up killing the birds, and making the bugs stronger.

After years of studying and teaching politics, I've concluded that politics is no different than trying to kill bugs. Its systems are complex, and cause and effect are seldom clearly linked. Political change is no more reducible to a simple technical fix than is pest control. The certainty that such fixes offer is misplaced and misleading. What works at one time and place is easily misapplied to another time and place, with disastrous results. The same goes for political ideologies: the simplest, most comforting explanations often are too simple.

Understanding these dynamics is perhaps easiest through a historical view of environmental politics. Consider the work of Rachel Carson, the author of *Silent Spring*, the book that in the 1960s sparked the environmental movement. Carson yanked much of the developed world into the beginnings of environmental awareness with a narrative, a dramatic, well-aimed story. She told us that unexpected effects, spread with technological ease and speed, could even stop birds from singing. Hers was the story of a trickster. It was a mental exercise, a *frame* in today's parlance, a brainteaser that aimed to (and did) produce conceptual change, which then led to considerable political change.

Politics is also narrative in the sense that it unfolds in time and space. Thus, *politics is uniquely contingent: what happens next is deeply conditioned, but seldom determined, by something that happened before.* I use the term *contingent* (rather than, say, *historical*) for an important reason: that chain of causes and effects may be hidden and hard to find, and it persistently resists being codified into simple formulas and routine technique. That's why the strategies and pathways found in this book cannot be reduced to "Fifty Surefire Ways to Stop Global Warming." Politics, like nature, is not that simple.

If this view of politics does sound a lot like how we view ecology, it might be that the sound of the birds not singing is becoming more audible. Environmentalists, as a group, are deeply committed to contingency and relational thought through their understanding of the complexities of ecologies, but they have been remarkably unable to do politics the way they do ecological science. How, you might ask, did that happen? As you might expect, it calls for a story.

The Birth of Green Politics

In natural ecosystems, environmentalists understand that interventions have consequences, not all of which are intended or are even understood to be related to the original intervention. In a political ecosystem, this deep relatedness is even more crucial. As in a classic ecosystem form, a sequence of events and conditions sets us on a path that we generally still follow. To understand how we arrived at this political moment in time for the new climate movement, with a long-delayed take-off period only now finally under way (see chapter 3), it is crucial to study the 1970s.

Although American greens revere earlier forebearers such as Henry David Thoreau and John Muir, the break symbolized by Earth Day 1970 was a massive disruption, a distinctively new beginning for contemporary environmentalism. That first Earth Day promised something that greens had never before even approximated: a mass movement. It is not too much to say that the entire contemporary canon of green thought took shape in the five or six years surrounding that first Earth Day (if we reach a bit, to let Rachel Carson into the mix).

Before the 1970s, throughout the early and middle twentieth century, the environment was a matter, in the political context anyway, that few cared about. It didn't rank on the policy agenda except when insiders inched some specific issue up higher on the agenda, year by grueling year. So the first generation of greens worked the only way they thought possible: through influence on elite leaders. Muir and Gifford Pinchot battled for President Theodore Roosevelt's approval. Years later, the Wilderness Act passed in 1964 because the Wilderness Society's director shepherded the process for ten years, almost entirely out of the public eye, lining up congressional and administration support.[1] It was hard to imagine that green politics could ever work any other way.

The first Earth Day broke that precedent in a way that was hard to miss, particularly for those who were there. Pat Williams, a retired member of U.S. House of Representatives from Montana, recounted to me that the gulf between the leadership on the stage and the audience watching could not have been larger; white males in white shirts and ties, the elites of their day, looked out on the Woodstock generation. It was the listeners that day who were soon leading the charge: as that new generation spread its wings in the 1970s, environmentalism became a dominant political issue. Arriving just in time for persistent oil shocks, burning rivers, and remarkably toxic urban air, the environmental movement was almost instantly successful.

That remarkable popularity coincided with a sea change in the U.S. Congress. Following Watergate and after a series of reforms that undermined seniority, a young, activist Congress passed environmental laws like there was no tomorrow. In short, environmentalism arrived with perfect timing. The

movement was well articulated in science and ethics, the barriers to building a social movement were low (amid a culture of activism that had yet to
meet the resentful response that has been so successful in recent decades),
and government was uniquely susceptible to green initiatives. Compared
with feminism, which had to recover from a long period of distraction after
the ultimately unsuccessful fight for the Equal Rights Amendment, greens
had a remarkable first act on the main stage of American politics.

As the 1980s soon unfolded, the legacy of that first Earth Day strongly
persisted. Environmentalists—no matter how much they became scientific, managerial, and legal insiders—preferred to stage highly visible, public controversy as outsider protest. In protests, public controversy translates
into ritualized moralism, which has as much to do with raising awareness
and confirming movement solidarity as with reaching out in any political
way. The protests reminded greens that they were outsiders and that they
weren't being heard, and served as a substitute for activity in the electoral
arena. Not insignificantly, that message got out to their adversaries and
to the public in general.

This unique mix of "insider" and "outsider" produced subtle effects,
which have not been well understood in the intermittent debates between
the "grassroots" and "Big Green" organizations. The insider part of the
green experience in the 1970s confirmed hopes of political power and control because surely an issue that emerges so forcefully and successfully must
be on its way to utterly reshaping society. The outsider element, though—
entirely understandable in the 1970s and confirmed by green ideology—
pushed greens away from the political institutions where actual control
is negotiated. Lobbying and filing lawsuits are potentially "insider"
approaches in that they involve important institutions. The ballot initiatives and cultural gestures of the movement, however, are "outsider,"
showing skepticism of political institutions and reflecting a single-issue
approach insulated from the compromise and cooperation typical of legislative and electoral action.

Soon, a sort of perfect political storm had been set in motion, even if
nobody much noticed it at the time. For although environmentalism had
opened with remarkable success in Congress, in the courts, and, crucially,
in public opinion, greens barely noticed that their initial rush of success

had the effect of tethering them to an odd set of moral and political commitments. American greens were clearly the reborn children of Ralph Waldo Emerson, Thoreau's patron, foil, and inspiration. They accorded personal moral commitment an incredibly high value, mystically depending on individual righteousness to change the world.

The packaging for 1970s green moralism, however, was not out of the pages of Emerson or Thoreau. Instead, it followed the pattern of another old New England religious tradition, the jeremiad. Loud, insistent, unwavering demands—often informed by an apocalyptic sense of doom about nature's capacity to adapt to human intervention—durably set the tone for green moralism. Thus the political terrain of environmentalism became caught between future and past, soldiering on with the moral and cultural composition of a cantankerous, hundred-year-old Protestant Bible-thumper, utterly convinced of its vision of the future, but still hampered with the self-image of an outsider who would never quite be welcome in King George's court. Add to the package the greens' scientific evidence that the actions of humans were bringing the end nearer. The perfect political storm was settling in.

From a political standpoint, the science-jeremiad-social movement combination informed an environmentalism that could be communicated as a culture, while still maintaining an evangelism that expressed the political goals it obviously continued to have. Without question, this cultural dimension served to consolidate the movement. There were organic gardens to grow, food co-ops to found, bicycles to tune up, and solar panels to futz with. Folk music. Central American crafts. Backpacking trips. Naturopathy. Recycling centers. Birth control. Nature centers for the local schools. Granola.

While other countercultures of the 1980s were conceptualizing themselves in the terms of identity politics, the politics of environmental culture retained its old New England roots. While other movements (at least in significant part) were founded on the insistence that institutions grant them respect and an opportunity to participate, greens persisted in issuing grim predictions and insisting that authority be ceded to them, implying not merely that they should have a voice in the conversation, but that the conversation should end, the sooner the better.

Green Politics Loses Its Footing

I've been telling my students for years that politics is more like wrestling than solo clarinet. Here's what I mean. As much as we tend to praise brilliant political leaders like Bill Clinton or Ronald Reagan—with the kind of praise we might otherwise reserve for a wonderful soloist—they both led political enterprises that engaged in an activity more closely resembling wrestling than solo clarinet. One wrestler moves, the other responds. Repeat as necessary. In the political ecosystem, responses are continual. No important move evades response. It is sometimes said of political operatives that they think like chess players, plotting several moves in advance. What is meant by that metaphor is that political folk are always anticipating their adversaries' responses at the same time that they look for openings and opportunities to launch initiatives of their own.

Although political life may seem like a policy debating society or a corrupt influence market, to cite two common interpretations, something other than policy or simple corruption is also going on. Perhaps the quintessential political activity involves anticipating and understanding the opposition one's own moves are helping to create. Yet, in the decades after Earth Day, this focus was precisely the capacity environmentalism had blocked itself from developing. The strategy was not anticipatory, but prescriptive. Environmentalists were not willing to enter a wrestling match; they played their clarinet solos and expected other Americans to be as intoxicated as they were by the tune.

Rather than strengthening their ability to anticipate the adversary's moves, though, greens, encouraged by the science and ethics on their side, often tended to do the opposite. From the Reagan days and on, greens tended to ridicule their adversaries, using them to promote fund-raising. The assumption seems to have been that all resistance to the green line was absurd, so the accumulating successes of anti-environmentalists were just irrational and didn't deserve serious attention. That strategy turns out to have been a disastrous choice because a counterrevolution was gathering, one that would last longer and succeed more wildly than anyone, even the counterrevolutionaries, could have imagined.

Resentment against "the 60s," antiwar radicals, feminists, and others was already starting to mobilize in the 1960s, as personified by George

Wallace, Barry Goldwater, Kevin Phillips's "culture war" strategy for Nixon's 1968 campaign, and a legion of hard hats, cowboys, and other "real Americans." Surprisingly, it took until the late 1970s for the reaction to focus on environmentalism. William Tucker made the counterbreakthrough in a late 1970s article in *Atlantic Monthly* (expanded in a successful 1982 book), charging environmentalists with elite, self-serving defense of their own private privilege.[2] Rachel Carson's breakthrough had been turned inside out.

Soon enough, greens were one of the prime targets for one of the most powerful recurrences of an age-old American political ritual, namely, a rowdy, populist politics of resentment. Reagan won the presidency after a campaign in which he uttered a steady stream of uninformed and condescending dismissals of environmentalism (and welfare, and affirmative action, and so on). The groundwork was laid for what would later become the wise use movement, made up of those bitterly opposed to environmental regulation as a signal of government's more general badgering of "real Americans." Before the 1980s ended, Rush Limbaugh would be carrying on about greens. Soon thereafter, the right would decide that global warming was a fiction.

In surprisingly short order, environmental politics shifted. Legislative triumphs were achieved less often, usually becoming possible when pollution issues were at stake and health effects were dramatic (as in the case of Love Canal) or federal pork barrel spending was enabled (as in the various iterations of the Clean Water Act). Reagan contested the future of the then-new Environmental Protection Agency, delaying many appointments and placing famously partisan appointees in some crucial offices. There were more successes in the courts, however. Court cases and congressional indecision "locked up" potential wilderness, an outcome greens could live with. Ecosystem-wise, however, these wins came at a terrible political cost because the politics of resentment could easily demonize the greens' new litigation strategy. The virulence of the new resentment in the rural West was particularly troubling. That region not only included crucial public lands of great interest to greens; it also contained enough U.S. Senate seats to throw the Senate to the Republicans, perhaps for generations to come.

Just as greens know that an ecosystem can mask indications of trouble, if one does not know precisely how and where to look, those more attentive to political ecosystems know that apparent stability can be misleading. A toxic event can harm relatively invisible organisms, and the threat to the more prominent ecosystem citizens might not be evident until the damage is irreversible.

By their own measures, greens could convince themselves that they were succeeding. Public support in polls remained high; group memberships and budgets grew; the courts remained generally friendly; and none of the hallmark legislation was actually dismantled, despite the vigorous criticism directed against such laws as the Endangered Species Act.

In classic ecosystem fashion, however, these optimistic indicators did not tell the whole story. A powerful opposition had formed in resistance to green proposals. That opposition was complex, including both an electoral dimension (the populist, angry anti-green element crucial to the right's electoral success) and a policy dimension (typified by Vice President Dick Cheney's secret meetings with energy lobbyists during the preparation of the George W. Bush administration's legislative proposals on energy). Although green values continued to poll well, they did so only in general terms. Few voters chose candidates on the basis of green issues, and few candidates—at any level—chose green issues as their defining trademark. Some who did—notably Sen. Frank Church of Idaho—lost their seats.

Lessons from the First Years of Climate Politics

When the climate change issue emerged on the global stage in the 1990s, nobody seemed to recognize that the issue would so thoroughly expose the weaknesses of environmentalism in the United States. Once the leadership of the Republican Congress under Clinton and then George W. Bush ignored dire warnings about climate change and allowed only minimal U.S. responses, a sort of political divide was reached. Environmental issues could now be scorned openly; bogus scientists, in cahoots with the carbon industry's well-heeled Global Climate Coalition, seemed to "balance" serious ones in the accounts of the popular media. Silly arguments demonstrated considerable political appeal, and ad hominem attacks from global warming deniers like Sen. James Inhofe (R-Okla.) (who in a 2003 speech declared that global warming is a hoax) were perceived as honest political discourse, replacing even the pretense of serious discussion. Somehow, the most dramatic environmental crisis ever articulated did not boost the American environmental movement; rather, it did the opposite, revealing the movement's many problems.

When could we begin to see the limits of the environmentalists' political potential? I believe the fulcrum moment actually arrived in 1993, early in the Clinton administration, when Clinton's economic plan—the first important legislative proposal made by his White House—was being formulated. If environmentalists were going to flex their political muscle, now was the time; Vice President Gore, after all, was the most prominent elected green in U.S. history. Yet even though Gore's bizarrely titled "Btu tax" would have forced conservation and helped balance the budget, goals that would have been consistent with both administration and environmentalist policy preferences, this version of a pollution tax, exactly what economists have advocated for years, never really made it out the door of the White House. In the judgment of the seasoned pols on the Clinton team and in Congress, it was a political "nonstarter." Treasury Secretary Lloyd Bentsen considered the tax to be "an administrative and political nightmare."[3] Having achieved its highest status in terms of elected sympathizers, the environmental movement lost out almost immediately. Subsequent, less public green successes during the Clinton years did not change the fundamental calculus that was set in place by the Btu tax's ill fate. If this condition needed confirmation, it came in the sad fate of Gore's own run for the White House in 2000, in which he deemphasized his own green credentials.

Only the persistent fund-raising expertise and professionalism of the environmental movement were left to mask the obvious: from its early triumphs in the 1970s, environmentalism had hit bottom. It was unable to move its most important issue, unable to elect its most prominent supporter, and unable to respond to the flood of resentment sent its way (notably in western states, where wilderness and species preservation issues were acute). Politically, the movement seemed utterly stalled. Success stories were few and far between.

Remarkably, environmentalism got a "last chance" it might not have deserved. Less than a year after George W. Bush's election, the September 11, 2001, attacks on New York City and the Pentagon reopened issues of politics in the Middle East. Although the focus was obviously on Islamic radicalism, there was an unmistakable environmental element to the story given that the region's geopolitical importance was largely determined by its petroleum reserves. It was as if a life raft had been sent to the greens. Politics is known for this sort of unexpected, even perverse development, precisely the sort of thing one wouldn't dare write into a novel because it was so improbable. Here, finally, was a frame for conservation that even a politically debilitated green movement could surely recognize and employ to rebuild itself. (See chapters 4, 5, and 7.)

You know the rest of the story: little or nothing happened. The evidence was now unavoidable. The environmental movement had expired. Even the miraculous green life raft sank.

Of course, echoes of the environmental movement still resound, but in my opinion, until we began to see the rise of the new climate movement, there had been little reason for optimism. Instead of a lively debate over how to rekindle the movement, we have seen in the last few years defensiveness and a resistance to change. If ever there were a movement that needed to be chided a bit about its own "death," this one's it. The hope of the new climate movement is the potential rebirth that will follow, but this movement must be composed thoughtfully, with attention to its political context.

Bringing Our Understanding of Ecosystems to the New Climate Movement

In most troubled ecosystems, environmentalists warn about quick fixes, reminding us that one intervention, even if it's the one they think most urgently necessary, might not solve the problem. One change sets off unpredictable effects, which then cause further dislocations, perhaps revealing even more relationships than had previously been understood. The political ecosystem is as complex as any natural ecosystem.

Yet into the early part of the twenty-first century, too many environmentalists who would scoff at any simple fix for a natural ecosystem were offering simplistic tactical solutions for the political ecosystem. One suggests that lobbying is the only viable option. Another argues that only grassroots activity can create change. Another suggests that institutions are hopeless and that only personal consciousness will work. One says we should work on poverty, while another says we should work on population. We must understand that there is no strong argument on behalf of elevating *any* of these tactical commitments to the level of a master green strategy. Each might be right in one setting, but wrong in others. Each produces responses from adversaries, some predictable and some not. It is easy to imagine that we need some mix of those elements, but that conclusion is of little help because it does not explain how the mix should be calculated, timed, and implemented.

The ecosystem metaphor suggests that we should look beyond the obvious effects because some pattern of relationships might be determining outcomes in ways not entirely obvious at first glance. The prominent role played by contingency in all politics means that grand, sweeping solutions—driven by ideologies—carry a heavy burden. Similarly, efforts to rely on scientific fact also get sidetracked in the political arena. The only way out of these traps is vigilant, savvy, and persistent attention to the political world.

How can the new climate movement learn from all that? Seemingly surefire ideologies represented the *modernist* approach to politics. In the wake of modernism's exhaustion, many social movements have reexamined and altered their political assumptions. This process is usually indirect, imprecise, and slow; intellectuals argue out the political theory, and their conclusions filter out, more or less efficiently, to activists and citizens. Feminists worked out the movement's attitude toward "essentialism," for example, as the civil rights movement had earlier worked out arguments about violence, nonviolence, and black nationalism. In a sense, all these discussions were about modernism, ideology, and certainty.

Alternative political movements across the board have had to rethink and reorient their political assumptions. In many cases, this change has involved rethinking the very basis of their political thought, especially as it relates to nature, the appeal to naturalism that has been so powerful during modernism's long run. It has been a particularly difficult discussion for environmentalism, which has, in fact, resisted the debate quite adamantly.[4] Perhaps fearing the kind of factionalism that has often typified the left, greens have steered toward the unanimity promised by science and a nearly monolithic ethical outlook, both of which are stands characteristic of modernist political thought. This commitment to a politics of certainty is deeply engrained in green political culture. By capturing nature and harnessing it to their cause, greens implicitly wagered that political success must be associated with certainty (which they believed science would underwrite).

Simply put, I believe that nature has become a problem for its best friends. Reliance on nature has rendered greens slow afoot, easy prey for even the youngest and least talented hawk. To make matters worse, the ethical framework that American environmentalism inherited from nineteenth-century New England further stymied its ability to rethink politics and shake itself free of habits that once worked but now clearly harm the movement. Too many environmentalists have treated politics as something simple and unimportant. Well, politics bit back.

So, what is to be done? As documented throughout this book, many people are working on this question. That's the good news. As the new climate movement takes off, I believe we can begin to see pathways forward through, let's call it, a pragmatist's top-ten list. I conclude this chapter with these brief suggestions and observations that, I believe, offer a better political approach for the new climate movement.

1. *Politics isn't a technique.* There is no set of tools at hand, guaranteed to work. Political life is more like an ecosystem, which calls for ongoing efforts at understanding and relationship.

2. Therefore, *green politics won't be fixed "once and for all."* It requires an ongoing conversation, a discussion or argument. Just as we need environmental chemists, we need green political intellectuals. We need more debates, including debates explicitly over political strategy.

3. *Green ethical thought* has been a remarkable development and nobody imagines it going away, but *it is not the same thing as politics.* We need to understand and debate the politics of change related to environmental issues in general and climate change in particular.

4. *The debate over the labels "global warming" and "climate change" probably doesn't matter.* Either label amounts to a demand that citizens and governments, in effect, shut up and listen to the scientists who will tell us all what nature demands. That approach has failed, and we have to replace it.

5. *Even organized labor is now debating big, dramatic change. If they can do it, surely we can, too.* Perhaps a megamerger between a green group and a group not identified as green is needed. Perhaps we should be talking about a serious effort to replace the Democratic Party or to put the weight of the movement behind some "change the rules" proposal that would, for example, alter the electoral structures that make third parties so hard to sustain in the United States. Let's seek out bold alternatives.

6. *Environmental studies students need to know as much about politics* (including, but not limited to the civil rights movement and subsequent identity politics movements) *as they are now expected to know about mathematics, chemistry, and biology.*

7. *Among our most important topics is the response to the resentment that has been aimed against greens.* Responding to it isn't easy, so it isn't surprising that it hasn't really started. The response could well go to the core of our politics, to the opening we granted our adversaries when we decided to claim authority in the name of nature as interpreted by science.

8. *Although the discussion about "framing" is useful—especially because it highlights the importance of political tactics—it isn't enough.* It only indirectly engages underlying assumptions and structures of green politics.

9. If biodiversity is a positive value in most natural ecosystems, *political diversity is even more important to the political world.*

10. *Maintaining a sustainable environmental movement is an insufficient goal. The goal must be far more ambitious.*

Telling Your Stories

How can climate warriors, you good readers of *Ignition*, put this top-ten list into action? Like Rachel Carson, you need to tell your stories, craft your tricks. They must be sufficiently seductive and disorienting to enable your audience to live in the newly realigned universe you are suggesting. Tricksters in this age of climate crisis now have to conjure up a second act. Citizens and activists have to generate the next move, and the one after that,

and the one after that, and none of these moves will be guaranteed to succeed, as if underwritten by the original conceptual change. The advice in
this chapter, in this book, is simply that: advice for getting our stories right
in hopes that some of them will change the world.

It's clear that to build a green future, we must change our politics. To begin,
we must recognize a simple truth: politics is distinctively narrative. It's done
with stories. Climate activists need to see that, because stories that have succeeded elsewhere—as literature or journalism or certainly as science—still
have to jump a boundary to generate political change. It's not enough to say
that climate scientists are predicting, say, a five degree Fahrenheit increase in
global temperatures by 2100. We need to ask, How can we climate tricksters
translate that prediction into stories that will bring about political change? In
addition, we need more than one story, for let's recognize that only a rare few
stories, like Carson's, carry conceptual breakthroughs. Many more stories are
of a second order; they work out the practices, understandings, and other
implications that follow the breakthroughs.

We need many stories, and better ones, too. And don't believe a sto-
ryteller who says her story "just came to her." That may be so, but it probably suddenly appeared after much effort to understand how stories work.
It's the sort of work we know; it's like studying an ecosystem. Then, all of
a sudden it seems, knowing what needs to be done. It's how the story goes.

14. Policy Pathways

CHRISTOPHER MCGRORY KLYZA

DAVID J. SOUSA

GLOBAL WARMING ACTIVISTS are rightly frustrated with the lack of forward movement on climate change policy in the U.S. Congress. Virtually nothing positive has come out of that body on the issue. Yet they shouldn't be surprised; such is the case in environmental policy making more generally. Since 1990, Congress has enacted only two significant environmental laws. It is a far cry from the golden era of environmental policy making of 1964 to 1980, when Congress passed more than twenty major laws dealing with the control of pollution and the management of private lands, public lands, and wildlife, laws such as the Clean Air Act, the Endangered Species Act (ESA), Superfund, and the Wilderness Act.

Congressional gridlock, though, does not mean policy gridlock. Indeed, policy making is flourishing through a set of five other pathways:

1. Appropriations and budget politics
2. Executive branch policy making
3. The courts
4. Collaboration-based politics
5. Prominence of the states

This chapter draws on material from *American Environmental Policy, 1990–2006: Beyond Gridlock* by Christopher McGrory Klyza and David J. Sousa (Cambridge: MIT Press, 2007). Copyright © 2007, The Massachusetts Institute of Technology. Published by permission of The MIT Press.

These nontraditional paths reveal a vibrant environmental policy arena at the beginning of the twenty-first century. Today, reform impulses confront the past and the present, the institutional and legal legacies of more than a century of state-building, and contemporary forces that have tied up Congress on environmental issues.

In this chapter, we examine the forces leading to congressional gridlock on the environment. We first discuss the significance of the *green state*—the set of laws, institutions, and expectations dealing with environmental policy. We then illustrate how to use these policy pathways in order to attack climate change in ways that will be useful to those in the policy arena.

Gridlock in Congress

Six main factors lead environmental policy making to become gridlocked in Congress: increased partisanship, a weakening of liberalism, trends in public opinion, increased interest group mobilization, more pervasive media, and the changing nature of environmental problems. Each factor is discussed in turn.

Increased Partisanship

There was remarkable bipartisanship on the environment in the golden era. For example, the vote on final passage of the ESA of 1973 was unanimous in the Senate and had only four dissenters in the House of Representatives. The bipartisanship soon began to change, however. According to the League of Conservation Voters, in the mid-1970s Democrats in Congress voted proenvironment 15 percent more often than Republicans. By the mid-1980s, that figure was in the low 30 percent range; it was more than 50 percent by 1994; and since 2000, Democratic voting for the environment regularly exceeds Republican scores by more than 60 percent.[1] What was once a low-conflict issue in Congress has become one of the nation's most partisan issues.

The Weakening of Liberalism as a Force in Political Life

Although there is now a lively debate about the future shape of the post-industrial Democratic Party, at least since 1980 the national party's liberal wing has been a frail political force. Its demography has changed. The competitive strengths of the parties have shifted. Organized labor declined, and the business community has become a dominant political actor. In addition, powerful intellectual assaults on some of the legacies of policy liberalism have combined to create a difficult political environment for activist liberalism, which has also been racked by internal divisions.

The wave of environmental laws that peaked in the 1970s followed hard on other major statutes that expanded the functions of the federal government, including Medicare and Medicaid, federal aid to education, and President Lyndon B. Johnson's Great Society. At that time, public trust in government was only beginning its steep descent, and it was easier then than now to make the case that large-scale federal intervention was necessary and was likely to alleviate pressing environmental problems.

The deterioration of trust has sharpened the right turn in policy debate, making major expansions of the federal government's domestic policy role—always difficult to achieve—even less likely. If expanded governmental power is needed to tackle global warming, the deterioration of trust and the weakness of the liberal impulse will limit the nation's ability to address those problems.

Trends in Public Opinion on the Environment

The electoral successes of Republicans have come despite, not because of, the Republican Party's positions on environmental issues. Public support for environmental protection remains strong. In a 2005 poll, 70 percent of Americans identified themselves as "active environmentalists" or "sympathetic to environmental concerns," and 24 percent described themselves as neutral. Only 4 percent called themselves "unsympathetic" to environmentalism.[2]

Although general support is high, environmental protection has low salience with voters. Few citizens rank environmental issues among the top concerns they carry into evaluations of government performance or candidates for office. Still, general levels of public support for environmental protection may be higher now than they were during the golden age of environmental lawmaking; certainly they are not lower. Public opinion seems generally supportive of the policy status quo, offering no strong support for new liberal initiatives or for conservatives seeking to amend laws such as the ESA and Superfund.

Indeed, in the 104th Congress (1995–1996), Republican leaders learned that citizens' general skepticism about government and the larger "right turn" in U.S. politics did not extend to support for rolling back the federal commitment to environmental protection. Citizens perceived the Republicans to be too extreme on environmental issues; claims that the green state was inefficient and too invasive had little effect, and the party was forced to moderate its rhetoric and its agenda. Likewise, to this point there has been no broad public outcry about the failure of successive presidents and sessions of Congress to act decisively to address global warming.

Thus, the environment seems to be a settled issue in public opinion. There is strong general support for the green state despite conservative complaints about costs and inefficiency and despite environmentalists' concerns that efforts at pollution control and conservation have been too weak. The barriers to dramatic policy change in the United States typically give way only when there is a perceived crisis. Today—despite increasing concern on global warming—there is no widespread sense of crisis on the part of the public, no overwhelming fears about continuing environmental degradation or deep concerns about the economic and social costs of environmental protection. Public opinion supports the status quo, feeding legislative gridlock.

Increased Interest Group Mobilization

Although public opinion on the environment has been stable for many years, the organizational politics surrounding these issues has changed dramatically. The environmental policy arena is thick with political organizations, and the intense mobilization of interests on all sides of key policy questions has limited opportunities for major legislative action. The explosion of environmental advocacy in the early 1960s and 1970s created a large interest group sector. Indeed, the environmental movement was "the largest, most visible, and fastest growing part of the citizen's sector" in the latter part of the twentieth century.[3] Christopher Bosso argued that "the breadth, density, and diversity of the environmental advocacy community give environmentalism itself greater resiliency and impact than are often recognized."[4] Environmental groups have been minor players in campaign finance, but their large memberships and staff resources, coupled with strong general public support for environmental protection, have made them formidable players in legislative politics.

The legislative successes of environmentalists triggered two significant reactions. First, business interests, knocked off balance by the environmental enthusiasm of the 1970s, quickly caught themselves and dug in against the expansion of the green state. Business political mobilization increased sharply in the 1970s, with significant increases in lobbying and campaign spending as well as support for policy research and public advocacy highlighting the costs of the new social regulation. One breathtaking development in this field has been the growth of corporate political spending, both in terms of direct contributions to candidates and soft money. The corporate sector's outsized fund-raising capacities give it ample resources to compete with a large and powerful environmental movement. Second, business mobilization has been joined by a grassroots "green backlash" movement incorporating diverse concerns, including outdoor recreationists, ranchers, farmers, property rights activists, and wise users. These backlash groups have achieved few significant legislative gains, but their activism has crystallized national discussions about the human costs of environmental protection and environmentally sensitive resource management.

Interest group mobilization has contributed to legislative gridlock on environmental issues, frustrating environmentalists and those seeking to roll back the laws of the 1960s and 1970s. Green groups are powerful enough to resist changes to the basic environmental laws favored by business and anti-green backlash groups. Yet environmentalists have been unable to overcome business resistance to green legislative proposals. Corporate campaign contributions, lobbying, and the capacity to summon angry grassroots support have hemmed in the environmental movement in Congress. The level of interest group mobilization on the environment could not have been dreamed of in 1970, and it has certainly contributed to legislative frustration for allies and enemies of the green state.

A More Pervasive Media

Since the 1970s, there have been several significant changes—often related to transformations in technology—in how the media cover government. First was the increase in satellite television linkages, leading to increased local television coverage. Local coverage influences how members behave, frequently leading to an increase in symbolic stands on issues and illuminating member behavior more clearly.

The rise of the Internet was a second important media change. The Internet made it easier for interest groups and individuals to track what members of Congress were doing on particular bills, to send e-mail action alerts to group members, and to deluge Congress with e-mail messages on issues (to a lesser degree, messages were sent by fax for a time). Activists and interested citizens seeking detailed information on what is happening in environmental policy can easily look beyond mainstream news sources and rely on releases from environmental organizations or economic interests that may offer up slanted versions of the issues at stake. There are also several environmental news services, such as the *Daily Grist*, *Headwaters News*, and *Greenwire*.

In addition, the increase in media outlets thanks to the Internet and the growth of cable TV led to more competition to break stories and to fill pages and time. These increased media outlets have also combined with the traditional mainstream media approach to reporting on contentious policy issues of presenting views from representatives of "both sides" of those issues. This practice has amplified the voices of the small minority in the scientific and policy communities who doubt that the global warming phenomenon is real or is linked to human activity. The result has created confusion for citizens where little should exist, making it more difficult to advocate for decisive action on this critical problem.

These changes in the media have combined with the well-known sensitivity of politicians to constituency interests, rising partisanship, and the explosion of interest groups. Thus, there is a reduction in the space available for members of Congress to engage substantive and wide-ranging legislation, especially legislation that alienates any significant population of groups.

The Changing Nature of Environmental Problems

In the early 1970s, pollution control policy focused primarily on curbing effluent and emissions from large, readily identifiable industrial sources.

Many of these sources are now reasonably well-controlled. Now we must look at more dispersed and widespread pollution sources.

What makes these problems even more difficult to address is that the politics of environmental policy change as the source of problems is defined as "us" (drivers of old cars, farmers, runoff from city streets, dry cleaners) instead of "them" (factory smokestacks). Developing national standards is difficult because of the complexities of the new problems; the prospects of high costs and palpable constraints on citizens' behavior change the politics of pollution issues. Legislators find it more difficult to support laws aimed at citizens and small businesses.

Taken together, these factors explain the difficulties Congress has had in dealing directly with environmental issues since 1990. This congressional gridlock, which has made it difficult for the political system to address new problems as well as concerns about existing laws and institutions, has been reinforced by the institutionalization of several layers of environmental policy commitments made over a hundred years of political development. These laws, institutions, and expectations dealing with conservation and environmental policy control strong points on the policy terrain and in many areas have held the status quo against drives for policy change. Yet the layering of the green state not only contributes to gridlock; it also energizes modern environmental politics and offers opportunities for policy to make its way up and down these layers and across the many alternative paths created by the green state and offered by the structure of the U.S. political system.

The Green State

The American green state consists of three major layers laid down over two hundred years: economic liberalism, conservation, and environmentalism and preservation. Over time, new impulses have come to dominate green state building, putting in place new laws, institutions, and political premises to guide policy. New impulses have not completely displaced the old, however; instead, they have layered new laws and built new institutions atop existing—and sometimes contradictory—structures. Because these past layers are not cleared away over time, there is no fresh start for new policies and institutions. Contradictions, conflict, and opportunity are built into the green state, with significant consequences for environmental policy making today.

The first layer of this green state, laid down from the founding of the United States through 1890, focused on developing the nation's resources, and its administrative footprint was light. The dominant ideas regarding natural resources at this time were economic liberalism and the belief that society would flourish if government transferred public lands to the private sector.

During the decades on either side of 1900, a concentrated flurry of activity created the second layer of the green state, a layer characterized by two impulses. The first focused on conservation, namely scientific management of natural resources, with Gifford Pinchot of the U.S. Forest Service its most noteworthy proponent. The foundational idea for conservation was technocratic utilitarianism: professionals should manage natural resources for society's greatest good. Preservation of scenic and natural areas was the focus of the second impulse, with John Muir and the Sierra Club leading the way.

The establishment of the second layer began a pattern for future green state building: rather than clearing away the earlier layer of the green state, reformers laid the second layer on top of the existing layer. In most cases, this method led to few problems because the first layer of the green state was thin and spotty and these new laws and institutions were laid down in open political space. Furthermore, because conservation was centered on resource development, it did not conflict fundamentally with the programs of the first layer. Over time, however, this layering of the green state led to major tensions that are at the core of modern environmental politics.

The period from 1964 through 1980 was the golden era of modern conservation and environmental policy making, when the third layer of the green state was created. During this time, Congress passed twenty-two major laws focused on pollution control, private lands, public lands, and wildlife management. Some new laws, such as the ESA and the Wilderness Act, were layered on top of the green state from the early twentieth century with, in hindsight, predictable results. The laws dealing with pollution, nearly half of the major laws, were largely forays by the federal government into open policy terrain at the national level. State and local governments had been dealing with pollution issues—under the rubric of public health—for many decades, but the federal government did not enter this arena in a significant way until 1970. Hence, the air pollution, water pollution, and hazardous chemical policies crafted during this decade fell on largely fallow soil. The original laws and the amendments that followed were far-reaching and complex, and the pollution portion of the green state quickly grew after its later beginnings. The Environmental Protection Agency (EPA), pulled together by collecting preexisting programs and agencies, also found open terrain as it began its work in 1970.

During this first decade of substantial national pollution control, almost all laws were based on a regulatory approach: government sets acceptable levels of pollutants and determines how firms will meet these levels. Even though other ideas have since flourished—market incentives, pollution prevention, risk management—it has proven nearly impossible to dislodge the regulatory programs at the heart of these pollution control statutes. Although these pollution control laws have not led to the same level of conflict within the green state, their broad economic and societal reach has made them quite controversial. The same is true for the National Environmental Policy Act, which introduced the environmental impact statement requirement for all significant federal actions. The once relatively narrow and economic development–oriented green state had changed dramatically.

With the election of Ronald Reagan and a Republican Senate from 1980 to 1986, congressional conservation and environmental policy making slowed, but still continued. President George H. W. Bush sought to reinvigorate environmental policy making when he was elected in 1988. Congressional environmental policy making under Bush culminated with the 1990 Clean Air Act amendments. Since then, Congress has passed only two significant conservation and environmental laws: the California Desert Protection Act (1994) and the Food Quality Protection Act (1996). Further building of the green state—at least at the national level—essentially stopped circa 1990.

This layering of multiple orders of policy regimes, without cleaning up past orders, has created a labyrinth in the green state. New policies often conflict with old ones; past ideas are embedded in policy regimes, creating policy patterns especially resistant to change. This labyrinth offers opportunities as well as constraints. Some of these opportunities are immediately apparent and pursued, and others became visible only over time.

As the green state has grown, it has become more and more of a labyrinth, especially because Congress has never taken the time—nor mustered the will—to clean up and reorder the green state. Congressional reform is unlikely to restructure the green state; it is far more likely that when it can act, Congress will add new layers atop past laws, building further complexity and contradictions into environmental policy. That is true even with a Democratic Congress.

The Policy Pathways

With this labyrinth in place and with Congress currently in gridlock mode on the environment, anyone who wants to reform, roll back, or extend the green state has to explore alternative pathways to have a real effect. These pathways have become the central arenas for environmental policy in the 1990s and the early twenty-first century. Some are built into the green state—appropriations politics, executive politics, the courts—whereas others can be viewed as ways to bypass the green state—collaboration, the states—but they are all ways for pent up policy to flow when "normal" legislative channels are gridlocked.

Appropriations and Budget Politics

With Congress unable to pass environmental policy through traditional means, members of Congress are increasing the use of the appropriations and budget process to make policy. Appropriations bills must pass each year or the government will not have money to operate. These "must pass" bills are attractive vehicles to tack on policies that might not be able to pass through normal legislative channels.

A relevant example dealt with Massachusetts' Cape Wind project, a proposed wind farm of 130 turbines located off the coast of Cape Cod. This offshore location has generated significant controversy, especially from such influential politicians as Massachusetts' then governor, Milt Romney (R), and Sen. Ted Kennedy (D). With the project moving toward approval and construction, Kennedy sought in 2006 to have Congress give Romney (and other coastal governors) the power to veto the project. Kennedy did not do so through an energy bill, but rather through the appropriations bill for the Coast Guard. After significant public pressure and criticism from other politicians, this proposal was dropped from the final appropriations bill.

Executive Politics

The president can make direct policy through existing discretionary laws, through executive orders, and through rule making. Neither Presidents Bill Clinton (D) nor George W. Bush (R) made use of these powers to advance significant climate change policy. Clinton did, however, issue several executive orders to improve energy efficiency at federal facilities.

Future presidents could make robust use of such executive orders and, even more important, of rule making to advance significant climate change policy. For instance, the president could determine that carbon dioxide is an ambient air pollutant under the Clean Air Act and require the development of regulations to reduce carbon dioxide levels.

The Courts

A group of primarily Northeast and West Coast states initiated two major lawsuits seeking to force the federal government to reduce national greenhouse gas emissions. The states, blocked in Congress, have not only acted on their own (through, for instance, renewable portfolio standards), but have also sought to use existing laws to achieve their goals. The first case seeks to have the EPA regulate motor vehicle emissions as greenhouse gases under the Clean Air Act. The Court of Appeals for the District of Columbia issued a complex split decision supporting the EPA's decision not to regulate these gases in *Commonwealth of Massachusetts v. Environmental Protection Agency* in July 2005. The Supreme Court heard oral arguments on the case in November 2006. The second case seeks to find several electric utilities responsible for their greenhouse gas emissions under public nuisance law. In September 2005, a federal judge dismissed the case (*State of Connecticut v. American Electric Power Company*), ruling that the case dealt with political questions that should be decided by the political branches, not the courts. The following month, the states appealed the decision. A victory—such as the Suprmeme Court decision on the first case—should have tremendous ramifications for climate change policy.

Collaboration

The collaborative pathway seeks to bypass, whenever possible, the conflict and inefficiencies of existing environmental policy and move in the direction of more efficient, pragmatic environmental policy. This approach goes by a variety of names—next generation, partnerships, reinvention—but they all seek what could be called "win-win" solutions. Supporters argue that collaboration can be achieved through increased reliance on flexibility, market mechanisms, and bargaining.

Among the leading examples of this approach in climate change policy are the following:

- Ceres, a network of investors and environmental groups seeking to reduce greenhouse gas emissions in partnership with industries
- The Pew Center on Global Climate Change, which works across the economic, political, and societal spectrum to advance pragmatic efforts to reduce greenhouse gas emissions
- The U.S. Mayors Climate Protection Agreement, in which U.S. cities seek to achieve Kyoto Protocol reduction targets

Although there are several promising cases of collaboration, the collaborative pathway faces a number of significant challenges, including determining who participates in the process, addressing the conflicts with existing laws and regulations that often constrain efforts at collaboration (the green state), and dealing with challenges to collaboration by opponents through other channels. Furthermore, the scope of the climate change challenge is such that it is unlikely that collaboration alone can effectively deal with the problem.

The States

As Barry Rabe points out in chapter 16, the states have been leaders in crafting climate change policy, especially through renewable portfolio standards. As noted above, however, the states have also not hesitated to turn to the courts in an effort to achieve policy goals.

Overall, two key factors appear to indicate when the states can serve as an innovative pathway. The first is when the states are acting in open policy terrain. That is very much the case with climate change policy, where there is no federal law analogous to the Clean Air Act. Second, state policy making is likely to succeed in areas in which the states have existing, secure policy responsibilities. Public utility regulation is an excellent example of this state-level opportunity.

These factors, of course, do not guarantee state action. There is also tremendous potential for contingency and conflict on the state pathway because of its intersections with federal policy making. Furthermore, conflict is never far removed from these state efforts. Policy advocates will pursue other venues, such as the courts and turning to Congress—thereby dragging opponents into the green state labyrinth—when such a course furthers their interests.

Congress is gridlocked on the environment, and the forces leading to gridlock will be difficult to overcome. Given the tremendous scope of the climate change challenge, we cannot afford to write off Congress as a place to make policy. Indeed, Congress must pass a comprehensive climate change policy at some point. At the same time, however, climate activists and others in the policy arena should continue to work on the alternative policy pathways.

Three of these pathways offer the most potential for significant and far-ranging policy: executive politics, the courts, and the states. With a sympathetic president in the White House, rule making could be used under existing law to regulate greenhouse gas emissions. A positive decision on one of the state-initiated cases working its way through the courts could dramatically alter the status quo, perhaps even requiring significant greenhouse gas reductions. Finally, the states have taken a leadership role on climate change and further successes seem likely there.

The American state has multiple access points. In seeking positive climate change policy, we should make use of all those pathways.

15. Climate Change and the Business Challenge

EILEEN CLAUSSEN

THIS BOOK, *IGNITION*, INCLUDES dozens of stories of individuals and groups who are taking responsibility in this age of global warming. At the Pew Center on Global Climate Change, which I have had the honor to lead since its inception in 1998, we have had a bird's-eye view of the growing realization, by so many Americans, that it's time to step up. In the last few years, from our perch inside the Washington, D.C., Beltway, we have been thrilled to collaborate with leaders of civic groups, businesses, and state governments who are taking the lead as the climate change movement comes into its own.

Alas, we have not seen such leadership from the White House in recent years. Indeed, the way the George W. Bush administration has shirked its responsibility on this issue reminds me of something I recently ran across on the Internet. It was a posting of actual comments on actual job applications. In one group of comments, people were asked why they had left their most recent jobs. One answered, "Responsibility makes me nervous." Another wrote that his former employer insisted he arrive at 8:45 every morning and that he—quote—"couldn't work under those conditions." Now just a word of advice to all you college-age readers: those are not the kinds of things you want to tell your future employers!

This chapter is partially based on the 2005 Scott Margolin Environmental Affairs Lecture, delivered at Middlebury College in April 2005.

Yet the attitude reflected in these comments is not all that different from the attitude toward climate change on the part of many of our nation's leaders: responsibility makes them nervous. It is not only the Bush White House. The Bill Clinton administration, for its part, seemed much more interested in appearing to take the climate change issue seriously than in actually doing something about it, which brings me to yet another actual quote from an actual job application. In this instance, the individual was asked about any unique skills or attributes he brought to the job. The answer: "I procrastinate—especially when the task is unpleasant."

Well, as chapter 2 makes clear, we can't procrastinate anymore. We need a groundswell, now. In this chapter, I focus specifically on policy levers that can enhance the role of the business community in building and maintaining this groundswell. Business participation, business action, and business innovation are all essential to reducing the very real threat that climate change poses to the world in the years and decades ahead.

Businesses Get on Board

A carbon-constrained world, a major goal of the climate change movement, is not an environmental fantasy, it's an inevitability. A world that is serious about addressing climate change will be a world that is serious about reducing carbon emissions. There is no other solution to this problem. The only question is how quickly it becomes a widely shared priority, and we all have an obligation to make it become a priority sooner rather than later.

Many business leaders understand and accept that things have to change. Consider this recent statement from Jim Rodgers, chief executive officer of Cinergy Corp., a major coal-burning energy company: "One day," he said, "we will live in a carbon-constrained world." Or look at this statement from John Rowe of Exelon: "There should be mandatory carbon constraints." You can't get more straightforward than that. Then there is a third quote, this time from Paul Anderson, chief executive officer of Duke Energy, one of the world's largest utilities and one that has historically been cautious on environment issues: he said that any action we take to address climate change must be "mandatory, economy-wide and federal in scope."[1]

Why is business coming around to the need to address this issue and beginning to accept the inevitability of carbon constraints? Well, to a large degree it is because of the facts: the science on this issue is no longer something you can dispute with a straight face, and some governments among are beginning to act. In 2006, for example, we saw real leadership from California with the passage of its Global Warming Solutions Act and from the nine-state Regional Greenhouse Gas Initiative.

In the years ahead, as policy makers begin to devise the rules and the strategies that will guide business action on these issues, companies will want a seat at the table. At the Pew Center, we recently commissioned Andrew Hoffman, professor of sustainable enterprise at the University of Michigan, to write a guide for corporate decision makers as they navigate rapidly changing global markets. The report was also designed to offer policy makers insight into corporate views on greenhouse gas (GHG) regulation, government assistance for technology advancement, and other policy issues.

One of the overarching themes to emerge from Hoffman's research is that company decision makers report the need to influence policy development as we move toward new forms of government regulation. Any policy that regulates GHG emissions will certainly constitute a major market shift, setting new "rules of the game" and changing the competitive landscape. Those cited in this report believe that they cannot leave the ultimate form of such regulations to chance.[2]

New Policy Directions for Businesses in a Carbon-Constrained World

So what kind of polices does the United States need? To achieve results—to promote the climate-friendly activity that will move us toward a clean-energy future—we need strong state-, regional-, and national-level policies that send a clear signal to business that companies are going to have to act on this issue in the years ahead. To get business more broadly engaged on this issue, government needs to focus on three Ps: predictability, price signals, and a portfolio of technologies that is broad and deep enough to make a real difference.

First, there's predictability. Businesses deal with a lot of uncertainty about all sorts of factors, so they crave greater certainty wherever possible about what affects their bottom line. They need to understand the direction and the ultimate goal of national and international climate policies, and they need to realize once and for all that we are not playing games here. Businesses in the United States and around the world need to know that climate change is a priority for governments. It is for real.

Knowing and understanding these things allows business to invest with confidence in the technologies and strategies that will get us where we need to be. For many industries, decisions with an effect on GHG emissions involve huge capital investments in power plants and technologies, investments that can have a life of a half-century or more. A bad decision can be economically disastrous.

Consider a company that makes a major investment right now in a traditional, coal-burning power plant with average efficiency. Then, in a few years, perhaps government puts in place constraints on carbon emissions, constraints that render the plant too costly to run. Or consider a company that substantially reduces its emissions right now, only to have government come along in a few years and require all companies to reduce their emissions, starting *now*. The company that has been reducing all along may have used up its easy, inexpensive reductions and will have to start spending more money on harder-to-achieve reductions, whereas its competitor, not as good a citizen, is able to subsist for the time being on the easy, inexpensive ones. Uncertainty can paralyze decision making and create perverse incentives to delay action, even when it is clear that acting now is in everyone's best interests.

The most important feature of the Kyoto Protocol is that it sends a signal of government resolve. It is a strong declaration of multilateral will to confront a quintessentially global challenge, but it is only a first step. In addition, with the United States and Australia outside the protocol and India, China, and Brazil without specific requirements to act, Kyoto covers only 55 percent of global GHG emissions, and only through 2012. It is a signal, but one that is not quite clear enough.

Today, only twenty-five countries are responsible for more than 80 percent of global GHG emissions. At the global level, businesses will not have the predictability they need until there is agreement among governments, including all the major emitting countries, on what happens after 2012, when Kyoto's current commitment period expires. Whatever the post-2012 framework looks like, it will likely include more than short-term obligations. Businesses around the world need to see a clear signal. They need to see a long-term objective and clear commitments to develop the technologies that will be required to meet it.

There is also the issue for U.S.-based companies that unpredictability may work against them competitively. It is hard to deny that a U.S. business that does not have to reduce its emissions may realize a short-term competitive advantage vis-à-vis, say, a European competitor. If you look at the long term, however, you see that the U.S. company's advantage may not last.

One important way to understand the effect of postponing emissions reduction requirements in the United States is to think of this delay as a certain kind of trade barrier. Delay protects a U.S. business in the short run against increased costs of power and transportation. In doing so, however, delay lets the business duck the reality of a permanent change in world markets, changes that will definitely result from pricing the costs of emissions reduction into the way we live and do business.

Instead, its European competitor is going to have to innovate and develop new, climate-friendly technologies and processes. That company may face greater costs in the short run, but these technologies and processes will ultimately become the basis for business success in a carbon-constrained world. Without some level of predictability and some level of incentive to innovate and develop the technologies of the future, U.S. companies will forever be playing catch-up, essentially relegating themselves to second-place status.

Of course, it is not just at the international level where business needs predictability. Many U.S. states are acting on this issue and, I hope, will continue to do so. Yet if I am a business, I do not want to be regulated under fifty different state policies. We need a national approach and national strategies to make sure there is uniformity and consistency in how businesses are treated.

The second of the "three Ps" that policy makers need to think about is pricing. Because emissions of carbon dioxide and other greenhouse gases come with a cost, businesses need not only predictability; they also need a price signal. Establishing a price signal is the only way to ensure that businesses act on a scale needed to reduce emissions across the board.

Right now, businesses in the United States continue to receive a mixed message—or no message at all—about how committed the nation is to reducing emissions. A price signal from the government would show all that we are very serious about this subject and that there is a clear economic case to be made for reductions.

In October 2004, the Senate voted on the Climate Stewardship Act, a measure that for the first time would place a national cap on U.S. greenhouse gas emissions. To ensure that emissions are reduced as cost-effectively as possible, the legislation would allow for emissions trading, the so-called cap-and-trade approach. Those who are able to reduce their emissions cheaply could sell credits to others for whom reductions might be more expensive to achieve. This cap-and-trade bill, the product of a bipartisan collaboration, attracted the support of forty-three U.S. senators in 2004.

In early 2007, committee leadership in the House and the Senate passed to Harvey Waxman and Barbara Boxer, respectively, both Democrats from California, who vowed to make climate legislation a priority. For leading businesses, cap-and-trade is a promising legislative approach to the climate problem because it sends a clear price signal: businesses that cannot reduce their emissions have to pay, whereas those that can do so more cheaply and efficiently have an incentive. Cap-and-trade also is based on the recognition that whatever we do, we need to create ample room for business to do what it does best.

The third "P" that should guide government thinking and policy as we weigh how best to engage business on this issue stands for the portfolio of technologies that will be required to protect the climate. Think for a moment about the amazing variety of activities that businesses can undertake to reduce their contribution to climate change. They can do everything from embracing green power programs and cogeneration projects to developing energy-saving processes and products, clean fuels, biomass energy, clean-burning vehicle engines and much, much more. Here are some examples from the companies we work with at the Pew Center:

- Air Products and Chemicals' larger hydrogen plants now function as cogeneration facilities, producing steam and power as by-products of the production process and exporting them to a nearby user.
- Boeing is on the verge of launching production of its new 7E7 aircraft. The 7E7 will be lighter because of the use of composite materials and will use 20 percent less fuel than comparable aircraft.
- American Electric Power has committed to building next-generation integrated gassification combined cycle, or IGCC, coal plants that will not only emit less greenhouse gas right away, but will also allow them to remove carbon dioxide from plant emissions in the future, once technologies improve for capturing and storing it.

The bottom line is that climate change is too big a challenge for any one solution. Meeting this challenge will require a range of technologies, from energy-efficiency and hydrogen to carbon sequestration, renewable fuels, coal bed methane, biofuels, and more.

The Role of Citizens in Promoting Climate-Friendly Business Leadership

We can play an important role in the policy arena by calling for legislation that promote the three Ps: predictability, price signals, and a balanced portfolio of technologies. Let me also suggest a fourth P to push businesses forward: shareholder pressure.

Consider companies that might not otherwise be inclined to make the climate issue a priority. In many instances, shareholders have pushed a company to at least acknowledge the problem and its part in it and to begin weighing options for addressing the problem. Corporate managements' main responsibility, as mainstream business principles go, is to maximize shareholder value. Managers, and particularly company officers, have a huge personal and professional interest in what the market thinks of their company. Shareholder decisions to buy and sell shares are one expression of those market views. A much more unambiguous expression is the direct communication of shareholders to the people charged with looking after their interests.

In early 2005, the Securities and Exchange Commission forced Exxon-Mobil to include two shareholder resolutions on the climate change issue in the proxy for the oil company's upcoming annual meeting. One resolution called on the company to detail how it plans to reduce its emissions in the Kyoto countries in which it operates. The other called on ExxonMobil to disclose the research data behind the questions the company has raised about the science of climate change. These actions lay the groundwork to the public request in December 2006, by Sen. Jay Rockefeller (D-W.V.) and Sen. Olympia Snowe (R-Maine), that ExxonMobil stop funding the last remaining climate naysayers.

ExxonMobil, of course, has not been alone in facing these kinds of shareholder demands. A recent study by Ceres found that oil and gas companies faced a record total of thirty-one shareholder resolutions on the climate issue in 2005.[3] The filers of these resolutions include some of the world's largest state and city pension funds, a foundation, socially responsible investment firms, and religious pension funds. In addition, an important focus of the resolutions is risk disclosure. In other words, to what extent are these companies preparing for looming constraints on their carbon emissions? To what extent are they managing to maximize shareholder value over the long term, taking into account those risks?

Increasingly, this type of information is exactly what investors are going to want to know so as to make sound judgments about how companies are managing risk and planning for the future. Two companies that have responded in good faith to shareholder resolutions are American Electric Power and Cinergy (which recently merged with Duke Energy and now goes by Duke). Both these utilities prepared good, solid analyses acknowledging climate change as a major issue for their businesses. Even more important is that the reports suggested that voluntary action alone was not sufficient to protect the climate. Rather, they suggest that some form of government regulation is inevitable and that the costs of compliance could be manageable.

Shareholder pressure will be an increasingly important factor in sparking business action on this issue in the years to come. As the climate change movement builds, we can take the lead and use shareholder pressure to compel businesses to do their part.

Shaping New Climate-Friendly Policies

Climate change is not only the most important global environmental challenge of the twenty-first century; it is one of the greatest challenges that the global community has ever faced. As the climate groundswell grows through the eight stages laid out in chapter 3, it is clear that we will need to bring fresh ideas and a fresh perspective to these issues. We need answers—workable strategies, integrated into forceful new policies—that will achieve real progress in reducing emissions right now.

What's the takeaway from the business sector? As we build the necessary policies, government should not be in the business of picking and choosing technologies or favoring one industry over another. Rather, we need to encourage the development of the full complement of technologies—some of which we may not even know about yet—that will begin to deliver real reductions in greenhouse gas emissions.

That means employing a wide-ranging portfolio of policies as well. Cap-and-trade alone is not enough. We also need aggressive research and development, government standards and codes, public infrastructure investments, public-private partnerships, and government procurement programs, and I am sure there are policies we haven't even thought of yet.

If we want to have businesses engaged on the climate change issue and do what's necessary to achieve real reductions in emissions, we need to focus on the three Ps: predictability, price signals, and a portfolio of technologies that get the job done. If we throw in enough of the fourth P, shareholder pressure, we can increase the odds that we can pave the way for a clean-energy future.

16. Taking It to the States

BARRY G. RABE

THE FAMILIAR TALE OF AMERICAN federal government inertia on climate change began to change by the middle of the current decade. The U.S. Senate went on record in 2005 with majority votes in favor of a national renewable portfolio standard and a State of the Senate resolution that endorsed future action. The U.S. Supreme Court rejected arguments from the George W. Bush administration and agreed to accept a case, *Massachusetts v. U.S. Environmental Protection Agency*, that would test whether the 1990 Clean Air Act Amendments could be interpreted to mandate regulation of carbon dioxide as an air pollutant. In turn, the 2006 midterm elections resulted in partisan shifts in both chambers of Congress, with the possibility of new legislative leaders attuned to climate policy action. It has become increasingly feasible to see at least some movement on climate change by federal institutions before 2010, notwithstanding the appropriate cautionary note about the prospects for extended federal gridlock provided in chapter 14.

Nonetheless, any future federal policy development will be able to draw on lessons and models generated from an ever-growing body of state government experience. During the past decade, state capitals as diverse as Sacramento, Carson City, Austin, Harrisburg, Albany, and Hartford, among others, have proven far more responsive to climate policy initiatives than Washington, D.C. This movement on the state level reflects diverse coalitions that have converged and secured approval of a wave of new policies designed to reduce greenhouse gases, ranging from renewable energy mandates to carbon cap-and-trade programs. Indeed, just about every imaginable climate policy that a future Congress might consider has one or more precedents already put into operation at the state level. These state policies have often cut across traditional constituency dividing lines, reflecting a broad base of political support in very diverse jurisdictions. Indeed, they may represent a long-standing pattern in U.S. government whereby state action ultimately sets the stage for federal policy and some long-term sharing of authority between federal and state governments for policy implementation. In this chapter, I explain the odyssey of state climate policy formation, offering both insights for future sub-national policy review and ideas that might prove useful in future rounds of federal or international policy development.

I have long been struck by the opportunities federal systems of government afford sub-national units such as U.S. states and cities to develop innovative approaches to a wide range of environmental challenges. In the late 1990s, I became intrigued by the question of whether states might take a lead role in policy development to reduce greenhouse gases. The rather widely held assumption then was that there was really nothing to this question. Some experts suggested that it was literally a waste of time to consider any state government role because it was assumed that any state efforts would be eclipsed by national and international action. Moreover, because it was presumed to not be in a state's immediate economic interest, conventional thinking suggested that it would be totally unrealistic to expect any state to examine climate change policy options, much less enact one or more policies.

These reactions did not convince me, though, especially because I found dozens of state policies that were already in operation and had essentially been ignored by most scholars and journalists writing about the evolution of U.S. climate policy. Consequently, much of my time in recent years has been spent exploring this policy evolution, attempting to understand the factors underlying state policy adoption and examining implementation as these policies mature. The debates over climate change and possible policy options have a fundamentally different feel once they move from national and international centers to a growing range of state capitals. They move beyond traditional partisan differences and blue state–red state dividing lines, suggesting a capacity to build unusually broad and diverse coalitions that are often guided by policy experts who work within state governmental agencies.

In the diverse reactions to my work, I hear regularly from people working on the issue of climate change at the state level as they attempt to distill lessons from other states. From outside the country, there is a near-disbelief that so little is happening in the United States. As one diplomat of a European Union member nation said to me after I gave a talk in late 2005 on the changing state role: "This cannot be. This is the United States and they do nothing on climate change." I responded then, and through this chapter, that one cannot begin to understand the U.S. response to climate change without some examination of the role of states.

Bottom-Up Policy

Many accounts of U.S. public policy are written as if the United States operated as a unitary system, whereby all innovations and initiatives emanate from the federal government. A more nuanced view of U.S. federalism indicates that states have often served a far more expansive and, at times, visionary role. By the middle of the current decade, the clear majority of states could be fairly characterized as being actively involved in climate change, with one or more policies that promised to significantly reduce their greenhouse gas emissions. Virtually all states were beginning to at least study the issue and explore very modest remedies. A growing number of them—such as California, Connecticut, New Jersey, New Mexico, and New York—were every bit as engaged as European capitals and far more active than all Canadian provinces except Manitoba and Quebec. These programs are beginning to have some effect on stabilizing greenhouse gas emissions from those jurisdictions. Indeed, many states are major polluters, with considerable potential for reduction. If the fifty states were to secede and become sovereign nations, thirteen would rank among the world's top forty nations in emissions, led by Texas in seventh place (ahead of the United Kingdom).

There are, of course, profound limitations on what the states, acting individually or collectively, can do to reverse the steady growth of U.S. greenhouse gas releases. States face enormous constitutional constraints, including prohibitions against the negotiation of international treaties and restrictions on commercial transactions that cross state boundaries. Yet actions at the state level offer considerable promise for reducing greenhouse gas emissions and in providing models for further policy development.

The potential for early and active state engagement on policy issues has only intensified recently. In many instances, the result has been dramatic increases in state revenue and expanding state agencies with considerable oversight in all areas relevant to greenhouse gases, including environmental protection, energy, transportation, and natural resources. Even in areas with significant federal policy oversight, states have become increasingly active and, in some cases, fairly autonomous in interpretation, implementation, and innovation.

Extending this power into the realm of climate change is fairly easy in situations such as electricity regulation, where state governments have been dominant for decades. Yet the burgeoning state role should be seen as a new movement, driven by three factors distinct to the issue of climate change.

1. *Costly weather-related damage.* Contrary to the rather acrimonious interpretations of climate science in national policy circles, individual states have begun to feel the effect of climate change in more immediate ways. Among coastal states, for example, concern is often concentrated on the consequences of rising sea level, particularly given the substantial economic development along many shores at relatively low sea levels. This dynamic has influenced state governments from Honolulu to Trenton. No two states have faced identical experiences, but individual states and regions have begun to face direct effects, thereby making climate change an issue that touches real-life experience and legitimizes a policy response.

2. *New job opportunities.* Virtually all states want both to reduce

greenhouse gas emissions and to simultaneously foster economic development. For example, active state promotion of renewable energy—through a combination of mandates and financial incentive programs—has focused on development of "home-grown" sources of electricity that promise to stabilize local energy supply and promote significant new job opportunities for state residents.

Many states with active economic development programs have concluded that investment in the technologies and skills needed in a less-carbonized society is a sound bet. In response, they have advanced many policy initiatives in large part in anticipation of economic benefits, often working collaboratively with firms that stand to benefit from shifts toward energy efficiency and renewable energy sources. Even some states that generate massive amounts of greenhouse gases, such as coal-intensive Pennsylvania, have begun to shift their thinking toward the opportunities for longer-term economic development presented by investment in renewable energy and related climate initiatives.

3. *State government innovation.* Many states worked intensively in recent decades to build in-house capacity to develop and administer new policies on energy, the environment, agriculture, and numerous other areas that have direct relevance to climate change. The result is that state agencies have proven to be increasingly fertile areas for "policy entrepreneurs" to develop ideas tailored to their state's needs and opportunities. These ideas can then be translated into legislation, executive orders, and pilot programs. Entrepreneurial officials have also proven to be effective in forming coalitions, often cutting across partisan lines in the legislature and engaging supportive interest groups where feasible.[1]

No two states have assembled identical climate policy constituencies, just as none have devised identical policies. Nonetheless, state agencies have been significant drivers of policy innovation.

Entering the Second Generation of State Climate Policies

The sheer volume and variety of state climate initiatives is staggering. Today the pace shows no sign of slowing and may actually be accelerating.

The clear majority of American states have enacted at least one piece of climate legislation or issued at least one executive order that set formal requirements for reducing greenhouse gases. More than half of the states have passed multiple laws designed to achieve such reductions, forty-seven have completed greenhouse gas inventories, and twenty-nine have set forth action plans to guide future policy. In twelve cases, states have formally established statewide reduction commitments over future years and decades, linked to policies designed to attain these reduction pledges. Renewable energy has been a particularly popular area of engagement, with twenty-three states and the District of Columbia having enacted so-called renewable portfolio standards (RPSs) that mandate a formal increase in the amount of electricity distributed in a state that must be generated from renewable sources. Twenty-two states have established their own versions of carbon taxes through so-called social benefit charges on electricity that allocate their revenues to renewable energy development or energy-efficiency projects. In transportation, twelve states have agreed to follow California in establishing the world's first carbon dioxide emissions standards for vehicles and thirty-six have programs designed to expand development and use of ethanol and other alternatives to oil. Moreover, fifteen states are engaged in some form of capping carbon emissions from electrical utilities.

Many states are also requiring more rigorous emissions reductions. Moreover, some are gradually shifting from voluntary initiatives to regulatory efforts. Most of these policies retain considerable flexibility in terms of compliance, consistent with the credit-trading mechanisms popular among most nations that have ratified the Kyoto Protocol, but their rigor is steadily increasing, along with their likely effect.

Policy Innovation Diffusion

Most state climate policies are individually tailored to the economic and energy circumstances of each particular jurisdiction. Often, however, policies enacted in one state are being replicated in other states in a process known as policy diffusion. In some cases, state policies spread across the nation and become, in effect, a de facto national policy, including numerous examples in the arena of taxation. Under such circumstances, states can simply negotiate interstate differences and implement interrelated programs. A tipping point at which the federal government concludes that it should respond by drawing from these state models and establishing a national policy may also come into play.

The policy tool that appears to be diffusing most rapidly is the RPS. The first RPS was enacted in 1991 in Iowa, with little if any attention to greenhouse gas emissions. Subsequently, the pace of adoption has intensified, with four new RPS programs approved in 2005 and three existing ones significantly expanded during that period.

Particular RPS features vary by state, but all such programs mandate a certain increase over time in the level of renewable energy that must be provided by all electricity providers in a state. For example, Nevada passed legislation in June 2005 that requires the state's utilities to gradually increase their supply of renewable energy, ultimately reaching 20 percent by 2015. Nevada, like virtually every other state that has enacted an RPS, provides regulated utilities considerable flexibility in finding ways to meet renewable mandates through so-called renewable energy credit programs. These programs permit off-site purchases of low-cost clean energy when the utility's own cost of providing comparable clean energy would be prohibitive.

RPS programs appear likely to continue to proliferate in coming years. Several states with established RPSs, such as Texas, have found them so successful that they have decided to build on the exponential rate of renewable energy growth of recent years with a substantial increase in future mandate levels.[2]

Ironically, this pattern coincides closely with the experience of the European Union, where a growing number of nations—Denmark, Sweden, and the United Kingdom among others—have adopted their own RPSs as central components of their plans for meeting greenhouse gas reduction obligations.[3] One major challenge will be harmonizing different state requirements, ranging from varied definitions of what constitutes renewable energy to state efforts to maximize generation of in-state renewable sources for economic development reasons. The former issue poses challenges for renewable energy market development in areas where generators serve multiple states, whereas the latter raises questions of state adherence to the commerce clause of the U.S. Constitution.[4]

Regionalism: Between Nation and State

American federalism allows states to work cooperatively on common concerns and, in some instances, formalize regional approaches involving two or more states. Some regional strategies take a permanent structure, such as interstate compacts, which involve a formal agreement ratified by participating states and, ultimately, Congress. Such strategies have been used extensively among states that share responsibility for an ecosystem or common boundary. Other approaches may entail establishing multistate organizations or commissions to facilitate ongoing negotiation over particular issues or less formal agreements outlining reciprocal policy commitments.

As state climate policies proliferate, certain clusters of states may become, in practice, regions even in the absence of formal agreements. Six neighboring southwestern states, for example, have an RPS, as do four contiguous Midwestern states. It is increasingly possible to envision interstate trading of renewable energy credits and other forms of cooperation that link these state programs.

More formal regional arrangements are also under consideration, perhaps most notably among northeastern states, whose relatively small physical size and dense population foster considerable economic and environmental interdependence. States in this region have a strong tradition of working together, whether campaigning for federal air emission standards to deter acid rain or common regional standards negotiated with the Environmental Protection Agency's New England office.

For decades, New England's governors have further formalized this partnership through an organization that links them in cooperative ventures with the five eastern provinces of Canada. The respective premiers and governors meet annually, with environmental and energy concerns often paramount. In 2001, the leaders of these jurisdictions, representing five different political parties, agreed to common greenhouse gas reduction goals, reaching at least 10 percent below 1990 levels by 2020 and followed by more significant reductions thereafter. These goals are not formally binding, even in Canada, which has been bound by Kyoto after its 2002 ratification of the protocol. Nonetheless, they have triggered exploration of common strategies and prodded some jurisdictions, particularly participating states, to take more aggressive steps on climate policy than ever before.

Perhaps the most vibrant regional initiative that involves states is the Regional Greenhouse Gas Initiative (RGGI). This program was launched in 2003, when New York's governor, George Pataki, invited his counterparts from ten neighboring states and the mayor of the District of Columbia to explore a regional plan. They looked at the possibility of establishing a regional cap-and-trade program for reducing carbon dioxide emissions from all fossil fuel-burning power plants located within the region. At this point, Massachusetts and New Hampshire had already taken formal action to cap greenhouse gas emissions from their own coal-burning plants, and similar steps were under consideration elsewhere. New York completed a multiyear review to confront climate change, which included a number of renewable energy initiatives and a pledge to reduce emissions 5 percent below 1990 levels by 2010 and 10 percent below 1990 levels by 2020. State policy analysts, however, concluded that a regional approach to cap-and-trade programs would be more cost effective rather than a state-by-state approach given the strong interstate linkages in regional electricity distribution.

New York reached agreement in December 2005 with six other states (Connecticut, Delaware, Maine, New Hampshire, New Jersey, and Vermont) on a regional cap-and-trade program. Maryland, Massachusetts and Rhode Island joined RGGI in 2007, and Pennsylvania, Illinois, and the District of Columbia began to give serious consideration to joining the group. Other entities, such as the Canadian province of New Brunswick, remain formal observers and could further expand the boundaries of the cap-and-trade region.

The RGGI would commence in 2009 and would cap regional emissions at 2009 levels through 2014, then reduce these levels 10 percent below that by 2018. The RGGI process entails a negotiation exclusively among states, without any input from federal officials, and it accommodates, to the extent feasible, the differences among individual states.

Yet another variant of a multistate approach involves an extension of regionalism to include states that are not necessarily contiguous with one another. Under federal air pollution legislation, for example, California enjoys unique status that it can parlay to establish a network of states with regulatory standards more stringent than those of the federal government. Congress concluded in the 1970s that California was so far ahead of the federal government in confronting air emissions that it could take any emerging federal air standard as a minimum from which it could establish its own regulations. The remaining states would then be free to adhere to federal standards or join forces with California, often unleashing "upward bidding" in air policy.

In 2002, California chose to revisit those powers, becoming the first western government to mandate carbon dioxide caps for motor vehicles. This legislation went to considerable lengths to characterize carbon dioxide as an air pollutant and therefore its regulation as a natural extension of the state's regulatory powers. The state has continued to assert that this policy does not encroach on fuel economy standards, which clearly remain under federal control.

Since enactment of these carbon dioxide caps, the California Air Resources Board has moved toward their implementation. These caps could achieve reductions of up to 30 percent in vehicle emissions in future fleets. This legislation has been a cornerstone of a larger California effort on climate change, which has resulted in some of the lowest per capita emission rates of any state and relatively modest emission growth since 1990.[5] In fact, under Republican Governor Arnold Schwarzenegger, the state has only intensified its efforts on climate. In June 2005, he signed an executive order that vowed to return California to 2000 emission levels by 2010, followed by a return to 1990 levels by 2020 and reductions that are 80 percent below current levels by 2050. This step was further formalized in September 2006 through the enactment of the California Global Warming Solutions Act.

The effects have been felt beyond state boundaries. Within two weeks of the Schwarzenegger executive order, New Mexico's governor, Democrat Bill Richardson, proposed comparable reductions through his own executive order authority. Perhaps more important is that twelve states— Arizona, New Mexico, Oregon, Washington, and eight northeastern states—have formally approved the California vehicle standards for carbon and others may follow suit. This set of new policies creates the very real possibility of two separate regional standards for vehicular emissions, including the "coastal strategy" (involving California and collaborating East Coast and West Coast states) at variance with the central states. Litigation involving automobile manufacturers and the Bush administration will likely determine whether this strategy can move forward. Nonetheless, this additional redefinition of regionalism illustrates how multiple states might pool their efforts and work collaboratively.

Taking It to the People

Direct democracy has been an alternative route for policy making in more than thirty states for nearly a century, reflecting its origins in the Populist and Progressive movements. Its use in the state context, however, has grown at an exponential rate since the 1980s, particularly in the controversial arenas of environmental and energy policy.[6] Indeed, state constitutions impose few if any restrictions on the kinds of policy questions that can be addressed through direct democracy, and a number of states, including California and Oregon, make extensive use of this provision.

For example, in November 2004, state climate policy moved from the exclusive realm of representative institutions into the arena of ballot propositions. Colorado voters, by a 54 percent to 46 percent vote, approved Proposition 37, which established an RPS for that state. This initiative set forth an ambitious target for steadily increasing the level of electricity in the state derived from renewable sources, from its current level of approximately 2 percent to 10 percent by 2015. Many other provisions in this legislation are comparable to RPSs elsewhere. What makes Colorado unique is that proponents turned to direct democracy after three similar efforts were narrowly defeated in the Colorado legislature. This time, a bipartisan group led by the Republican speaker of the state assembly and a Democratic member of the U.S. House assembled a very broad coalition, attracting agricultural, environmental, and public health interests as well as manufacturers of renewable energy systems that stood to gain from the legislation. Most major media outlets in the state offered strong endorsement for Proposition 37. The law survived a massive opposition campaign led by the state's dominant utility, Xcel Energy, and has since moved through an extensive rule-making process.

Other environmental cases suggest that once one state turns to the ballot on a salient issue others often follow suit. Ironically, the RPS issue continues to move apace in many jurisdictions, with Montana following Colorado—through conventional methods—shortly thereafter. This linked set of events further underscores the possibilities for expanding the state role in climate policy development. Indeed, Washington State voters in November 2006 endorsed a ballot proposition for an RPS very similar to the one enacted in Colorado.

Taking It to the Courts

Alongside citizen-driven policy, states also have turned increasingly to litigation against their neighbors or the federal government for actions—or inactions—seen to cause environmental harm to their states and citizenries. The vast majority of state attorneys general are elected officials, many of who become very prominent figures in state governance.[7] These leaders often possess considerable independence from their respective governors and have proven increasingly bold in expanding the definition of their roles. Huge shifts in policy have followed interventions led by attorneys general in such areas as regulation of the tobacco and financial services industries.[8] Strong signals indicate that climate policy is emerging as the next target for this type of engagement.

In recent years, a loose coalition of attorneys general has formed that explores ways in which states might develop litigation to force the federal government to act. For example, in February 2003, attorneys general from California, Connecticut, Illinois, Maine, Massachusetts, New Jersey, New Mexico, New York, Oregon, Rhode Island, Vermont, and Washington filed suit in federal court challenging a Bush administration decision to exclude carbon dioxide as a pollutant regulated under the 1990 Clean Air Act Amendments. The U.S. Supreme Court heard oral arguments on this case in December 2006. Other legal challenges, contending that climate change is posing a significant threat to state residents and seeking a judicial remedy that would force some degree of active federal engagement, have followed. Such steps have often been endorsed and supported by coalitions of environmental groups and state regulatory agencies, which often supply expertise in developing the litigation strategy.

It is much too soon to discern what effect, if any, these respective approaches might have because they move the federal courts into new policy terrain and are likely to receive very different hearings in respective federal judicial districts. Nonetheless, taking it to the courts represents yet another strategy that states appear increasingly willing to employ in assuming a lead role in U.S. climate policy formation. This approach appears particularly unique in that it is designed not to result in intrastate action or interstate cooperation. Instead, the focus is finding state-based policy levers that might compel a recalcitrant federal government to take action on the climate issue.

The Second Generation and Beyond

There is no sign whatsoever of a slowing pace in state engagement on climate change. Long-active states are expanding their efforts and elevating their reduction commitments. Long-dormant states are, in some instances, showing signs of engagement. Consequently, one could increasingly envision a U.S. climate policy system emerging on a bottom-up basis, with an expanding and perhaps permanent role for states to play in continued policy development and implementation. Indeed, many of the proposals for federal climate policy introduced into the 110th Congress include provision for a two-tier system, whereby states could continue to pursue policies that were more ambitious than those that might be established under any future federal law. In certain respects, this behavior appears to parallel the experiences of other federal or federated systems, whether or not they have the ratified the Kyoto Protocol.

In Europe, for example, striking parallels to the U.S. case exist. The European Union remains formally bound to meeting Kyoto reduction targets, which led to the launch of the emissions trading scheme, or ETS, in 2005 and the first volley of cross-national carbon credit trading. Each European Union member country, however, has a different reduction target and is free to establish its own internal policies. This situation has resulted in a tapestry of different strategies and wide variation in individual nations' degrees of success in approaching their pledged reductions. Just as some states lead while others lag in the United States, it is increasingly clear that a similar dynamic operates among European nations.

Australia appears to be following the U.S. pattern, with growing state involvement amid federal disengagement. This phenomenon, though, is not universal in federal systems, as is reflected in the glacial pace of climate policy development in Canada and its provinces despite federal ratification of Kyoto.[9]

At the same time, there are challenges facing state involvement on climate policy.[10] Although these challenges have not yet had any demonstrable effect on state policy, they potentially could.

The first challenge emerges from a consortium of well-heeled organizations hostile to any U.S. government action to reduce greenhouse gases. These organizations have become increasingly vocal in the state policy-making process. Organizations such as the Heartland Institute and Competitive Enterprise Institute have published reports that portray state-based initiatives as posing dire economic and social consequences. Such releases routinely condemn state climate policies as "mini-Kyoto regimes" and offer catastrophic estimates of future economic consequences. Perhaps most important is the American Legislative Exchange Council's aggressive campaign to reverse or rescind existing state climate laws, even though it has had little demonstrable effect on state policy thus far.[11]

The second issue is that various interest groups and the executive branch of the federal government may join forces to bring legal or administrative challenge, on constitutional grounds, to many state climate policy initiatives. This threat is somewhat ironic given the long-standing emphasis in the Republican Party on the virtues of decentralization and given that so many Bush administration leaders, including the president himself, were leaders in climate policy development when they worked in their respective statehouses.[12] Nonetheless, there are growing indications that serious challenges may ensue. Perhaps the most prominent confrontation will focus on the California vehicle emissions program, but other challenges are also possible through the route of preemption via legislative or administrative action. Indeed, in early 2007 the National Association of Manufacturers endorsed broad federal preemption of existing state policies as a key condition to enactment of any federal climate policy.

Finally, as a growing number of states become active players in climate policy development and implementation, inevitable questions emerge regarding interstate collaboration. These questions are most apparent in cases such as the RGGI, which requires considerable cooperation between multiple states in agencies in which turnover of elected officials is constant. Despite the substantial body of agreement reached among RGGI states, a number of questions remain concerning the long-term viability of such a regional cap-and-trade program. Issues such as the governance structure for overseeing implementation remains a point of contention, even before moving into even trickier issues such as defining acceptable offsets, addressing "carbon leakage" from energy imports outside the RGGI zone, and whether to allocate allowances without charge or through an auction. California and four neighboring states will face similar challenges, following a February 2007 agreement among their governors to follow the RGGI model and possibly connect trading programs across the continent.

Despite these potential impediments, all indicators suggest that climate policy has not only reached the agenda of most state capitals but is actively moving ahead with fairly broad political support. Continued state climate policy engagement can be envisioned in coming years, giving a growing set of states a level of climate commitment and expertise that rivals the most aggressive nations pursuing the Kyoto Protocol.

All this work at the state level suggests that the U.S. context for climate policy is far more complex—and far less fruitless—than many conventional depictions would suggest. Consequently, there is ample reason to suspect that states will remain central players in the evolution of U.S. climate policy, with considerable potential for achieving emission reductions and providing lessons and models worthy of consideration in the nation's capital and around the world.

My decade-long scrutiny of the evolving state role in climate policy was founded on a long-standing recognition that a federal system afforded states unique opportunities in many areas of environmental and energy policy. In some respects, the proliferation of state innovations follows a familiar and historic pattern, opening a number of questions of possible effects on

U.S. climate policy and long-term collaboration between state and federal levels. Moreover, this state-level experience forces a rethinking of the common characterization of U.S. citizens and their political institutions as indifferent toward climate change and incapable of collective action. Diverse states with every conceivable pattern of partisan control of elected institutions suggest a very real possibility for assembling broad coalitions and enacting policies designed to reduce greenhouse gas emissions. The strategies and tactics employed in these states complement those discussed in other chapters of this book, including the chapter 3 discussion of movement building. Indeed, as states such as California and New York begin to explore the prospect of working cooperatively not only with each other but also with foreign governments, the possibilities for intergovernmental learning and collaboration on climate change are endless.

17. Let's Cause Trouble, Good Trouble, Necessary Trouble

JOHN PASSACANTANDO

NOT LONG AFTER SEPTEMBER 11, 2001, I went to see Congressman John Lewis (D-Ga.), the giant of the civil rights movement. His memoir of those years, *Walking with the Wind*, will make you want to be an activist just the way spending a day at the Monterey Bay Aquarium will make you want to be a marine biologist.

I went to see him with no real agenda in mind, but I was getting plenty of blowback about Greenpeace's nonviolent direct actions, peaceful protests, which we borrowed from other peaceful movements. From the Quakers came the witnessing of a wrongful act both to create some moral suasion against the act as well as to drive change within yourself to resist the act; from the civil rights activists came the training in nonviolence to prepare yourself to physically stand up to wrongdoing and to simultaneously not only not hate, but love your opponent. I was tired of hearing so many people say that the time for protest was over, that it was all about fighting terrorists now. So I made an appointment and, with trepidation, went to meet with the congressman.

It's usually better not to meet your heroes. When you speak with them face to face, their stature may be diminished, but not so with John Lewis. Sitting alone in his office as he told me stories about the movement and about the hostility to the lunch counter sit-ins, the marches, the boycotts inspired me anew. His voice and elocution are unusual; there is something

239

magical about the way he sounds. His voice was building to a crescendo, and as he reached the climax, he said, "You have to go cause trouble, good trouble, necessary trouble."

That evening, with that voice still ringing in my head, I realized that it was time to cause some new trouble. And the trouble we need to cause in the twenty-first century is about global warming.

Now why would someone want to be a troublemaker, an activist on global warming? Masochism comes to mind. If that's all we've got, though, we're not going to attract all the new people this movement needs. How about joy, or even love?

We must love something deeply before we can defend it, yet you can't love the earth. That's too abstract. I'm talking about love like the feel of your lover's hair, the clasp of a child's hand, a jazz riff, the tug of a fish on a line, an Adirondack snowstorm, the curl of a wave caught perfectly, growing tomatoes, peeling garlic: now that's where power is born.

Think about the great environmental leaders. Rachel Carson's childhood experience exploring tide pools in Maine planted the seeds for her to ultimately write the environmental epic *Silent Spring*. Ed Abbey's love of the Southwest's redrock country gave us his raging defense of desert country. John Muir, founder of the Sierra Club, loved the high Sierras to a point of near ecstasy. Time spent in the company of whales drove the founders of Greenpeace to put themselves between the harpoons and the whales. Once we know what we love, we can then, if we are to be activists, become enraged when we see our love threatened. Anger without love is not activism, it's someone who needs therapy.

Love, followed by anger, can be the inspiration to develop the skills of activism, the craft. It's not an elite craft either, it's a folk craft. It's something that can be developed over a lifetime, but also something that anyone sufficiently motivated can learn.

People often ask me, "What should I do about global warming?" I tell them that we must start with our heart. That's the love, that's knowing what inspires you and empowers you to act. What do you love? Almost everything that is loved in this world connects to maintaining climate stability and averting climate change. Put words to what you love. Make the connection to climate and keep the connection clear as inspiration to action.

Then look at your spheres of influence: children, schools, communities, colleagues, clubs. They are always larger than you initially think. People have been organizing mayors, states, and businesses; they've been pushing back on ExxonMobil's lies about global warming (lawyers will play a nice part here someday, too). So many—whistleblowers within the government and industry, scientists, religious leaders, doctors, economists—have gotten the message about global warming and are doing their part. It's all in play, but if we simply focus on Hollywood stars and Al Gore making a fantastic movie about global warming, we'll miss the larger point. These folks are elites. That's great. They are deploying in their spheres of influence. They can raise huge sums of money, they can make and promote a movie. Maybe you and I can't. Yet our role is even more important now.

The game is now almost won at the elite level. The television networks get it. Newspaper editors get it. Few journalists worth their salt who write about global warming still quote the industry-paid skeptics anymore. Most politicians operating at a national level, such as senators John McCain (R-Ariz.), John Kerry (D-Mass.), Chuck Hagel (D-Oreg.), and Hillary Clinton (D-N.Y.), acknowledge the need to stop global warming. All but the most retrograde companies are at least starting to say the right things.

So what's missing? Why does the United States remain the industrial world's most powerful holdout to taking real measures to reduce its carbon dioxide emissions? The answer lies in the lack of any real, ongoing concern throughout the country—expressed in coffee shops, in sports stadiums, in PTA meetings, or anywhere that Americans meet and talk—about climate change. Without such ongoing buzz, and clear demand for action, no broader action will happen within the U.S. Congress. It's that simple.

Although the Senate is bad enough, the U.S. House of Representatives has still not voted on a single measure to deal with global warming. There are still prominent members who call global warming a hoax. Despite gains by Democrats in the House in the 2006 midterm elections and large majorities of people in the country saying they support strong action to stop global warming, resistance remains.

Politics for House members, with few exceptions, is still local. Elite media, national and international TV networks, and national newspapers are all irrelevant to them. They are dependent on voters in their districts, and those people read local papers and watch local TV stations.

Even though these representatives raise money from elites far outside their districts and those people might read the *Wall Street Journal*, it's essentially a local game. No member of Congress has yet been punished for being bad on global warming. And even though people worry about global warming, they have not yet pushed this interest at their representatives the way people have voiced opposition to the war or lamented the need for health care or protection of social security. When pushed, though, members of Congress and candidates for Congress listen to what the voters are saying back home in their districts.

To test this point, Greenpeace ran an experiment in the 2006 midterm elections. Could global warming be an important issue in those elections?

A number of environmental groups are engaged in the political process, and the results of the midterm elections show that the environment can be a salient issue. The environmental community's work in defeating some of whom it considers the worst members of Congress, such as Rep. Richard Pombo (R-Calif.), was extremely important. Organizations used energy independence (as the focus groups instructed them to) or a broader agenda of Democratic issues, but Greenpeace chose to organize in the field specifically around global warming. The Greenpeace experiment was to see if global warming could be a top-tier political issue that candidates of both parties must address. We went into six congressional districts, twelve politicians total, in the midterm races. Ultimately, we moved seven of the twelve candidates to commit to action compatible with Greenpeace's platform to stop global warming, a plan that gets the nation on track to achieve an 80 percent reduction in global warming pollution emissions by 2050. We worked in a wide range of places to learn as much as possible from this experiment. In Vermont, for example, there are natural constituencies, with folks like Bill McKibben and Jon Isham already working, so our organizers could hit the ground running. We also worked in more challenging places like Washington, Florida, Colorado, Pennsylvania, and Michigan, where many people weren't as far along. Nevertheless, several core factors remained consistent throughout.

The biggest factor is that people generally believe that global warming is coming. The problem is that they believe the threat to be far in space and time, such as flooding in Bangladesh in fifty years. The more you can do to bring the issue home, here and now, the greater resonance you will have and consequently the easier it will be to build a base of people to go at politicians. You can talk about maple trees in Vermont, wildfires in Colorado, hurricanes in Florida; unfortunately, every week the science community seems to be rolling out research that you can use in various localities. Seasons are changing, snowpacks are shrinking, ocean currents are moving from normal patterns, weather patterns are turning upside down. Just stick to the science. The public is ready for you when you make it locally relevant. We are now going to be working in a much larger way in districts through the 2008 election.

You may know Greenpeace for its work stopping Japanese whalers in the southern oceans, or you may have seen the Greenpeace explorers who became the first people to walk and canoe to the North Pole in summertime to document the meltdown from global warming. Greenpeace has all the ships, satellite phones, helicopters, airdrops, and attention-getting wow-that-is-cool stuff. Nonetheless, organizers working in U.S. congressional districts right now have more power to break the world's biggest logjam on global warming than all that "stuff," without ships or survival suits. We didn't use satellite phones in the districts. (Yes, we did use one helicopter, but that was simply to photograph five hundred volunteers who came out in Florida two days before the election to spell "Save Our State" along a half-mile of beach that global warming will soon swallow.) The bottom line is that there is nothing we did that you can't do.

Organizing, whether in congressional districts with Greenpeace or at a PTA meeting, putting together a house party for a local political leader, and moving a vote at the United Nations are all much the same. You find what you love. You get enraged when you see it suffering harm. Power wells up. You start developing the skills, friends, and support groups, and then you deploy. Just like John Lewis.

In my experience, there are few things more fun that moving a stuffy, double-talking congressman by organizing everyone he talks to. Progressive guru Jim Hightower says it's the most fun you can have with your clothes on.

It's pretty trendy to be cynical about politics. It keeps you out of the position of being let down by a politician. So I'm not asking you to look at Congress as a bunch of Abraham Lincolns and George Washingtons. Be as cynical as you like.

I can, though, promise you that if there is something you love about this sweet earth that global warming is going to harm—if you can't find something, you're not looking—you can make change happen in a completely peaceful, nonpartisan, and *relevant* way that will make a difference in this fight of our generation.

There is joy in that, and when we all get together to do it, it's actually fun. It's good trouble, necessary trouble, and, I'll add, fun trouble.

Afterword

JARED DUVAL

NATHAN WYETH

> We have at most ten years—not ten years
> to decide upon action, but ten years to alter
> fundamentally the trajectory of global greenhouse
> emissions. . . . Such an outcome is still feasible
> in the case of global warming, but just barely.
>
> Dr. James Hansen, director, NASA Goddard Institute for Space Science

We two, the authors of this afterword, are in our early twenties. We are of the generation that came of age on September 11, 2001. Yet the lesson our leaders told us they learned that day—that they would never again ignore a gathering threat to U.S. security—rings hollow when we reflect on the challenge of global warming. If anything, the lesson young people have learned is that when the fate of the world is truly at stake—from a problem that is so simple you can teach it to a second-grader—the president is going to call for more scientific studies, for baby steps, or will try to scare Americans into thinking that nothing can be done about it.

We believe, along with all the other authors of this book, that a moment of truth is now upon us. As stated by the country's preeminent climate scientist, NASA's James Hansen, global greenhouse gas emissions must peak and decline by 2015 or today's youth will be face life on a radically different planet than the one we now inhabit.[1] Our leading

245

scientists predict that this different planet would be marked by sea levels up to eighty feet higher than today, the extinction of up to 60 percent of species currently on this planet, and hundreds of millions of human refugees from drought and flooding of the coasts where over half of the world's population lives. Leading economists predict the costs to run into the trillions of dollars. Those are Great Depression numbers.

That, though, is not our world, nor does it have to be.

The year 2015 may seem like a distant deadline, but for global emissions to begin to decline then, the United States must take bold and urgent action now. The task will require massive effort from individuals, government, and corporations, a new New Deal on a national and global scale. As the generation that would face some of the worst consequences of a destabilized climate, we must work to ensure that the policy responses to global warming now being formulated by political leaders live up to this task. So far, most policy responses put forth in Congress do not live up to this. If solving global warming is approached merely as a technical matter rather than the moral challenge that it is, we fear that our political system will produce a lowest common denominator solution that might slow carbon emissions but would not solve the problem.

Think about it: to avoid a catastrophe in our generation, we need to start changing fundamentally the way the whole world produces and consumes energy in less than eight years. It took us nine years to put a man on the moon after President John F. Kennedy announced it as a national goal. This second Apollo project is larger and more profound in what it demands of us.

Yes, climate destabilization is probably the biggest danger that has ever faced humanity. Overcoming it may be our greatest challenge. Perhaps it is our youth, but we also see it as today's greatest opportunity for a better tomorrow.

Architect William McDonough said that "design is the manifestation of human intent."[2] An examination of today's energy economy, a fundamental aspect of our civilization, reveals little conscious design outside the interests of fossil fuel producers. Our intent is a society and energy economy in line with ecological precepts and reality, whose design will better provide for human needs. We see it as a chance to correct many inequalities and right many wrongs. We just need to go back to the drawing board and be willing to think big.

We believe that we have the chance to put together a global compact that recognizes historical inequalities while setting countries on a path to correct them. We see technologies and change that will reinvigorate the U.S. economy, create cleaner air and healthier communities, and make clean energy available to world's citizens who today don't even have electricity. Climate protection solutions will free us from a national security strategy based on securing oil from the world's most dangerous and sometimes most oppressive places, and pull the rug out from under the despots who writer Thomas Friedman calls "petro-fascists." Clean energy development doesn't oppress and poison lower-income, largely minority communities in the way that fossil fuel production currently does. Together, we can create more just and sustainable ways of life that will not only protect the climate but also reinvigorate the wellsprings of human potential. As Thomas Paine reminded us during a trying time for the country, "the harder the conflict, the more glorious the triumph."[3]

As we go about the work of building a climate movement, we draw on visionary individuals and organizations from the twentieth century in the United States. We find inspiration in the civil rights movement, the clear moral choice laid down to the country at a time when a fundamental shift in society was needed. Today, a similar moral choice is needed about whether we base our society and economy on the logic of fossil fuels, or the logic of clean energy and sustainability.

We build our political strategy on the wisdom from David Brower, Sierra Club's first executive director and a founder of the modern environmental movement. He reminded us that "politicians are like weather vanes, our job is to make the wind blow."[4]

We draw strength from the ACT-UP! activists working against AIDS in the 1980s. After years of scientific evidence accumulating and thousands of unnecessary deaths, on an issue that challenged deeply held views in U.S. society, the Reagan Administration's response was tepid and ultimately inadequate. We know in hindsight that it failed to stem the worldwide crisis we see today. AIDS activists from ACT-UP! responded to inadequate policies with appropriate outrage, taking to the streets and demanding a response commensurate with the threat. We see too many parallels between AIDS in the 1980s and global warming in the 1990s to ignore. We won't accept half measures during the coming critical decade.

We draw on John Kennedy's Apollo project of the 1960s for certainty that we can overcome this challenge with the promise of American ingenuity. We draw on Robert Kennedy's admonishment that "this world demands the qualities of youth: not a time of life or a state of mind, a temper of the will, a quality of imagination, a predominance of courage over timidity."[5]

The environmental movement has tried and failed for years to make the U.S. political system respond to this issue. From the inspiration above, however, we draw clarity for what we must demand and work for during the coming months and years. We must take a hard look at scientific reality and ecological need, take the moral road, and advocate for what is necessary: policies that will have emissions peak and decline by 2015 and reduced by 80 percent below 1990 levels by 2050. Given the increasingly clear consequences of global warming, we see no moral alternative. This clarity is necessary because, unlike almost every other issue on the political agenda, there actually is a *last chance* to avoid the destabilization of the climate. If we don't enact bold and comprehensive policy to cut our emissions now, the carbon we would emit until 2015 cannot be brought back down. As much as our generation would be willing to take action to stabilize the climate in twenty or thirty years, our ability to do so will have already been taken away from us.

A social movement based on moral values (which this movement must be) cannot win if the principle upon which it is based is compromised. If our future is in danger, a movement or a leader will have no credibility advocating for a policy that will simply slow carbon emissions and prolong the status quo rather than create a new clean energy economy.

We cannot wait for Washington. More than three hundred U.S. cities are taking local action to stop global warming. New Mexico has just become the twelfth state, joining California, New York, and others, in adopting clean car legislation that will dramatically reduce global warming pollution. In 2006, two U.S. campuses, the University of Florida and the College of the Atlantic, became the first to commit to climate neutrality: *no net carbon emissions*. Within a year, they have been followed by commitments to work toward climate neutrality by the presidents of over 100 institutions of higher education, from community colleges to major state universities as part of the American College and University Presidents Climate Commitment. In addition, students at over five hundred high schools and colleges in the United States and Canada are working under the banner of the "Campus Climate Challenge" to call on their schools to set the emissions reductions goals demanded by science: 80 percent by 2050. Religious communities are responding to the call to preserve Creation, and have organized more than four thousand local showings of Al Gore's *An Inconvenient Truth*.

On the path to growing a movement that demands a moral choice from our political leaders and dramatic action in the immediate future, the march across Vermont in September of 2006 that culminated with more than a thousand citizens filling the streets in the state's largest city (as also detailed in Bill McKibben's introduction) was a dramatic first step and a preview of what is to come. What was remarkable about that five-day, fifty-mile trek was that it asserted the proper balance of power, with politicians responding to citizens, not the other way around. For too long, we've compromised our future by letting politicians tell us what they think is feasible. In Vermont, we told candidates for office what was demanded of them and they signed on. The two of us are now leading plans to replicate the Vermont march in states across the country, coming-out parties for the grassroots strength that has been built by local campaigns for clean energy at the church, campus, and city level.

Already, among the young people working on global warming can be found the rumblings of a approach that deploys tactics up to the task, such as sit-ins, fasts, and marches, and our generation must lead the charge. In fact, the first acts of civil disobedience have already happened: the 2006 spring semester at Penn State University culminated with a student sit-in at the university president's office advocating for a comprehensive global warming policy that will result in decrease of 80,000 metric tons of carbon emission by 2012.

The 2006 midterm election was the first one when stopping global warming made its way into the top ideas that progressive politicians advocated. Energy issues dominated campaign ads to an unprecedented degree, and a Zogby poll indicated that among young people, and Latinos especially, global warming was a "sleeper issue" that helped clinch voters' decisions.[6]

Beginning in 2007, students in early primary states will make the climate crisis a topic that every aspiring presidential candidate must address. In 2008, twenty years after the threat was first discussed on Capitol Hill, we will translate global warming into an issue that finally gains attention in presidential campaigns. We expect that the new U.S. president will enter the White House in 2009 ready to make climate change a national priority.

Far from being wary of such bold action, we believe that the U.S. public is waiting for this kind of leadership on global warming. According to a 2006 poll, 76 percent of Americans believe that it is "necessary to take steps to counter global warming's effects right away," and 81 percent of youth (ages 13 to 24) say the same thing.[7] In some polls, young people have even ranked the environment as the most important problem their generation will have to deal with, ahead of the economy, education, health and diseases, and terrorism and war.[8]

We've learned, partly in frustration, partly by necessity, that the politics of half measures and division is not worthy of our generation. So tell us that revamping our approach to energy will be costly, and we'll remind you that it will cost us far more to not do anything. Tell our generation that it will be a great challenge to redesign our energy economy, and we'll tell you to look at our peers sent to patrol deadly streets in the Middle East and the marginalized communities most at risk from extreme weather. Look at the people losing their livelihoods because U.S. companies have fallen behind competitors in producing the most efficient technology possible. Look at the communities still suffering from the "traditional" externalities of fossil fuels, the smog, soot, and toxins that harm human health. In our experience, young people are ready to make the bold changes that can solve these problems.

When we think of the task before us, it is easy to be overwhelmed by the enormity of it all. Yet there are sources of inspiration. We are moved to act by our responsibility to the youngest or future generations, those who have the most to lose and the least ability to change our course. We can be moved by the more than ten thousand generations that have come before us. We can be driven by a faith in God, not daring to be held responsible for destroying Creation. We can approach the clean energy solutions to global warming as a critical piece of creating the twenty-first-century resolutions to global poverty and oppression. We can be moved because we yearn to live up to our human potential. Sometimes we are moved simply by thinking about our childhood and the special natural places we've known and by the desire for our children to one day have the same opportunities. We can be moved by all these things.

The important thing is to join the movement. As Dr. Martin Luther King Jr. said, "There is an invisible book of life that faithfully records our vigilance or our neglect." During this time more than any other, we must err on the side of vigilance, and we must be unwavering in our dedication to make bold and inspirational solutions to global warming a defining act of our generation.

ENDNOTES

Chapter 1: Igniting Action for a New Movement

1. National Religious Partnership for the Environment. Available at www.nrpe.org/whatisthepartnership/index.html.

2. Evangelical Climate Initiative, Feb. 8, 2006. Available at www.christiansandclimate.org/statement.

Chapter 2: Groundswell

1. F. Baumgartner and B. Jones, *Agendas and Instability in American Politics* (Chicago: University of Chicagoo Press, 1993), pp. 9–21.

2. Baumgartner and Jones, pp. 235–236.

3. Paul R. Ehrlich, *Human Natures: Genes, Cultures, and the Human Prospect* (Washington, DC: Island Press, 2000), p. 330.

4. T. Friedman, "States of Discord: Techno Logic," *Foreign Policy* (March–April 2002): 64. See generally T. Friedman, *The Lexus and the Olive Tree: Understanding Globalization* (New York: Farrar, Straus and Giroux, 1999).

Chapter 3: Shaping the Movement

1. B. Moyer, with J. McAllister, M. L. Finley, and S. Soifer, *Doing Democracy: The MAP Model for Organizing Social Movements* (Gabriola Island, BC: New Society Publishers, 2001).

2. R. Gelbspan, *Boiling Point: How Politicians, Big Oil and Coal, Journalists, and Activists Have Fueled the Climate Crisis and What We Can Do to Avert Disaster* (New York: Basic Books, 2004), p. 138.

3. National Research Council, *Carbon Dioxide and Climate: Report of an Ad Hoc Study Group on Carbon Dioxide and Climate* (Washington, DC: National Academy of Sciences, 1979), p. viii. Cited in J. G. Speth, *Red Sky at Morning: America and the Crisis of the Global Environment* (New Haven, CT: Yale University Press, 2004), p. 3.

4. B. Rabe, *Statehouse and Greenhouse: The Emerging Politics of American Climate Change Policy* (Washington DC: Brookings Institution, 2004), p. 43.

5. Gelbspan, *Boiling Point*, p. 12.

6. D. Vergano, "The Debate's Over: Globe *Is* Warming," *USA Today,* June 13, 2005, p. 1A.

7. T. Friedman, "Run, Dick, Run, *New York Times,* June 22, 2005, p. A27.

8. D. Kirkpatrick, "Senate Passes Amendment to Combat Climate Change," *New York Times,* June 22, 2005, p. A12.

9. J. Cook. "Biodiesel Company Gets Huge Infusion," *Seattle Post-Intelligencer,* Feb. 22, 2007, p. E1.

10. T. Friedman, "The Energy Mandate," *New York Times,* Oct. 13, 2006, p. A27.

11. Associated Press, "Global Warming Gases Seep Out of Thawing Permafrost," *Seattle Post-Intelligencer,* Sept. 7, 2006, p. A7.

12. J. Connelly, "West Can't Beat Heat of Global Warming," *Seattle Post-Intelligencer,* Aug. 23, 2006, p. B1.

13. "Extraordinary Rise in Warming Is Seen,"*New York Times,* Sept. 26, 2006, p. A15.

14. G. Dauncey with P. Mazza, *Stormy Weather: 101 Solutions to Global Climate Change* (Gabriola Island, BC: New Society Publishers, 2001).

15. C. Komanoff, "Whither Wind? A Journey through the Heated Debate over Wind Power," *Orion* 25, no. 5, (Sept./Oct. 2006): 37.

16. T. Anathasiou and P. Baer, *Dead Heat: Global Justice and Global Warming* (New York: Seven Stories Press, 2002), back cover.

17. D. C. Korten, *The Great Turning: From Empire to Earth Community* (San Francisco: Berrett-Koehler / Bloomfield, CT: Kumarian Press, 2006).

18. J. Lovelock, *The Revenge of Gaia: Earth's Climate Crisis and the Fate of Humanity* (New York: Perseus Books, 2006), p. 11; M. Hertsgaard, "The G-8's Risky Nuclear Embrace," *The Nation* 283 (July 31, 2006) (available online only).

19. B. Deming. "On Revolution and Equilibrium," in *Revolution and Equilibrium* (New York: Grossman, 1971), p. 207. Cited in D. Cortwright, *Gandhi and Beyond: Nonviolence for an Age of Terrorism* (Boulder, CO: Paradigm, 2006), p. 127.

Chapter 4: Irrationality Wants to Be Your Friend

1. J. Diamond, *Collapse* (New York: Viking, 2005), p. 434.

2. Diamond, *Collapse,* p. 436.

3. Pew Research Center for People and the Press, "Partisanship Drives Opinion: Little Consensus on Global Warming," July 12, 2006. Available at www.people-press.org.

4. Pew Research Center, "Partisanship Drives Opinion."

5. Pew Research Center for People and the Press, "Global Warming: A Divide on Causes and Solutions: Public Views Unchanged by Unusual Weather," Jan. 24, 2007.

6. J. Diamond, *Why Is Sex Fun? The Evolution of Human Sexuality* (New York: Harper-Collins, 1997); J. Diamond, *The Third Chimpanzee: The Evolution and Future of the Human Animal* (New York: Harper Perennial, 1992).

7. D. Gilbert, "If Only Gay Sex Caused Global Warming," *Los Angeles Times,* July 2, 2006. Available at www.latimes.com/news/opinion/sunday/commentary /la-op-gilbert2jul02,0,4254536.story?coll=la-sunday-commentary.

8. K. Ellison, "Turned Off by Global Warming," *New York Times,* May 20, 2006.

9. A. Gore, *An Inconvenient Truth* (Emmaus, PA: Rodale, 2006), p. 286.

10. Pew Research Center, "Partisanship Drives Opinion."

Chapter 5: Communication Strategies to Mobilize the Movement

1. G. Lakoff, *Don't Think of an Elephant! Know Your Values and Frame the Debate* (White River Junction, VT: Chelsea Green Publishing, 2004), p. 144.

2. L. Saad, "Americans Still Not Highly Concerned about Global Warming, Though Record Number Say It's Happening Now," *Gallup Poll*, April 7, 2006.

3. Pew Research Center for People and the Press, "Global Warming: A Divide on Causes and Solutions: Public Views Unchanged by Unusual Weather," Jan. 24, 2007.

4. See the account of this debate at *Grist*, www.grist.org/news/maindish/2005/01 /13/doe-intro/.

5. M. Gladwell, *The Tipping Point: How Little Things Can Make a Big Difference* (Boston: Back Bay Books / Little Brown, 2000).

Chapter 6: Coming Home to Roost

1. E. Asimov, "The Paradox of Global Warming," *New York Times*, Aug. 6, 2003, F1.

2. See, for instance, B. English, "A Groundswell Against SUVs King-Size Vehicles Stir Some Large Resentment," *Boston Globe*, Feb. 10, 2003, B7.

3. These figures come from my conversations with M. Dowie, author of *American Foundations: An Investigative History* (Cambridge: MIT Press, 2001), in 2003.

4. See, for instance, C. Saillant, "Ventura County Supervisors Assail President Bush's Energy Plans," *Los Angeles Times*, Sept. 21, 2005, B4.

5. See www.grassrootsfund.org.

6. B. McKibben, personal conversation, March 2, 2007.

7. D. Quammen, "Planet of Weeds: Tallying the Losses of Earth's Animals and Plants," *Harper's Magazine*, Oct. 1998.

Chapter 7: Focus on Health

1. J. Patz and others, "Impact of Regional Climate Change on Human Health," *Nature* 438 (Nov. 17, 2005): 310–317; see also J. Eilperin, "Climate Shift Tied to 150,000 Fatalities," *Washington Post*, Nov. 17, 2005, p. A20.

2. Physicians for Social Responsibility, Washington, DC. PSR/Ozone Action, *Heat Waves and Hot Nights*, July 26, 2000.

3. Physicians for Social Responsibility, *A Breath of Fresh Air: How Smarter Energy Choices Can Protect the Health of Pennsylvanians* (Washington, DC: Author, Sept. 2004), p. 5.

Chapter 8: Binding Life to Values

1. The published work on lived religion in American religious history began with D. D. Hall, ed., *Lived Religion in America* (Princeton, NJ: Princeton University Press, 1997), followed by R. A. Orsi, *Between Heaven and Earth* (Princeton, NJ: Princeton University Press, 2004), and R. K. Gould, *At Home in Nature* (Berkeley: University of California Press, 2005), among others.

2. M. Shellenberger and T. Nordhaus, "The Death of Environmentalism," *Grist* Jan. 15, 2005. Available at www.grist.org/news/maindish/2005/01/13 /doe-reprint. Originally released by Shellenberger and Nordhaus to the Environmental Grantmakers' Association in October 2004.

3. K. Breslau and M. Bryant, "God's Green Soldiers," *Newsweek*, Feb. 13, 2006.

4. "Forces of Faith Enter Fray over Energy Policy," *Christian Science Monitor*, Feb. 27, 2002, p. 3.

5. "'Greens' and Churches Join Hands in Environmental Mission: Sometimes-Uneasy Alliance a Decade in Making, Fights Alaska Drilling, Global Warming," Politics and Policy section, *Wall Street Journal*, March 26, 2002.

6. P. W. DeVous, "The Unholy Alliance: Radical Environmentalism and the Churches,"Acton Institute for the Study of Religion and Liberty, April 2002. Available at www.acton.org.

7. C. T. Whitman, Memorandum to President George W. Bush, March 6, 2001. A photocopy of the memorandum was supplied to the author by the National Religious Partnership for the Environment.

8. Rabbi L. Troster, interview with author, May 2006. Italics reflect vocal emphasis.

9. Interview with "Joshua," COEJL Leadership Training Institute, 2004. Source of quotation from participant of training institute.

10. COEJL, "Building a Jewish Environmental Movement," 2002, 5–7; emphasis mine.

11. R. Gottlieb makes a similar claim in his *Religious Environmentalism* (Oxford: Oxford University Press, 2005).

Chapter 9: Climate Justice

1. UNFCCC United Nations Framework Convention on Climate Change. This precursor treaty to the Kyoto Protocol entered into force in 1994. For more information, see www.unfccc.int.

2. J. Karliner, "Climate Justice Summit Provides Alternative Vision." Nov. 21, 2000. Available at www.corpwatch.org/article.php?id=977.

3. *Bali Principles of Climate Justice*, Aug. 29, 2002. Available at www.corpwatch.org /article.php?id=3748.

4. A. Revkin, "Eskimos Seek to Recast Global Warming as a Rights Issue," *New York Times*, Dec. 15, 2004.

5. *Greenhouse Gangsters vs. Climate Justice* (Oakland, CA: CorpWatch, 1999); *What's Fair? Consumers and Climate Change* (Oakland, CA: Redefining Progress, 2000).

6. A. Miller, personal communication, Dec. 12, 2005.

7. See www.ejcc.org/aboutus.html.

8. Miller, pers. comm.

9. Miller, pers. comm. At the 2002 World Summit on Sustainable Development in Johannesburg, the organization released a series of *10 Principles for Just Climate Change Policies in the U.S.*

10. J. Gearon, personal communication, Nov. 6, 2005.

11. I. Lobet, "Latino Power," *Living on Earth*, NPR Radio, Oct. 6, 2006.

12. Miller, pers. comm.

13. V. Jones, "In 'Green' Coverage, Are Blacks Being Left Out?" May 31, 2006. Available at www.alternet.org/story/36980.

Chapter 11: Your Mission: Focus the Nation

1. J. Hanson, "Climate Change on the Edge, Greenland Ice Cap Breaking Up at Twice the Rate It Was Five Years Ago, Says Scientist Bush Tried to Gag," *The Independent (UK)*, Feb. 17, 2006. Emphasis added.

2. www.focusthenation.org.

Chapter 12: Practical Steps to Create Change in Your Organization

1. Personal communication, Buddy Hay, Vice President, Sustainable Operations, Interface Research Corporation, August 9, 2005.

2. Hay, pers. comm.

3. These concepts were developed by Barry Oshry in Seeing Systems (San Francisco: Berrett-Koehler, 1996).

4. Hay, pers. comm.

Chapter 13: The Sound of Birds Not Singing

1. C. Allin, *The Politics of Wilderness Preservation* (Westport, CT: Greenwood, 1982); D. Zaslowsky, *These American Lands: Parks, Wilderness, and the Public Lands* (New York: Holt, 1986).

2. W. Tucker, *Progress and Privilege* (Garden City, NY: Doubleday, 1982).

3. B. Woodward, *The Agenda: Inside the Clinton White House* (New York: Simon and Schuster, 1994).

4. W. Chaloupka, "Jagged Terrain: Cronon, Soulé, and the Struggle Over Nature and Deconstruction in Environmental Theory," *Strategies* 13, no. 1 (2000): 23–38.

Chapter 14: Policy Pathways

1. League of Conservation Voters, "Past Environmental Scorecards." Available at www.lcv.org/scorecard/.

2. Harris Poll, "Three-Quarters of U.S. Adults Agree Environmental Standards Cannot Be Too High and Continuing Improvements Must Be Made Regardless of Cost," Harris Interactive, Sept. 13, 2005. Available at www.harrisinteractive.com /harris_poll/index.asp?PID=607.

3. F. Baumgarter and B. Jones, 1993, *Agendas and Instability in American Politics* (Chicago: University of Chicago Press, 1993), p.184.

4. C. J. Bosso, *Environment, Inc.: From Grassroots to Beltway* (Lawrence: University Press of Kansas, 2005), p. 82.

Chapter 15: Climate Change and the Business Challenge

1. P. Anderson. Quoted at www.nrdc.org/globalWarming/fwait.asp and http://www.commondreams.org/views05/0711-05.htm.

2. A. Hoffman. Available at www.pewclimate.org/global-warming-in-depth /all_reports/corporate_strategies/index.cfm.

3. www.ceres.org/news/news_item.php?nid=95.

Chapter 16: Taking It to the States

1. B. Rabe, *Statehouse and Greenhouse* (Washington, D.C.: Brookings Institution, 2004); M. Mintrom, *Policy Entrepreneurs and School Choice* (Washington, DC: Georgetown University Press, 2000).

2. Texas Public Utility Commission, *Scope of Electricity Market Competition in Texas.* Austin: Author, 2005.

3. Ian Rowlands, "The European Directive on Renewable Energy: Conflict and Compromises," Energy Policy, vol 33 (2005), pp. 965-974.

4. B. Rabe, "Racing to the Top: The Expanding Role of State Renewable Portfolio

Standards" (Washington, DC: Pew Center on Global Climate Change, 2006). Available at no charge at: www.pewclimate.org.

5. S. Brown, *Global Climate Change and California* (Sacramento: California Energy Commission, 2005).

6. D. Guber, "The Ballot Box II," pp. 125–152 in *Grassroots of a Green Revolution* (Cambridge: MIT Press, 2003).

7. C. Provost, "State Attorneys General, Entrepreneurship, and Consumer Protection in the New Federalism," *Publius* 33 (Spring 2003): 3753.

8. Provost, "State Attorneys General."

9. B. Rabe, "Beyond Kyoto: Implementing Greenhouse Gas Reduction Pledges in Federal Governance Systems," *Governance: An International Journal of Policy, Administration and Institutions* 25 (July 2007).

10. B. Rabe and P. Mundo, "Business Influence in State-Level Environmental Policy," in *Business and Environmental Policy*, eds. S. Kamieniecki and M. E. Kraft (Cambridge: MIT Press, 2007).

11. American Legislative Exchange Council, *Energy, Environment, and Economics* (Washington, DC: Author, 2006).

12. C. T. Whitman, *It's My Party Too*(New York: Penguin, 2005).

Afterword

1. J. Hansen, "The Threat to the Planet," *New York Review of Books* 53, no. 12 (July 13, 2006).

2. From speech delivered at the centennial celebration of the Church or St. John the Divine in New York City, 1993.

3. T. Paine, "The American Crisis," Dec. 19, 1776.

4. D. Brower, *Let the Mountains Talk, Let the Rivers Run* (New York: HarperCollins, 1995), p. 27.

5. R. F. Kennedy, "Day of Affirmation Address" (news release text version), University of Capetown, Capetown, South Africa. June 6, 1966.

6. Zogby Post-Election Poll, "Dems Gained From Global Warming Debate," Zogby International, Nov. 16, 2006. Available at www.zogby.com/News /ReadNews .dbm?ID=1194.

REFERENCES

Agyeman, J. *Sustainable Communities and the Challenge of Environmental Justice*. New York: New York University Press, 2005.

Agyeman, J., B. Doppelt, K. Lynn, and H. Hatic. "The Climate-Justice Link: Communicating Risk with Low Income and Minority Audiences." Pp. 119–138 in *Creating a Climate for Change: Communicating Climate Change and Facilitating Social Change*, edited by S. Moser and L. Dilling. Cambridge, UK: Cambridge University Press, 2007.

Agyeman, J., and B. Evans. "'Just Sustainability': The Emerging Discourse of Environmental Justice in Britain?" *Geographical Journal* 170, no. 2 (2004): 155–164.

Alinsky, S. *Rules for Radicals*. New York: Random House, 1971.

Allin, C. *The Politics of Wilderness Preservation*. Westport, CT: Greenwood Press, 1982.

Alston, D. Speech Delivered at the First National People of Color Environmental Leadership Summit. Washington, DC, Oct. 1991.

American Legislative Exchange Council. *Energy, Environment, and Economics*. Washington, DC: Author, 2006.

Anderson, V., and L. Johnson. *Systems Thinking Basics: From Concepts to Casual Loops*. Waltham, MA: Pegasus Communications, 1997.

Andrews, C. *Slow Is Beautiful*. Gabriola Island: New Society Publishers, 2006.

Andrews, R. N. L. *Managing the Environment, Managing Ourselves: A History of American Environmental Policy*. New Haven, CT: Yale University Press, 1999.

Apollo Alliance. *New Energy for Cities: Energy Saving and Job Creation Policies for Local Governments*, 2006. Available at www.apolloalliance.org/docUploads /new%5Fenergy%5Fcities%2Epdf.

Arctic Climate Impact Assessment (ACIA). *Impacts of a Warming Arctic: Arctic Climate Impact Assessment.* Cambridge, UK: Cambridge University Press, 2004. Available at www.acia.uaf.edu/pages/overview.html.

Baer, P., J. Harte, B. Haya, A. V. Herzog, J. Holdren, N. E. Hultman, D. M. Kammen, R. B. Norgaard, and L. Raymond. "Equity and Greenhouse Gas Responsibility." *Science* 289 (2000): 2287.

Bali Principles of Climate Justice. Aug. 29, 2002. Available at www.corpwatch.org/article.php?id=3748.

Bator, R. J., and R. B. Cialdini. "The Application of Persuasion Theory to the Development of Effective Proenvironmental Public Service Announcements." *Journal of Social Issues* 56, no. 2 (2000): 527–41.

Baumgarter, F., and B. Jones. *Agendas and Instability in American Politics.* Chicago: University of Chicago Press, 1993.

Bord, R. J., R. E. O'Connor, and A. Fisher. "In What Sense Does the Public Need to Understand Global Climate Change?" *Public Understanding of Science* 9 (2000): 205–218.

Bosso, C. J. *Environment, Inc.: From Grassroots to Beltway.* Lawrence: University Press of Kansas, 2005.

Boston Globe Staff. "As Support Widens, Environmental Groups Get Religion." *Boston Sunday Globe*, July 8, 2001, p. A1.

Bostrom, A., M. G. Morgan, B. Fischhoff, and D. Read. "What Do People Know about Global Climate Change? 1. Mental Models." *Risk Analysis* 14 (1994): 959–70.

Brechin, S. R. "Comparative Public Opinion and Knowledge on Global Climatic Change and the Kyoto Protocol: The U.S. versus the World?" *International Journal of Sociology and Social Policy* 23, no. 10 (2003): 106–134.

Breslau, K., and M. Bryant. "God's Green Soldiers." *Newsweek*, Feb. 13, 2006.

Brewer, T. L. "U.S. Public Opinion on Climate Change Issues: Evidence for 1989–2002." Paper prepared for conferences on climate change issues at McDonough School of Business, Georgetown University, Washington, DC. Available at www.ceps.be.

Brown, S. *Global Climate Change and California.* Sacramento: California Energy Commission, 2005.

Bulkeley, H. "Governing Climate Change: The Politics of Risk Society?" *Transactions of the Institute of British Geographers* 26, no. 4 (2001): 430–447.

———. "A Changing Climate for Spatial Planning?" *Planning Theory and Practice* 7, no. 2 (2006): 203–214.

Bulkeley, H., and M. Betsill. *Cities and Climate Change: Urban Sustainability and Global Environmental Governance.* London: Routledge, 2003.

Bullard, R. *Confronting Environmental Racism: Voices From The Grassroots.* Cambridge: South End Press, 1993.

Chaloupka, W. "Jagged Terrain: Cronon, Soulé, and the Struggle over Nature and Deconstruction in Environmental Theory." *Strategies* 13, no. 1 (2000): 23–38.

Chertow, M. R., and D. C. Esty, eds. *Thinking Ecologically: The Next Generation of Environmental Policy.* New Haven, CT: Yale University Press, 1997.

Christian Science Monitor Staff. "Forces of Faith Enter Fray over Energy Policy." *Christian Science Monitor,* Feb. 27, 2002, p. 3.

Clear the Air/Physicians for Social Responsibility. *Children at Risk: How Air Pollution from Power Plants Threatens the Health of America's Children.* Washington, DC: Author, May 2002. Available at www.cleartheair.org/fact/children /children_at_risk.pdf.

Climate Justice Now! "The Durban Declaration on Carbon Trading." Signed Oct. 10, 2004. Available at www.carbontradewatch.org/durban /statementeng.pdf.

Colburn, T., D. Dumanoski, and J. P. Myers. *Our Stolen Future: How We Are Threatening Our Fertility, Intelligence and Survival—A Scientific Detective Story.* New York: Dutton, 1996.

Cole, L., and S. Foster. *From The Ground Up: Environmental Racism and the Rise of the Environmental Justice Movement.* New York: New York University Press, 2001.

Commonwealth of Massachusetts. *Massachusetts Climate Protection Plan.* Boston: State House, Executive Department, 2004.

Congressional Black Caucus Foundation, Inc. *African Americans and Climate Change: An Unequal Burden.* Washington, DC: Author, 2004.

Corbett, J. B. "Altruism, Self-Interest, and the Reasonable Person Model of Environmentally Responsible Behavior." *Science Communication* 26, no. 4 (2005): 368–389.

Dauncey, G., with P. Mazza, *Stormy Weather: 101 Solutions to Global Climate Change.* Gabriola Island, BC: New Society Publishers, 2001.

De Young, R. "Expanding and Evaluating Motive for Environmentally Responsible Behavior (ERB)." *Journal of Social Issues* 56, no. 3 (2000): 509–526.

Debbané, A., and R. Keil. "Multiple Disconnections: Environmental Justice and Urban Water in Canada and South Africa." *Space and Polity* 8, no. 2 (2004): 209–225.

Derthick, M. *Up in Smoke.* Washington, DC: Congressional Quarterly Press, 2005.

Dewey, J. 1916. *Democracy and Education.* New York: Macmillan, 1916. Available at www.ilt.columbia.edu/publications/dewey.html.

Doppelt, B. *Leading Change Toward Sustainability: A Change Management Guide for Business, Government and Civil Society*. Sheffield, UK: Greenleaf, 2003.

Downs, A. "Up and Down with Ecology—The 'Issue-Attention Cycle.'" *Public Interest* 28 (1972): 38–51.

Duffy, R. J. *The Green Agenda in American Politics: New Strategies for the Twenty-first Century*. Lawrence: University Press of Kansas, 2003.

Dunion, K., and E. Scandrett. "The Campaign for Environmental Justice in Scotland as a Response to Poverty in a Northern Nation." Pp. 311–322 in *Just Sustainabilities: Development in an Unequal World*, edited by J. Agyeman, R. Bullard, and B. Evans. London: Earthscan, 2003.

Spitzer. E, Letter to the U.S. EPA. *Notice of Intent to Sue under Clean Air Act*. Office of New York Attorney General, 2003.

Engel, K. "The Dormant Commerce Clause Threat to Market-Based Environmental Regulation." *Ecology Law Quarterly* 26 (1999): 243–349.

FrameWorks Institute. *Talking Global Warming* (Summary of Research Findings). Washington, DC: FrameWorks Institute, 2001.

Friends of the Earth International. *Climate Debt: Making Historical Responsibility Part of the Solution*. Amsterdam: Author, 2005.

Gardner, G. T., and P. C. Stern. *Environmental Problems and Human Behavior*. 2nd ed. Boston: Pearson Custom Publishing, 2002.

Gärling, T., S. Fujii, A. Garling, and C. Jakobsson. "Moderating Effects of Social Value Orientation on Determinants of Proenvironmental Behavior Intention." *Journal of Environmental Psychology* 23 (2003): 1–9.

Gelbspan, R. "Katrina's Real Name." *Boston Globe*, Aug. 30, 1005.

Gelobter, M., M. Dorsey, L. Fields, T. Goldtooth, A. Mendiratta, R. Moore, R. Morello-Frosch, P. Shepard, and G. Torres. *The Soul of Environmentalism: Rediscovering Transformational Politics in the 21st Century*. Oakland, CA: Redefining Progress, 2005.

Gladwell, M. *The Tipping Point: How Little Things Can Make a Big Difference*. Boston: Back Bay Books/Little, Brown, 2000.

Goffman, E. *Frame Analysis*. New York: Harper, 1974.

Goodstein, L. "Evangelical Leaders Join Global Warming Initiative." *New York Times*, Feb. 8, 2006, p. A12.

Gorman, P. "Paul Gorman: Making Spiritual Connections." *E: The Environmental Magazine*, Nov.–Dec. 2002: 8–9.

Gottlieb, R. *Religious Environmentalism*. Oxford: Oxford University Press, 2005.

Gough, R. "Indigenous Peoples and Renewable Energy: Thinking Locally, Acting Globally—A Modest Native Proposal for Climate Justice from the Northern Great Plains." Paper prepared for the Second National People of Color Environmental Leadership Summit, 2002, Washington, DC.

Gould, R. K. *From Environmental Practices to Religious Practices: Boundary Negotiation and Future Prospects in the Greening of Institutional Religion.* Society for the Scientific Study of Religion, 2002.

———. *At Home in Nature: Modern Homesteading and Spiritual Practice in America.* Berkeley: University of California Press, 2005.

Graham, M. *The Morning after Earth Day: Practical Environmental Politics.* Washington, DC: Brookings Institution, 1999.

Grandjean, P., P. Weihe, R. F.White, F. Debes, S. Araki, K. Yokoyama, K. Murata, N. Sorensen, R. Dahl, and P.J. Jorgensen. "Cognitive Deficit in 7-Year Old Children with Prenatal Exposure to Methylmercury." *Neurotoxicology and Teratology* 19, no. 6 (1997): 417–428.

Grubb, M. "Seeking Fair Weather: Ethics and the International Debate on Climate Change." *International Affairs* 71, no. 3 (1995): 463–496.

———. *The Kyoto Protocol: A Guide and Assessment.* London: Royal Institute for International Affairs and Earthscan, 1999.

Guber, D. L. *The Grassroots of a Green Revolution: Polling America on the Environment.* Cambridge: MIT Press, 2003.

Hansen, J. "The Threat to the Planet." *New York Review of Books* 53, no. 12, July 13, 2006.

Harper, D. *Online Etymology Dictionary,* 2001. Available at www.etymonline.com/.

Hatic, H. "Creating a Climate Justice Action Plan: Securing the Link between State Climate Policy and Environmental Justice." Unpublished master's thesis. Department of Urban and Environmental Policy and Planning. Tufts University, 2005.

Hays, S. P. *Conservation and the Gospel of Efficiency: The Progressive Conservation Movement, 1890–1920.* New York: Atheneum, 1975.

———. *Beauty, Health, and Permanence: Environmental Politics in the United States, 1955–1985.* New York: Cambridge University Press, 1987.

Hessel, D. *Theology for Earth Community.* Maryknoll, NY: Orbis, 1996.

Houghton, J. *Global Warming: The Complete Briefing.* 2nd ed, Cambridge, UK: Cambridge University Press, 1997.

Ikeme, J. "Equity, Environmental Justice and Sustainability: Incomplete Approaches to Climate Change Politics."*Global Environmental Change* 13 (2003): 195–206.

Immerwahr, J. *Waiting for a Signal: Public Attitudes toward Global Warming, the Environment and Geophysical Research.* Washington, DC: American Geophysical Union, 1999.

Jones, V. "In 'Green' Coverage, Are Blacks Being Left Out?" May 31, 2006. Available at www.huffingtonpost.com/van-jones/in-green-coverage -are-_b_21950.html.

Kaplan, S. "Human Nature and Environmentally Responsible Behavior." *Journal of Social Issues* 56, no. 3 (2000): 491–508.

Karliner, J. (2000). "Climate Justice Summit Provides Alternative Vision." Nov. 21, 2000. Available at www.corpwatch.org/article.php?id=977.

Karliner, J., K. Bruno, and C. Brotsky. "*Greenhouse Gangsters vs. Climate Justice.*" San Francisco: Transnational Resource and Action Center, 1999.

Kasser, T. *The High Price of Materialism.* Cambridge: MIT Press, 2003.

Kearns, L. "Saving the Creation: Christian Environmentalism in the United States." *Sociology of Religion* 57, no. 1 (1996): 55–70.

———. "Noah's Ark Goes to Washington." *Social Compass* 44 (1997): 349–366.

Kempton, W. "How the Public Views Climate Change." *Environment* 39, no. 9 (1997): 12–21.

Kennedy, J. F. *Public Papers*, 1963, pp. 459–464. Available at www.presidency.ucsb.edu/ws/.

Kim, D. *Introduction to Systems Thinking.* Waltham, MA: Pegasus Communications, 1999.

King, M. L., Jr. *Stride Toward Freedom: The Montgomery Story.* New York: Harper and Row, 1958.

Klyza, C. M. *Who Controls Public Lands? Mining, Forestry, and Grazing Policies, 1870–1990.* Chapel Hill: University of North Carolina Press, 1996.

Klyza, C. M., and D. J. Sousa, *American Environmental Policymaking, 1990–2006: Beyond Gridlock,.* Cambridge: MIT Press, 2007.

Kolbert, E. *Field Notes from a Catastrophe: Man, Nature, and Climate Change.* New York: Bloomsbury, 2006.

Kruger, J., and W. Pizer. "Regional Greenhouse Gas Initiative." *Resources,* Winter 2005: 4–6.

Lakoff, G. *Moral Politics: How Liberals and Conservatives Talk.* 2nd ed. Chicago: University of Chicago Press, 2002.

———. *Don't Think of An Elephant: Know Your Values and Frame the Debate: The Essential Guide for Progressives.* New York: Chelsea Green, 2004.

Leiserowitz, A. "American Opinions on Global Warming." Project report, University of Oregon, 2003.

Lobet, I. "Latino Power." *Living on Earth,* NPR Radio, week of Oct.6, 2006.

Lohmann, L , ed. *Carbon Trading. A Critical Conversation on Climate Change, Privatisation and Power.* Uppsala: Dag Hammarskjold Foundation, Durban Group for Climate Justice and The Corner House. 2006.

McAdam, D., J. McCarthy, and M. Zald, eds. *Comparative Perspectives on Social Movements: Political Opportunities, Mobilizing Structures, and Cultural Framings.* New York: Cambridge University Press, 1996.

McCright, A. M., and R. E. Dunlap. "Challenging Global Warming as a Social Problem: An Analysis of the Conservative Movement's Counter-Claims." *Social Problems* 47, no. 4 (2000): 499–522.

McKibben, B. *The End of Nature.* New York: Random House, 1989.

McNeill, J. R. *Something New under the Sun: An Environmental History of the Twentieth Century.* New York: Norton, 2000.

Melnick, R. S. "Risky Business: Government and the Environment after Earth Day." Pp. 156–184 in *Taking Stock: American Government in the Twentieth Century*, edited by M. Keller and R. S. Melnick. New York: Cambridge University Press, 1999.

Meyer, D., and N. Whittier. Social Movement Spillover." *Social Problems* 41, no. 2 (1994): 277–298.

Miller, A., and P. Brown. *A Fair Climate for All.* Oakland, CA: Redefining Progress, 2000.

Miller, A, G. Sethi, and G. Wolff. *What's Fair? Consumers and Climate Change.* Oakland, CA: Redefining Progress, 2000.

Mintrom, M. *Policy Entrepreneurs and School Choice.* Washington, DC: Georgetown University Press, 2000.

Morgan, M. G.,B. Fischhoff, A. Bostrom, and C. J. Atman. *Risk Communication: The Mental Models Approach.* New York: Cambridge University Press, 2001.

Moser, S. "More Bad News: Emotional Responses to Climate Change Information." Pp. 64–80 in *Creating a Climate for Change: Communicating Climate Change and Facilitating Social Change*, edited by S. Moser and L. Dilling. Cambridge, UK: Cambridge University Press, 2007.

———. "In the Long Shadows of Inaction: The Quiet Building of a Climate Protection Movement in the United States." *Global Environmental Politics* special issue edited by H. Bulkeley and S. Moser, forthcoming.

Moser, S., and L. Dilling. "Making Climate Hot: Communicating the Urgency and Challenge of Global Climate Change." *Environment* 46, no. 10 (2004): 32–46.

———, eds. *Creating a Climate for Change: Communicating Climate Change and Facilitating Social Change.* Cambridge, UK: Cambridge University Press, 2007.

Moyer, B., J. McAllister, M. L. Finley, and S. Soifer. *Doing Democracy: The MAP Model for Organizing Social Movements.* Gabriola Island, BC: New Society Publishers, 2001.

Novotny, P. (2000) *Where We Live, Work and Play: The Environmental Justice Movement and the Struggle for a New Environmentalism.* Westport, CT: Praeger, 2000.

Okereke, C. "Global Environmental Sustainability: Intragenerational Equity and Conceptions of Justice in Multilateral Environmental Regimes." *Geoforum*, forthcoming.

Olson, R. L. "Sustainability as a Social Vision." *Journal of Social Issues* 51 (1005): 15–35.

Orren, K., and S. Skowronek. *The Search for American Political Development*. New York: Cambridge University Press, 2004.

Oshry, B. *Seeing Systems*. San Francisco: Berrett-Koehler, 1996.

Page, E. "Intergenerational justice and climate change." *Political Studies* 47 (1999): 53–66.

Physicians for Social Responsibility, PSR/Ozone Action. *Heat Waves and Hot Nights*. Washington, DC: Author, July 26, 2000.

Program of International Policy Attitudes. "Americans on Climate Change: 2005. Program on International Policy Attitudes." University of Maryland and Knowledge Networks, Menlo Park, CA, 2005. Available at www.pipa.org/Online Reports/ClimateChange/Report07_05_05.pdf.

Provost, C. "State Attorneys General, Entrepreneurship, and Consumer Protection in the New Federalism." *Publius* 33 (Spring 2003): 37–53.

Rabe, B. G. *Statehouse and Greenhouse: The Emerging Politics of American Climate Change Policy*. Washington, DC: Brookings Institution, 2004.

———. *Racing to the Top: The Expanding Role of State Renewable Portfolio Standards*. Washington, DC: Pew Center on Global Climate Change, 2006.

———. "Beyond Kyoto: Implementing Greenhouse Gas Reduction Pledges in Federal Governance Systems." *Governance: An International Journal of Policy, Administration and Institutions* (in press).

Rabe, B, and P. Mundo. "Business Influence in State-Level Environmental Policy." Pp. 265–298 in *Business and Environmental Policy*, edited by S. Kamieniecki and M. E. Kraft. Cambridge: MIT Press, 2007.

Rabkin, S., and D. Gershon. "Changing the World One Household at a Time: Portland's 30-Day Program to Lose 5000 Pounds," 292–302 in *Creating a Climate for Change: Communicating Climate Change and Facilitating Social Change*, edited by S. Moser and L. Dilling. Cambridge, UK: Cambridge University Press.

Revkin, A. "Eskimos Seek to Recast Global Warming as a Rights Issue." *New York Times*, Dec. 15, 2004. Available at www.nytimes.com/2004/12/15 /international/americas/15climate.html?ex=1260853200&%2338;en =3ea45328a3358d4b&%2338;ei=5088&.

Rogers, E. *Diffusion of Innovations*. 5th ed. New York: Free Press, 2003.

Saad, L. "Americans Still Not Highly Concerned about Global Warming." *Gallup News Service*, April 7, 2006.

Schell, J. *The Unconquerable World: Power, Nonviolence, and the Will of the People.* New York: Holt / Metropolitan Books, 2003.

Scholsberg, D. "Reconceiving Environmental Justice: Global Movements and Political Theories." *Environmental Politics* 13, no. 3 92004): 517–540.

Schultz, P. W. 2002. Knowledge, Information, and Household Recycling: Examining the Knowledge-Deficit Model of Behavior Change. Pp. 67–82 in *New Tools for Environmental Protection: Education, Information, and Voluntary Measures,* edited by T. Dietz and P. C. Stern. Washington, DC: National Academy Press, 2002.

Seacrest, S., R. Kuzelka, and R. Leonard. "Global Climate Change and Public Perception: The Challenge of Translation." *Journal of the American Water Resources Association* 36, no. 2 (2000): 253–263.

Sharp, G., and J. Paulson. *Waging Nonviolent Struggle: 20th Century Practice and 21st Century Potential.* Boston: Extending Horizons Books/Porter Sargent, 2005.

Shellenberger, M., and T. Nordhaus. *The Death of Environmentalism: Global Warming Politics in a Post-Environmental World,* 2004. Available at www.thebreakthrough.org and www.evansmcdonough.com.

Shipan, C. R., and W. R. Lowry. "Environmental Policy and Party Divergence in Congress." *Political Research Quarterly* 54 (2001): 245–263.

Shue, H. "Global Environment and International Inequality." *International Affairs* 75, no. 3 (1999): 531–545.

Speth, J. G. *Red Sky at Morning: America and the Crisis of the Global Environment.* New Haven: Yale University Press, 2004.

Stamm, K. R., F. Clark, and P. R. Eblacas. "Mass Communication and Public Understanding of Environmental Problems: The Case of Global Warming." *Public Understanding of Science* 9 (2000): 219–237.

Stern, N. *The Economics of Climate Change* . Cambridge, UK: Cambridge University Press, 2007.

Stern, P., and T. Dietz. "The Value Basis of Environmental Concern." *Journal of Social Issues* 50, no. 3 (1994): 65–84.

Stern, P. C. "Toward a Coherent Theory of Environmentally Significant Behavior." *Journal of Social Issues* 56, no. 3 (2000): 407–424.

Sturgis, P., and N. Allum. "Science in Society: Re-evaluating the Deficit Model of Public Attitudes." *Public Understanding of Science* 13 (2004): 55–74.

Switzer, J. V. *Green Backlash: The History and Politics of Environmental Opposition in the U.S..* Boulder, CO: Lynne Rienner, 1997.

Texas Public Utility Commission. *Scope of Electricity Market Competition in Texas.* Austin: Author, 2005.

Tol, R., T. Downing, O. Kuik, and J. Smith. "Distributional Aspects of Climate Change Impacts." *Global Environmental Change* 14 (2004): 259–272.

Toth, F., ed. *Fair Weather? Equity Concerns in Climate Change*. London: Earthscan, 1999.

Traister, R. *The F Word*, July 5, 2005. Available at www.truthout.org/issues _05/070705WA.shtml.

Tucker, M. E., and J. A. Grim, eds. *Religions of the World and Ecology* (multivolume series). Cambridge: Harvard University Press, 1998–2003.

Tucker, W. *Progress and Privilege*. Garden City, NY: Anchor/Doubleday, 1982.

United Church of Christ Commission for Racial Justice. *Toxic Wastes and Race in the United States*. New York: Author, 1987.

Walker, G., and H. Bulkeley. "Geographies of Environmental Justice." *Geoforum* 37, no. 5 (2007): 655–659.

Wall Street Journal Staff. "'Greens' and Churches Join Hands in Environmental Mission: Sometimes-Uneasy Alliance a Decade in Making, Fights Alaska Drilling, Global Warming." *Wall Street Journal*, March 26, 2002.

Wantanabe, T. "The Green Movement Is Getting Religion." *Los Angeles Times*, Dec. 25, 1998.

Waskow, A. *Torah of the Earth*. Woodstock, VT: Jewish Lights, 2000.

Whitman, C. T. *It's My Party Too*. New York: Penguin, 2005.

———. Memorandum to President George W. Bush, March 6, 2001.

Wilbanks, T. J.,S. M. Kane, P. N. Leiby, R. D. Perlack, C. Settle, J. F. Shogren, and J. B. Smith. "Integrating Mitigation and Adaptation: Possible Responses to Global Climate Change." *Environment* 45 (2003): 28–38.

Wilkinson, C. F. *Crossing the Next Meridian: Land, Water, and the Future of the West*. Washington, DC: Island Press, 1992.

Wittner, L. S. *Toward Nuclear Abolition: A History of the World Nuclear Disarmament Movement, 1971 to the Present*. Stanford, CA: Stanford University Press, 2003.

Woodward, B. *The Agenda: Inside the Clinton White House*. New York: Simon and Schuster, 1994.

Zaslowsky, D. *These American Lands: Parks, Wilderness, and the Public Lands*. New York: Holt, 1986.

Zimmerman, J. *Interstate Cooperation*. Westport, CT: Praeger, 2002.

ABOUT THE EDITORS

JONATHAN ISHAM JR. is the Luce Professor of International Environmental Economics at Middlebury College, where he teaches classes in environmental economics, environmental policy, introductory microeconomics, social capital in Vermont, and global climate change. Since early 2005, he has spoken widely throughout the nation about building the new climate movement. He serves on advisory boards for Focus the Nation, Climate Counts, and the Vermont Governor's Commission on Climate Change. He was the corecipient, representing Middlebury College, of the 2005 Clean Air–Cool Planet Climate Champion Award for advancing campus solutions to global warming. In January 2006, he was featured on National Public Radio's Radio Open Source program "Global Warming Is Not an 'Environmental Problem.'" In January 2007, he was trained in Nashville, Tennessee, as a member of Al Gore's Climate Project. Isham has published articles in *Economic Development and Cultural Change, Journal of African Economies, Nonprofit and Voluntary Sector Quarterly, Quarterly Journal of Economics, Rural Sociology, Social Science Quarterly, Society and Natural Resources, Southern Economic Journal, Vermont Law Review*, and *World Bank Economic Review*. He was the coeditor of *Social Capital, Development, and the Environment* (Edward Elgar, 2002) and has coauthored chapters in books published by Oxford University Press, Cambridge University Press, and New England University Press. He holds an AB in social anthropology from Harvard University, an MA in international studies from Johns Hopkins University, and a PhD in economics from the University of Maryland.

SISSEL WAAGE is an independent consultant on environmental issues focusing on sustainable business and products, markets and payments for ecosystem services, community-based conservation, and conservation-based economic development. Prior to consulting, Sissel launched and directed the research and development program at the Natural Step, an international advisory services and research organization focused on sustainable business. She served as core staff with the Natural Step's Services Group, advising Fortune 500 companies on integration of sustainability into strategy, operations, reporting, and philanthropy. She has also worked with Sustainable Northwest and the World Wildlife Fund's East and Southern Africa Program, and she has served as a consultant to the Garfield Foundation, Packard Foundation, Biodiversity Support Program, Forest Trends, a forest research station, and several other international conservation and development organizations. Sissel received her BA from Amherst College and completed her PhD at the University of California, Berkeley in the Department of Environmental Science, Policy and Management. She has studied at the University of Oslo, in Norway, as a Fulbright scholar and at the National University of Singapore. She has published articles in *Corporate Environmental Strategy*, *Society and Natural Resources*, *Political Geography*, and *Journal of Sustainable Forestry* and has edited *Ants, Galileo, and Gandhi: Designing the Future of Business through Nature, Genius, and Compassion* (Greenleaf, 2003).

ABOUT THE AUTHORS

JULIAN AGYEMAN is associate professor of urban and environmental policy and planning at Tufts University, Boston-Medford. His research interests are in the nexus between environmental justice and sustainability. He is cofounder and coeditor of the *Local Environment: The International Journal of Justice and Sustainability*. He has written more than 120 publications, including the books *Local Environmental Policies and Strategies* (Longman, 1994), *Just Sustainabilities: Development in an Unequal World* (MIT Press, 2003), *Sustainable Communities and the Challenge of Environmental Justice* (NYU Press, 2005), and *The New Countryside? Ethnicity, Nation and Exclusion in Contemporary Rural Britain* (Policy Press, 2006). He is a fellow of the U.K. Royal Society of the Arts and a member of the U.S. National Academies' Board on the Transportation of Nuclear Waste, and he serves on the editorial boards of *Environmental Communication: A Journal of Nature and Culture*; *Sustainability: Science, Practice and Policy*; *Journal of Environmental Education*; and *Australian Journal of Environmental Education*.

HARRIET BULKELEY is a lecturer in the department of geography at Durham University, U.K., with a focus on environmental governance. She has written extensively on the responses of municipalities to the challenges of climate change and is coauthor, with Michele Betsill, of *Cities and Climate Change: Global Environmental Governance and Urban Sustainability* (Routledge, 2003). Her research interests also encompass understanding the processes of environmental policy, urban sustainability, and environmental justice. She is currently engaged in a research project at the Tyndall Centre for Climate Change Research in the United Kingdom that examines the prospects for climate governance post-2012.

WILLIAM CHALOUPKA is a professor of political science at Colorado State University, where he also chairs the department. His books include *Everybody Knows: Cynicism in America*; *In the Nature of Things: Language, Politics, and the Environment* (coedited with Jane Bennett; 1993); and *Knowing Nukes: Politics and Culture of the Atom* (1992), each published by the University of Minnesota Press. Until recently, he was coeditor of *Theory and Event*, an international journal of political and social thought published online through Project Muse and Johns Hopkins University Press.

EILEEN CLAUSSEN is president of the Pew Center on Global Climate Change and Strategies for the Global Environment. She is the former assistant secretary of state for Oceans and International Environmental and Scientific Affairs and has also served as a special assistant to the president and senior director for Global Environmental Affairs at the National Security Council. Claussen has also served as chairman of the United Nations Multilateral Montreal Protocol Fund and was director of Atmospheric Programs at the U.S. Environmental Protection Agency, where she was responsible for activities related to the depletion of the ozone layer; Title IV of the Clean Air Act; the Clean Air Accord with Canada; and the EPA's energy efficiency programs, including the Green Lights program and the Energy Star program. She also served as the Timothy Atkeson Scholar in Residence at Yale University.

BOB DOPPELT is director of Resource Innovations, a sustainability research and technical assistance institute, and the Climate Leadership Initiative, a climate-change research and technical assistance program, and is a principal in the consulting firm Factor 10 Inc. He is also a courtesy associate professor of planning, public policy, and management at the University of Oregon and teaches at Bainbridge Graduate Institute. He is the author of *Leading Change Toward Sustainability: A Change-Management Guide for Business, Government and Civil Society* (Greenleaf, 2003). Doppelt's work focuses on assisting organizations in implementing sustainability and global warming change management, governance, and leadership development programs. He founded the University of Oregon Sustainability Leadership Academy and spearheaded efforts that led the governors of both Oregon and Washington to sign executive orders requiring state agencies to adopt sustainability plans. He has also assisted numerous local governments and private firms in adopting sustainability and climate-change action plans. Most recently, he has led efforts to analyze the economics of climate change in the Pacific Northwest. He is a graduate of the International Program on the Management of Sustainability, Ziest, Netherlands.

JARED DUVAL is director of the Sierra Student Coalition, the national student chapter of the Sierra Club. He also cochairs the Steering Committee of Energy Action, the international coalition for the youth climate movement that runs the Campus Climate Challenge campaign. Duval started organizing when he was a junior in high school and led a successful campaign to protect the Great Hollow Wetlands of Lebanon, New Hampshire, from a large-scale construction project. Since then, he has led many other campus and community campaigns, served as the energy and environmental policy intern for Howard Dean's presidential campaign, and taught at St. Mary's High School in Dar es Salaam, Tanzania, working with students on HIV/AIDS awareness and prevention. He graduated from

Wheaton College in 2005, with majors in political science and in economics, and has received the Brower Youth Award, Morris K. Udall scholarship, and Harry S. Truman scholarship.

MARY LOU FINLEY became interested in social movements in the mid-1960s when she was on the staff of Martin Luther King's Chicago Project. In the 1970s, she spent two years in a nonviolence training community in Philadelphia and has led nonviolence trainings for activist groups. She has been active in environmental movements, peace movements, the women's movement, and movements for economic justice. She has published work in the fields of medical sociology, public health, social movements, and higher education and is a coauthor with Bill Moyer, JoAnn McAllister, and Steve Soifer of *Doing Democracy: the MAP Model for Organizing Social Movements* (New Society Publishers, 2001). Finley holds graduate degrees in sociology and public health (master's of public health from the University of Washington and PhD from the University of Chicago) and is currently on the faculty of Antioch University Seattle.

EBAN GOODSTEIN is professor of economics at Lewis and Clark College in Portland, Oregon, and author of the college textbook *Economics and the Environment* (John Wiley, 2004), now in its fifth edition, as well as *The Trade-off Myth: Fact and Fiction about Jobs and the Environment* (Island Press, 1999). His articles have appeared in *Journal of Environmental Economics and Management, Land Economics, Ecological Economics,* and *Environmental Management*. Goodstein's research has been featured in the *New York Times, Scientific American, Time, Chemical and Engineering News, Economist,* and *Chronicle of Higher Education*. He is also director of Focus the Nation, a national educational initiative on global warming solutions for the United States. Goodstein received a BA from Williams College and a PhD from the University of Michigan.

BEN GORE is a freelance writer and novelist based in Washington, D.C. He is a 2005 graduate of Middlebury College and founded the Sierra Student Coalition's Student Action on Global Economy program, which promotes fairness, sustainability, and justice in free trade and development issues. During his work with the coalition, he also served as communications director, founder, and editor of the magazine *Live from Earth,* and chair of the executive committee. At Middlebury College, he was active in many environmental issues as well as local antiwar protests. His work has appeared in *The Leader, Middlebury Magazine,* and *Grist*. He is currently writing about bicycle touring in northern Canada.

REBECCA KNEALE GOULD is an associate professor of religion and environmental studies at Middlebury College, where she teaches courses on religion and nature, environmental ethics, religion and social change in America, simplicity in American culture, and American religious history. Her book, *At Home in Nature: Modern Homesteading and Spiritual Practice in America* (University of California Press, 2005), an ethnographic and historical study of the spiritual dimensions of back-to-the-land experiments, was based on research she conducted while living and working at the homestead of Helen and Scott Nearing. She is currently engaged as cowriter and scholarly consultant for *Heaven on Earth: A Documentary Film Project on Spirit and Nature*, a project that dovetails her ongoing research project "Religion on the Ground: Environmentalism and Religious Institutions," which has received funding from the Louisville Institute, Lily Endowment, and Mellon Foundation. Gould is a recent fellow in the Young Scholars Program of the Center for American Religion at Indiana University–Purdue University Indianapolis. She writes and speaks on a variety of topics, primarily religious environmentalism. She is a board member of two national nonprofit initiatives, the Simplicity Forum and Take Back Your Time, and serves on the boards of advisors for Green-Faith, the Society of Religion, Nature and Culture, and the Good Life Center.

KENTON DE KIRBY is a research analyst in the department of framing and cognitive analysis at American Environics. He was formerly a research associate at the Rockridge Institute, where he worked with Pamela Morgan and George Lakoff on environmental and other issues. He holds a BA in linguistics from the University of California, Berkeley.

CHRISTOPHER MCGRORY KLYZA is the Robert '35 and Helen '38 Stafford Professor in Public Policy and a professor of political science and environmental studies at Middlebury College, where he has taught courses on U.S. conservation and environmental policy and American politics and has served as the director of the environmental studies program. He is the author or editor of five books on conservation and environmental policy: coauthor, with David Sousa, of *American Environmental Policymaking, 1990–2006: Beyond Gridlock* (from MIT Press, forthcoming); editor of *Wilderness Comes Home: Rewilding the Northeast* (University Press of New England, 2001); coauthor, with Steve Trombulak, of *The Story of Vermont: A Natural and Cultural History* (University Press of New England, 1999); author of *Who Controls Public Lands? Mining, Forestry, and Grazing Policies, 1870-1990* (University of North Carolina Press, 1996); and coeditor, with Steve Trombulak, of *The Future of the Northern Forest* (University Press of New England, 1994). He is currently at work on a book tracing green state buildings in the United States, a quixotic project that involves trips to every state library in the country. Klyza serves on the board of directors of the local conservation organization Vermont Family Forests.

BILL MCKIBBEN is the author of ten books on the environment and other topics. His first book, *The End of Nature*, was also the first book for a general audience on global warming; today it is available in more than twenty languages. A former staff writer and editor for the *New Yorker*, his work appears in *Harpers*, *Atlantic*, *New York Review of Books*, and a variety of other national publications. A scholar in residence at Middlebury College, he is the recipient of Guggenheim and Lyndhurst fellowships and the Lannan Prize in Nonfiction Writing. His most recent book is *Deep Economy: The Wealth of Communities and the Durable Future* (Times Books, 2007.) He is a graduate of Harvard University.

PAMELA MORGAN is vice president of framing and cognitive analysis at American Environics. She was the first director of the Strategic Framing Project, was a fellow at the Rockridge Institute and the Longview Institute, and has worked on projects with the FrameWorks Institute. Morgan has taught cognitive linguistics, American studies, classics, and medieval studies at the University of California, Berkeley and elsewhere. Her publications have appeared in edited volumes and include "Competition, Cooperation, and Interconnection: 'Metaphor Families' and Social Systems," in *Cognitive Sociolinguistics*, ed. G. Kristiansen and R. Dirven, forthcoming; "Framing Social Issues: Does 'The Working Poor' Work?" (co-authored with George Lakoff, in *Public Obligations: Giving Kids A Chance: A Report from a Conference on the State Role in Early Education*, Kennedy School of Government, Harvard University, 2002), and "The Semantics of an Impeachment: Meanings and Models in a Political Conflict" (in *Language and Ideology*, vol. 2, ed. R. Dirven, R. Frank, and C. Ilie, 2001). She holds a PhD in linguistics from the University of California, Berkeley and a PhD in history from the University of California, Santa Barbara.

SUSANNE MOSER is a research scientist at the Institute for the Study of Society and Environment at the National Center for Atmospheric Research in Boulder, Colorado, and a geographer by training (PhD 1997, Clark University). Moser's research foci have been the human dimensions of global change. She has focused on uncertainties in the human dimensions of global change (causes, vulnerability, effects, and adaptive responses), particularly on coastal areas and human health. She has worked for the Heinz Center in Washington, D.C., on a congressionally mandated project on coastal erosion and management and for the Union of Concerned Scientists as its staff scientist for climate change. Her current research includes effective climate-change communication and social change, science-stakeholder (particularly decision makers) interactions, coastal effects of climate change, and effective adaptation strategies. She is coeditor, with Lisa Dilling, of a major anthology on climate-change communication, *Creating a Climate for Change: Communicating Climate Change and Facilitating Social Change* (Cambridge University Press, 2006). She also has published papers in *Mitigation and Adaptation Strategies for Global Change, Science, Journal of Geography in Higher Education, Environment, Proceedings of the National Academy of Sciences, Global Environmental Change, Global Environmental Politics*, and *Environmental Research Letters*, as well as chapters in many books.

ROBERT MUSIL is former executive director and chief executive officer of Physicians for Social Responsibility, a national organization concerned with global security and health that shared the 1985 Nobel Prize for Peace. He is adjunct professor at the American University School of International Service, where he teaches courses on global climate change and nuclear weapons and democracy. Musil holds degrees from Yale, Northwestern, and the Johns Hopkins School of Hygiene and Public Health. He has been a visiting fellow at the London School of Hygiene and Tropical Medicine and at Pembroke College, Cambridge, and is a Woodrow Wilson visiting scholar. He is an award-winning journalist who has produced, among many public radio and television documentaries, the public radio documentary series *One Blue Sky: Health and the Human Environment.*

ADITYA (ADI) NOCHUR, a recent graduate of Tufts University, currently sits on the executive committee of the Sierra Student Committee. He has been active in the growing youth climate movement for more than three years, working with numerous student groups such as Energy Action Coalition, EnviroCitizen, and the Climate Campaign, focused on issues of environmental and climate justice. Nochur has also organized climate summits, promoted days of action, and helped build strong state networks in Massachusetts and the Northeast in efforts to empower his fellow youth to become advocates around climate and energy policy.

TED NORDHAUS is an author, researcher, and political strategist. He is coauthor, with Michael Shellenberger of *The Death of Environmentalism and the Politics of Possibility* (Houghton Mifflin, 2007). In October 2004, Shellenberger and Nordhaus published an essay by the same name, which created an international debate over the future of progressive politics. He is a managing partner of American Environics, a research and consulting firm created to bring cutting-edge research and methodologies used to understand the evolution of American social values to progressive political projects. He has run campaigns and initiatives for many environmental and progressive political causes, including the Public Interest Research Groups, Sierra Club, Environmental Defense, and Clean Water Action. Nordhaus also served as campaign director for Share the Water, a coalition of environmentalists, anglers, farmers, and urban water agencies advocating reform of federal water policies in California; as executive director of the Headwaters Sanctuary Project; and as a partner and political strategist with Next Generation, a political consulting firm serving environmental organizations and campaigns. He has also been a pollster and vice president of Evans McDonough Company, an opinion research firm based in Oakland. He holds a BA in history from the University of California, Berkeley.

JOHN PASSACANTANDO is executive director of Greenpeace USA, leading a team of more than two hundred people and overseeing an organization with a 250,000 members in the United States and a budget of $26 million. Prior to joining Greenpeace, he was cofounder and executive director of Ozone Action and rallied the grassroots movement to stop global warming. Prior to that, Passacantando was executive director of the Florence and John Schumann Foundation and helped focus its grant-making programs on the grassroots renewal of democracy. He also worked as director of marketing for Polyconomics, Inc., where he provided economic analysis to managers of the country's largest institutional investment portfolios, distilling tax law, interest rate, and commodity price changes. Before joining Polyconomics, he sold computer systems throughout New York, New Jersey, and Connecticut for Triad Systems Corporation. He received a BA from Wake Forest University and an MA from New York University, both in economics.

BARRY RABE is a professor of public policy in the Ford School of Public Policy at the University of Michigan, where he also holds faculty appointments in the School of Natural Resources and Environment, and the Program in the Environment. Rabe is also a nonresident senior fellow at the Brookings Institution, with which he has published three books. One of them, *Statehouse and Greenhouse: The Emerging Politics of American Climate Change Policy*, received the 2005 Lynton Keith Caldwell Award from the American Political Science Association as the best book published on environmental policy in the past three years. In 2006, in recognition of his body of scholarly work examining the role of state governments in climate policy formation and implementation, Rabe became the first social scientist to receive a Climate Protection Award from the U.S. Environmental Protection Agency. His work has been cited in many contexts, including by National Public Radio, *Wall Street Journal*, *Washington Post*, and *Economist*. Rabe holds a BA in history from Carthage College and a PhD in political science from the University of Chicago.

MICHAEL SHELLENBERGER is codirector of the Breakthrough Institute, a think tank, and cofounder of American Environics, a research and strategy firm. He works on and writes about subjects ranging from politics to energy to changing social values, including articles for the *Los Angeles Times*, *American Prospect*, *Philadelphia Inquirer*, and *Glamour*. He is coauthor, with Ted Nordhaus, of *The Death of Environmentalism and the Politics of Possibility* (Houghton Mifflin, 2007). In October 2004, Shellenberger and Nordhaus published an essay by the same name that created a national debate over the future of environmentalism and progressive politics. In 2003, Shellenberger cofounded the Apollo Alliance, an umbrella organization of Greens and trade unionists. He is also author of *Race to the Top*, a report on nongovernmental organizations' ethical business campaigns. He received his MA in cultural anthropology from the University of California, Santa Cruz.

WILLIAM SHUTKIN is an attorney, educator and social entrepreneur. He has led three pioneering environmental organizations and taught environmental law and policy in the Department of Urban Studies and Planning at MIT, where he is currently a research affiliate. Shutkin was an adjunct professor of law at Boston College Law School from 1993 to 2004 and is the author of *The Land That Could Be: Environmentalism and Democracy in the Twenty-First Century* (MIT Press, 2001), which won a Best Book Award from the American Political Science Association and was selected as one of *Time* magazine's 2002 "Green Century" recommended books. Shutkin earned an AB in history and classics from Brown University and an MA in history and a JD from the University of Virginia, and he completed doctoral studies in jurisprudence and social policy as a Regents Fellow at the University of California, Berkeley. He was also a law clerk to Federal District Court Chief Judge Franklin S. Billings Jr. in Vermont.

DAVID SOUSA is a professor in the Department of Politics and Government at the University of Puget Sound. He received his BA from the University of Rhode Island and his PhD from the University of Minnesota. He has written about trade union politics, congressional elections, and environmental policy. He is coauthor, along with Christopher McGrory Klyza, of *American Environmental Policymaking, 1990–2006: Beyond Gridlock* (MIT Press, forthcoming).

GUS SPETH is dean and a professor in the practice of environmental policy and sustainable development at Yale University. He holds a BA and a JD from Yale University and an MLitt from Oxford University. Speth has served as administrator of the United Nations Development Programme and chair of the UN Development Group, founder and president of the World Resources Institute, professor of law at Georgetown University, chairman of the U.S. Council on Environmental Quality, and senior attorney at and cofounder of the Natural Resources Defense Council. His publications include *Red Sky at Morning: America and the Crisis of the Global Environment* (Yale University Press, 2005); *Worlds Apart: Globalization and the Environment* (Island Press, 2003), and articles in *Foreign Policy, Foreign Affairs, Environmental Science and Technology*, and *Columbia Journal World of Business* as well as other journal articles and books.

JULIA WEST, a graduate of Middlebury College, has been involved with campus and national student organizing since 1998 through student-oriented groups, including the Sierra Student Coalition, Energy Action, Amnesty International, and a wide array of campus organizations and informal collections of students. Her involvement has grown from writing letters on behalf of political prisoners of conscience to a variety of leadership roles within the student activist movement. In the summer of 2006, she began teaching math to grade-school students on the island of Pohnpei in the Federated States of Micronesia.

NATHAN WYETH is an undergraduate student at Brown University in Providence, Rhode Island, with a concentration in development studies. He is also a veteran organizer with the Sierra Student Coalition, the student-run arm of the Sierra Club, where he has led national grassroots campaigns to promote environmentally responsible trade policies; end the World Bank's subsidizing of oil, gas, and mining industries; and protect the Arctic National Wildlife Refuge. He currently serves as the youngest member of the Sierra Club's board of directors. Wyeth is a 2002 winner of the Brower Youth Award, and his writing has appeared in *Grist*.

INDEX